THE PASSAGE OF TIME

STORIES OF NICHOLAS COUNTY, WEST VIRGINIA

ANNA L. AND ROBERT B. CAMPBELL SR.

ISBN: 978-1-64184-399-7 (Paperback)
        978-1-64184-400-0 (ebook)

Dedication

To the brave pioneer families who risked their lives to travel and settle in the mountains of Nicholas County, West Virginia

In memory of heroic men and women who served during the wars for our freedom

For the encouragement given by family and friends that made this book of stories possible

TABLE OF CONTENTS

The stories in this book originally were published as newspaper articles in the Nicholas Chronicle. The chapters in the book are presented in the order they appeared in the newspaper. Also, the editors made a few revisions to the text of the articles. The editorial decisions were made to maintain the authenticity of the original stories.

INTRODUCTION

Pioneer life and local Nicholas County, West Virginia history have been a passion for Robert and Anna Campbell for many years. We were amazed how the Irish, English, and Scottish ancestors survived in the mountains for generations. Many people heard Robert's detailed account of his grandfather William H. Campbell's first dynamo built to produce electricity for the mills "20-watt lights" on Muddlety Creek, Nicholas County, West Virginia.

At a social gathering, the owner of The Nicholas Chronicle approached the Campbell's about writing stories for the weekly newspaper. Robert replied, "We shall give it some thought. I'm a storyteller; my wife, Ann, is a writer and historian." After much consideration, Ann consented to write for the newspaper with help and research from her husband, Robert. We received positive response with several requests that our stories be published in a book.

Our daughter, Martha Jane Larkin, PhD and her husband, Richard Larkin, PhD expressed the possibility of a published book of the Nicholas County pioneering after Robert passed away March 7, 2015. They made that a reality with their expertise and technology.

The stories with pictures portray the culture, character, creativity, Christian values, and the caring people that made Nicholas County, West Virginia a unique place to live for generations.

Anna (Ann) L. Campbell

1

STARBUCK FAMILY

We begin a new series today about our pioneering Nicholas County families, written by well-known Summersville residents, Robert B. and Ann Campbell. Edward Starbuck was the first Starbuck to settle in the United States about 1635 in Dover, New Hampshire. He was born Feb. 16, 1604 in Leicester, England. At the age of 55 years, Edward went on an exploring trip, where he met Thomas Macy, James Coffin and Isaac Coleman. They set out in an open boat for Nantucket. In the spring, Starbuck went back to Dover to fetch his family and 10 other families. Thus, began the two and- a-half centuries long residence of Starbucks on the island that became, after his demise, a leading whaling base, until kerosene lamps replaced whale oil lamps in the 1850's. Starbuck built a house on land deeded to him by the Indians. This deed is the oldest Nantucket document in existence. Edward died April 12, 1690.

Six children were born to Edward and Katherine Reynolds Starbuck. One of these was Nathaniel Starbuck, born about 1635. He later married Mary Coffin and they had 10 children. Nathaniel (3) born Aug. 9, 1668, married Dinah Coffin who was born in 1674. This union produced 10 children in Nantucket. This Nathaniel (3) was probably the first Nantucket millionaire. His father, Nathaniel (2) provided financing from the whale fishery and Nathaniel (3) supplied the harpoons and other hardware.

Paul Starbuck, born Oct. 29, 1694, was the son of Nathaniel (3) and married Ann Tibbetts, born July 8, 1697, who also lived on Nantucket. This union produced nine children, the oldest being Edward, who was born Nov. 28, 1719 and who later married Damaris Worth of Nantucket. This union created five children, including Matthew, born Jan. 6, 1750. Matthew Starbuck married Rose Barnard and they had one son. Rose died in 1776. Then Matthew married Lydia Barney in 1776 and they had 14 children. Later, Matthew married wife number three, Anna Swain, and they had no children. He then married wife number four, Dinah Macy.

Matthew was disowned by the Quakers for "being with armed men" when, unlike most Starbucks of the time, he actively supported the revolutionary cause. He was an able seaman on John Paul Jones. After the war, he captained the whaling ship, "Hope," which he took from Nantucket to Dunkirk, France in 1791. He moved to Guilford County, North Carolina in 1795 and took up farming, where he died in 1815. His fourth wife, Dinah, died in 1830.

The 14th of Matthew's 15 children was Benjamin Starbuck, born Nov. 2, 1798 in North Carolina. Benjamin married Anna Gardner on Sept. 30, 1819. Nine children were born to this union. Anna died June 25, 1841 in Salem, Indiana. Benjamin married his second wife, Julia Ann Hubbard on March 28, 1844. They had a family of seven children. Benjamin and Anna Gardner Starbucks second son, Oliver Perry Starbuck, born Aug. 30, 1822, was the eighth generation of Starbuck family in the United States.

Next will be about what brought the Starbuck family to West Virginia.

2

STARBUCK FAMILY MOVES TO VIRGINIA (WEST VIRGINIA)

T his is the second part of a new series about our pioneering Nicholas County families, written by well-known Summersville residents, Robert B. and Ann Campbell After Benjamin Starbuck's first wife, Anna Gardner, died June 25, 1841, following the birth of a son, in Salem, Indiana, the oldest daughter, Matilda Starbuck Hobbs cared for some of the children. In Elmira Starbuck Lindley's obituary, it stated she was nine years old when her mother, Anna G. Starbuck died. She lived with her older sister and attended Friends Church Schools in Indiana.

It isn't known what brought Benjamin Starbuck to Braxton County, Virginia (WV) following his wife's death. In Sutton, he established a Saddler Shop on the corner of Main Street and Bridge Road. A good saddler was in demand at that time to make and repair saddles. Oliver Perry Starbuck, an older son, moved from Indiana to Sutton, leaving friends and some family members in Salem, Ind. He also worked with his father, Benjamin, in the saddler business.

Benjamin Starbuck married a second wife, Julia Ann Hubbard (B Dec. 13, 1813) on March 28, 1844. They had seven children: John (B 1845), Martha (B 1848), Adeline (B 1850), Benjamin

Barney (B 1853), George (B 1855), David (B 1858) and Mary Elizabeth (B 1860).

The seven children, in the second family produced by Benjamin and Julia Ann Starbuck, settled and married in the Braxton County area. George married Mary Armstrong in 1886 and Benjamin Barney married Mary E. Skidmore in 1887. Adeline married Addison Shaver and David married Martha Barnette in 1886. Blanch married Fred Bennet in 1910 and Rose married Brontie Harris in 1910.

Children born to Benjamin Barney and Mary Skidmore Starbuck were Ellis (1878-1883), Daisy (1885-1886) and Grover Cleveland Starbuck (1888-1959). (There will be more information on the life of Grover C. Starbuck).

Julia Ann Starbuck died (no date available) and is buried along with many family members in the Benjamin Skidmore Cemetery, Franklin Road, Sutton, West Virginia.

In August 2004, we, along with our daughter, Martha Campbell Larkin, researched Court House Records and Genealogical records in Braxton County. There were no Starbucks living in Braxton County, West Virginia.

A Stitching Horse, used by the Starbucks, is also known as a Saddler Bench. A combination stool and hands-free clamp, it allowed the user to hand-stitch a saddle or harness parts.

3

OLIVER PERRY STARBUCK COMES TO NICHOLAS COUNTY

This is the third part of a series about our pioneering Nicholas County families, written by well-known Summersville residents, Robert B. and Ann Campbell. Oliver Perry Starbuck was born August 30, 1822 in Stokes County, North Carolina, to Benjamin and Anna Gardner Starbuck. At the age of seven, he moved with his family to Salem, Indiana, a place where he grew into manhood. He moved to Braxton County, Va. (WV) with his father after his mother died.

He learned the trade of a saddler from his father in Sutton, Va. (W.Va.). Being a man of many talents, Oliver Perry Starbuck was also a photographer and rode horseback, taking and producing tintype pictures. It has been stated that he took pictures during the Civil War at Carnifax Ferry in Nicholas County.

Mills were of great interest to Oliver Perry, as his first mill was built below Harpers Ferry on the Gauley River, which ground all kinds of grain and also spun wool into yarn. After operating this mill for years, he selected a site on "Mumble-the-Peg" Creek. (now known as Muddlety Creek)

He married Deborah Brock (born 1827) daughter of Daniel David and Catherine Brock. Mr. Brock was also a miller by trade. Oliver P. and Deborah Starbuck had three sons, Edgar (B 1856 - D 1902) who married Rowena Rusk and after she died, married Eva Legg; Grafton Starbuck (B 1858) married Madora Ann Walker. Fielding M. Starbuck was born Sept. 1852. Deborah Brock Starbuck, who died at the age of 34 years on April 5, 1862, is buried in the Methodist Episcopal Church, South Cemetery on Broad Street in Summersville, WV.

Grafton Starbuck built the first frame schoolhouse in 1896 at Jodie, Fayette County, WV. and operated a grist mill in Jodie. He was the owner and operator of a grist and planing mill near Belva, Fayette County, WV.

Edgar was owner and operator of a grist mill and a sawmill at Tipton, Nicholas County. He and his wife, Rowena had three sons, Willie L. (B 1884), Guy Starbuck (B 1893), and Omer Starbuck (B 1898 - D 1899). Edgar married Eva Legg after Rowena died (1893) and their sons Omer and John B. are also buried in the Methodist Episcopal Church, South Cemetery to the left of the cemetery steps.

More is known about Fielding M. Starbuck, born 1852, who married Henrietta J. Harrow on Sept. 18, 1877. They had a son, Harry Ashton Starbuck, born Nov. 11, 1884 at Fayette Station, WV who lived and died in Hinton, WV on Dec. 1948.

Fielding M. Starbuck, an inventor, had several patented inventions as listed: Fielding M. Starbuck of Ansted, WV, Washington DC and Summersville, WV:

Dinner Pail - May 8, 1883, Carburetor Attachment Aug. 15, 1916.

Vaporizer for Internal Combustion Engines May 6, 1924.

Air Brake - Sept. 28, 1926.

Part of his inventing took place in an old garage building located where Hardman's Hardware, Summersville, WV is presently located. Fielding owned and operated a foundry in Hinton, WV where some of his inventions were created. He also had a photography business known as F.M. Starbuck

Photography Pavillion. While living in Ansted, WV, he was publisher of the "Ansted West Virginian," a local newspaper published in 1890. He lived in a house known as the Starbuck

House, which later became the Gauley Mountain Hotel. Fielding moved to Hinton, WV, where he lived his remaining years.

More information will be next about Oliver P. Starbuck's second wife and family on the "Mumble-the-Peg Creek."

Grafton Starbuck and one of his wives, Electra Starbuck. He was a carpenter and built the first frame schoolhouse in 1896 at Jodie, Fayette County, WV.

Fielding M. Starbuck was born 1852, the son of Oliver
P. and Deborah Starbuck. He was a photographer,
publisher, inventor, and foundry owner.

4

OLIVER P. STARBUCK

In researching property in the Nicholas County Courthouse for deeds made to Oliver Perry Starbuck, the following deed information was recorded in Book 11 page 115. "This deed made seventeenth day of December in the year 1856 between John Bell and Emeline, his wife, Winston Shelton and Mary Ann, his wife and John H. Robinson and Roweena his wife of the first part and Oliver P. Starbuck of the second part all of the county of Nicholas, state of Virginia. Witnessed that the above named party of the first part for and in consideration of the sum of four hundred dollars to them in hand by the said Oliver P. Starbuck the where of is hereby acknowledged to grant unto the said Starbuck two certain tracts of or lots of land lying and being in the town of Summersville, Nicholas County, Virginia designated as lots number 6 and 15 containing one-half acre each and being the same now in possession of said Starbuck and the same deed to Bell, Shelton and Robinson by Robert Kelly, serving Executor of John Hamilton deceased the said Starbuck to have and to hold the same."

Oliver Perry Starbuck was a widower in 1862 with three young sons, Fielding, Edgar, and Grafton, to care for while running his mills. On October 30, 1862, Oliver married Susan Ellen Herold (born April 30, 1838), daughter of Henry S. and Elizabeth Lockridge Herold. During the marriage of Oliver P. and Susan Ellen, they had five daughters: Florence Elizabeth (born

March 28, 1864), Anna Starbuck (born March 16, 1866), Lillie who died young, Virginia (born 1873), and Etta Alice (born 1879). With the two families to raise, Oliver P. and Susan Ellen Starbuck were busy caring for the children and establishing and expanding the mills and carding business.

A deed from Book II page 117, records that on the 26 day of January 1870 between Madison Hughes and Miriam R. his wife of the first part and Oliver P. Starbuck of the second part both parties of the county of Nicholas, State of West Virginia witnesseth for and in consideration of one hundred dollars paid in hand the party of the second part a certain part tract or parcel of land containing seventy-five acres lying in the county and state afore said on the North side of Gauley River beginning at a spruce tree above the mouth of Hominy Creek leaving said river down 324 poles to a chestnut and spruce opposite the mouth of Hominy Creek leaving said river N. 8 poles to a stake N. 50 E to the beginning which said tract of land embraces the mill-carding machine house and other improvements made and occupied by Starbuck and is known by the name of STONEWALL BOTTOM and the party of the first part generally to the party of the second part and title to the above tract of land between the following seals. Madison Hughes (Seal) Miriam Hughes (Seal)

This information documents the location for Oliver Perry Starbuck's business of the gristmill and carding machine house in the 1870s.

The second family of Oliver Perry Starbuck and Mumble-the-Peg property will be continued in the next article in The Passage of Time.

Note the spelling of Mumble-the-Peg, later known as Muddlety Creek, is recorded on the deeds.

Susan Ellen Starbuck

5

THE STARBUCK FAMILY AND MUMBLE-THE-PEG PROPERTY

On Jan. 8, 1883, Oliver P. Starbuck entered an agreement with William and Rebecca Dotson for the sum of one hundred fifty dollars for certain tract or parcel of land lying in Nicholas County, Summersville District on both sides of Mumble-the-Peg Creek, being the same land on which O. P. Starbuck's Grist Mill and dwelling house now stands. Beginning at a large spruce tree on West bank of Mumble the Peg about two poles from the creek and about one fourth of mile from the Jones Spinning Factory thence down the creek along the hillside E. 60 poles to a maple and pointers at the edge of the Laurel thence 75 E 22 poles to a spruce and maple on the East bank of Mumble-the-Peg Creek cover to Harris on Dotson and with one of his lines East 30 poles to a said maple and birch growing on a hillside. N 6 W 56 poles to a small Chestnut and pointers N. 29 poles to a small white oak and pointers. To have and to hold the aforesaid tract of land with its appurtenances unto the said O. P. Starbuck his heirs or assignees forever with covenants of general warranty. And the said parties of the first part hereby grant to the said O. P. Starbuck, his heirs and assignees forever the right of way for a good wagon road to the land hereby conveyed through their other land on a good grade as can be gotten through said land not to exceed 5 degrees. Signed: William Dotson (seal) Rebecca Dotson (seal).

Oliver P. Starbuck built a large mill to house the gristmill, two carding machines and picker and an open shed on the upper slope at the edge of Mumble-the-Peg Creek. In an area under the floor he placed the turbine to be run by waterpower.

It was necessary to build a dam across the creek and far enough above the mill to supply waterpower to turn the turbines. The base of the creek was solid rock which made it necessary to chisel square holes to set posts in to support a stringer across the top. Wooden boards were secured on the stringer and placed at an angle up the creek. The force and weight of the water held the boards in place.

On the side above the mill, a canal was excavated to carry the water to the turbine. A gate was constructed which could be raised when water was needed to turn the turbine. Also, a spillway was built to let any excess water flow over and continue downstream.

To apply power to the different machines, belts from the turbine shaft to each machine were installed with wooden leaver to tighten the belt on the desired machine.

By this time, the Starbuck Mill Complex had become a "hub of activity" for Summersville, West Virginia. Oliver P. Starbuck had two carding machines, a picker, gristmill, and a sawmill located on "Mumble-the- Peg Creek."

The carding machine, brought to Nicholas County about 1830 by Andrew J. Jones, was purchased about 1865 by Oliver P. Starbuck, following the death of Henry J. Jones. Oliver P. moved the mill from Muddlety to a site on Gauley River, but because of high water and other problems, soon had to move it back to Mumble-the-Peg area. Carding of wool was done by hand before the invention of a carding machine. The wool was fed into carding machines to blend the fibers into a straight band. A web of carded wool was passed through a set of carding rollers that press dust, seed, and other foreign matter from the wool. A picker is used to remove larger objects from raw wool.

The gristmill turned out corn meal from corn, flour from wheat, and buckwheat flour. The farmers brought the grains to be milled. The sawmill turned out lumber from logs and virgin timber in Nicholas County, West Virginia.

Starbuck's Grist Mill

The carding machine

6

FLORENCE ELIZABETH STARBUCK

The first daughter born to Oliver P. and Susan Ellen Starbuck was Florence Elizabeth, born March 28, 1864, near Summersville, Nicholas County.

As a young girl, Florence rode with her father, Oliver P., on horseback to take tintype pictures. It is suspected that on a trip to Braxton County she may have met her husband, William Henry Campbell, of Burnsville, W.Va. They were married on July 6, 1889. The following announcement from the newspaper stated, "One of the most pleasant events of the season was the marriage of Mr. Henry Campbell of Burnsville, Braxton County, and Miss Florence Starbuck, daughter of O. P. Starbuck, ESQR, of the County (Nicholas) at the residence of the bride's father, about two miles East of this place. Rev. W. R. Chambers of Braxton County was the officiating minister and the attendants were Mr. M. W. Heffner, a Miss Annie Starbuck, Mr. L. B. Burk and Miss Maggie Campbell, sister of the groom. A number of the most intimate friends of the contracting parties were present to witness the nuptial ceremonies. Prof. Vidalette presided at the organ and rendered Mendelssohn's Wedding March in his inimitable style on the entrance of the wedding party. After the ceremony, the party and invited guests reported to the dining hall, where a wedding feast had been prepared as only Mrs. O. P. Starbuck can prepare one, and after all had partaken to their heart's content, the tables literally groaned under the loads of untasted viands.

The newly married couple departed for their home at Burnsville in the afternoon, accompanied by Miss Annie, sister of the bride. Mr. Campbell is a popular young man of Braxton County, and his wife has a host of friends in Nicholas County, who will unite with us in wishing that earth's choicest blessings may attend them through a long useful and happy life."

Florence and William Henry Campbell resided in Burnsville, W.Va., where they had four sons: Howard Blackburn Campbell, born Sept. 23, 1890; Herbert M. Campbell, born May 30, 1892; Russell Herold Campbell, born Sept. 20, 1894; and Eugene Leslie Campbell, born April 13, 1896.

Late in the year of 1896, Oliver Perry Starbuck was in failing health and sent word to his daughter, Florence, and husband, William Henry Campbell, that he needed them to move to Nicholas County and help run the mills. They moved their young sons and settled at the Starbuck Complex to help with the business. Two daughters were born in Nicholas County. Lottie Jean was born Dec. 27, 1897, and Elizabeth Campbell was born Oct. 20, 1900.

On Feb. 2, 1888, a deed between Oliver P. Starbuck first part, and F. M. Starbuck, Florence E. Starbuck, Annie Starbuck, Virginia Starbuck and Etta Starbuck, parties of the second part for the consideration of one dollar in hand for a parcel or tract of land conveyed from Rebecca and William Dotson on Jan. 8, 1883 in Book 2 page 147 being the said party of the first part now resides together with the mill and the fixtures and appurtenances of every kind and the carding machine and its necessary fixtures, tools, appurtenances for a non particular description of the land by mills and bounds or fences has been had to the deed from Rebecca Dotson and before mentioned the intention of this conveyance bring to convey to the parties of second part the land aforesaid with buildings the new carding machine with its fixtures appurtenances as well as the mill its appurtenances to have and to hold until parties of second part, their heirs and assignees forever. Signed: O. P. Starbuck (seal)

Back row (l-r) Howard B., Eugene L., Herbert M., Russell
H. Campbell Front – Elizabeth, Florence Starbuck, Lottie
Jean and William Henry Campbell, circa 1906 – 08

7

ANNA, LILLY, AND VIRGINIA STARBUCK

Oliver P. and Susan Ellen Starbuck's second daughter, Anna Starbuck, was born March 2, 1866 in Nicholas County, West Virginia, near Summersville. Anna was a talented artist. She painted several paintings that were displayed in homes. Fancy needlework was also a favorite hobby of hers.

On Oct. 30, 1890, Anna married M. W. Hefner of Burnsville, W.Va., where they lived their short married life together. Anna was an avid gardener. A true Christian woman, Anna was converted at a protracted meeting in 1885 in Summersville. Soon after her conversion, she joined a Presbyterian Church and remained a faithful member until Feb. 18, 1899 when she was received by letter from her pastor, the Rev. W. H. Wilson, into the Methodist Episcopal Church, South.

Anna died on Aug. 26, 1899, after a brief illness of three days. She was 33 years old and was the granddaughter of Henry S. and Elizabeth Lockbridge Herold.

Another daughter, Felia F. "Lilly" Starbuck, born Sept. 10, 1868, died young. She is buried in Methodist Episcopal Church, South Cemetery, Summersville.

Virginia Othelia Starbuck was born in 1873 near Summersville in Nicholas County, to Oliver P. and Susan Ellen Starbuck. She was educated in public schools and attended Summersville Normal

School. She married Clint West and resided in Clarksburg. They had two children, William West and Bessie West. William O. West lived in Vincennes, Ind., and had two sons, William Martin and Robert Thomas West of Vincennes.

Daughter, Bessie, married Arthur Venicia and they had one son, Arthur Venicia Jr., who was an accomplished musician at the organ. Later, in Florida, after Arthur Venicia died, Bessie married a Mr. Fischer whom she met in St. Petersburg. In her latter days, she lived near her son, Arthur, near Miami, Fla. Tragedy came to both Arthur and his mother when some trusted employees at Arthur's International House of Pancakes became greedy, hired killers to first kill Arthur, their wealthy boss, and assumed his identity and possessions. When the 84-yearold mother became suspicious, she was killed. The 44-year-old son and mother were buried on their 5-acre plot of land. A little dog belonging to the Venicias kept going to the gravesite and that gave a clue and one employee who had been involved had information that finally let to the arrest. The trial lasted five weeks and the jury found the four defendants guilty of first-degree murder and recommended death by electrocution. This tragedy took place on Father's Day, June 1983. Bessie Venicia Fischer was killed three weeks later. Some family members had a proper burial for Arthur Venicia Jr., and mother Bessie West Venicia Fischer in St. Petersburg.

Fortunately, the mother and grandmother, Virginia Starbuck West Cotton, passed away in February 1956, so she wasn't aware of the tragic events in her family.

Anna Starbuck Hefner 1866–1899

Virginia Othelia Starbuck 1873–1956

8

ETTA ALICE STARBUCK

The youngest daughter born to Oliver P. and Susan Ellen Starbuck was Etta Alice Starbuck, born 1879 near Summersville, Nicholas County, W.Va. She was educated in public schools and attended the Summersville Normal School in 1894 – 1895. Etta was an accomplished organist and played in many churches most of her adult life.

She married Dr. Robert Petty and lived in Huntington, W.Va. They had no children. After Dr. Petty passed away, Etta lived many years in St. Petersburg, Fla., where she met and married Dr. Thomas Houston. They enjoyed a busy social life and she continued to play the church organ and for other events. After Mr. T. Houston passed away, Etta continued to drive her car even though her advanced years and poor eyesight became a problem. On one occasion, her nephew, Eugene L. Campbell, went with Etta to renew her driver's license. When the driver's test was over, the nephew asked his Aunt Etta, "Did you pass the test?" She replied, "No! I thought I could fool them one more time." Thus, ended the driving for a very independent person, which was difficult for her. Etta Alice Starbuck Petty Houston died at the age of 97 years on March 17, 1976. Many nieces and nephews survived her. She was buried in Asheville, N.C.

The wedding of Etta Alice Starbuck and Dr. Robert Petty was recorded in The Nicholas Chronicle, August 1990 as follows, "One of the pleasant social events of last week was the marriage of Dr. Robert Petty of Mason County and Miss Etta A. Starbuck of Summersville, which took place at the residence of Mr. W. H. Campbell on Saturday, Aug. 25, with the Rev. M. V. Bowles officiating. The groom is a prominent young dentist and the bride one of the accomplished young ladies of Summersville. May happiness be theirs through life." Even though Oliver Perry and Susan Ellen Starbuck were successful with their mills and carding machine business, and raised two families, there was tragedy. A son, granddaughter and a great-grandson were murdered. There are descendants but no Starbuck name listed in the area. A street (road) called Starbuck Road in Summersville is named for the Starbuck family.

Etta Alice Starbuck

9

GROVER CLEVELAND STARBUCK

The youngest child of Benjamin Barney and Mary Elizabeth Skidmore Starbuck was Grover Cleveland Starbuck, born March 15, 1888, in Sutton. When Grover Cleveland was 1 year old, his mother died and his father brought him to the home of relatives in Summersville to be raised. Oliver P. and Susan Ellen Starbuck had their young family and the mills to operate and were unable to care for Grover Cleveland. The young Grover was adopted by Robert P. and Nora Groves Reynolds in Summersville. They gave him affection and tenderness of real parents. Also influencing his life was his foster uncle, Thomas O. Reynolds, one of nature's true gentlemen, whose homely philosophy gave inspiration to all who were privileged to know him. After attending local schools, Grover C. Starbuck started training as a printer, but in 1910 accepted a position as the assistant cashier in the newly formed Farmers and Merchants Bank where he worked for seven years. The brick building on Main Street, Summersville, formerly Mrs. E. J. Walker's 10-cent store, was secured and arranged for a bank. Wallace P. Kincade was the cashier. Also, in 1910, Grover Cleveland and Myrtle Dixson, daughter of R. J. Dixson of Birch River and Sarah "Ma" Dixson of Summersville were married. They purchased lots in Alderson addition in 1912 and had a two-story frame house built on the corner of Main Street and Route 39 West in Summersville. A daughter, Anna Lee Starbuck, was born March 2, 1911, and a son, Grover Cleveland II, was born May 21, 1916, in Summersville.

In 1913, the Nicholas Chronicle reported the following social event. "An enjoyable social event was the New Year party at the home of Mr. and Mrs. G. C. Starbuck Tuesday night. The guests, about 50 in number, assembled about 8 o'clock and were royally entertained at games, social chat and music until near the midnight hour when a sumptuous lunch was served, after which the New Year was greeted with a considerable display of fireworks. The guests then departed with many expressions of thanks for the pleasant evening."

In 1917, the Starbuck property was sold to Lee Fitzwater who sold the same property to Joseph Hill in 1925. The Starbuck property was passed on to Mr. Hill's son, Ira Hill, in 1925. The heir of Ira Hill, daughter Willa Hill Boso, passed the property on to her three Boso grandsons, who are the present owners. Many Summersville people refer to the Hill House, which was the Starbuck house.

In 1918, Grover Cleveland Starbuck arranged to actively selling and installation of Delco Light Systems. Mr. A. N. Breckenridge was the factory representative and Grover C. Starbuck was the agent for Delco Light and Service. Their goal was to place lights on every farm.

Grover C. Starbuck accepted a position as cashier of the First National Bank of Mt. Hope, W.Va. He later resigned and accepted management of Kings Daughters Hospital of Staunton, Va., where Grover, Myrtle and family resided for about 27 years. Myrtle Starbuck operated a B&B known as the Dutch Inn on U.S. 11 in Verona, Va.

Believing that his health required shorter hours with less responsibility, Mr. Starbuck resigned his position in Staunton and moved to Arlington, Va., where he operated as a realtor. After an illness of several months, Grover Cleveland Starbuck died Sept. 4, 1959. At that time, he was survived by wife, Myrtle Dixson Starbuck; daughters, Anna Lee Starbuck Stockton of Roanoke,

Va., and Mary Frances Starbuck Cable of Strasburg, Va.; and a son, Grover Cleveland Starbuck D.D.S. of Arlington.

Grover Cleveland was buried at Thornrose Cemetery in Staunton.

Grover Cleveland Starbuck and wife, Myrtle Dixson Starbuck

Back: Nellie Skaggs, Fannie Bays Burdette, Ella
Lambert; front, Grover G. and Myrtle Dixson Starbuck;
daughter, Anna Lee Starbuck (Born March 2, 1911)

10

GROVER THOMAS STARBUCK

For the past several weeks, we have shared some history and genealogy of the Starbuck Family in the Passage of Time printed in the weekly issues of the Nicholas Chronicle. The more research we do, spurs more interest and enthusiasm in learning more about the pioneer families. What is equally as exciting is the discovery of another descendent from the family line.

A late Sunday afternoon, on a warm summer day, we were returning to our home walking on Starbuck Road. We looked toward Webster Road and saw a small red convertible with the canvas roof down, stopped at the corner of Starbuck and Webster Roads. A woman sat in the passenger side of the car, while the driver, a man, stepped out to photograph something. He returned to his car and drove toward us, stopped near Ann and said, "Starbuck Road — are there any Starbucks living here?" She replied, "no, " but he (pointed toward Bob) is related to the Starbucks." The man asked another question, "Have you heard of Grover Starbuck? I am his Grandson, Tom Starbuck."

We were totally surprised and very excited to hear the name STARBUCK. We invited the couple to please turn the car around and enter the driveway across Webster Road so that we could talk to them, as we have been doing research on the Starbuck Family because Bob's grandmother was Florence Starbuck.

Grover Thomas and wife Gina Starbuck were just as interested in finding new relatives as the Campbells. We sat on the porch and shared as much information as their time would permit. We asked if they would like to see the house that his grandfather, Grover Cleveland Starbuck had built about 1912 and the Methodist Cemetery where the Starbuck Family members were at rest. We drove our newly acquainted relatives to those locations.

Tom Starbuck took many pictures of the house, cemetery, the bank where his grandfather, Grover C. Starbuck had helped to organize as an assistant cashier and of course pictures of each other. Darkness started to befall us and we invited them to spend the night with the Campbells, but they had been traveling and needed to return to their home in Winchester, Va. This was the beginning in 2004 of more visits, letters and phone calls from Grover and Gina Starbuck, our new relatives.

Grover Thomas Starbuck, an architect with the U.S. Army Corps of Engineers, traveled to many countries until his retirement. Grover Thomas and Gina Starbuck have five children: daughter, Susan, and sons, Tom, Mark, Dean and Sean Starbuck.

In an earlier writing about Grover Cleveland Starbuck, the grandfather of Grover Thomas, it was mentioned the influence on his life by a foster Uncle Thomas O. Reynolds. In a family scrapbook, Tom's mother wrote the explanation of his name "Thomas" in memory and honor of the gentleman who influenced the grandfather's life. It was of special interest for Grover Thomas to visit the grave of Thomas O. Reynolds (1865–1935) in Summersville.

This concludes stories of the Starbuck Family from the period of 1635 when Edward Starbuck settled in the United States to the present time, 2008. There are no known Starbucks still living in the area, only descendents. The next series will be of descendents, the Campbell Family and the first Electric-Hydro Power Plant, located on the Starbuck property on Muddlety Creek, Summersville.

Grover Thomas and Gina Starbuck stand near the
house built by his grandfather, Grover Cleveland
Starbuck, in 1912 (Now known as the Hill House)

G. Thomas Starbuck Family — left, Susan, Tom (father),
Todd (back), Mark (front), Dean and Sean Starbuck,
great-grandchildren of Grover C. Starbuck

11

THE CAMPBELL FAMILY

The Campbell family is among the 49 "best families" selected by the American Historical Genealogical Society for whom the Society has published family histories. The Campbell family has been prominent in the British Empire and the United States. Its members having played important roles in war and peace. The oldest spelling of Campbell (dates back 1296) is Cambel or Kamel. Campus-bellus from which as derived Campbellus and finally Campbell, the spelling used at this time.

The Campbell Coat of Arms is the Arms of the Dukes of Argyll who are the chieftains of the Campbell clan. The hereditary insignia of this family stands for splendid honor, noble lineage and true aristocracy.

The first generation of Campbells to migrate to the United States was Thomas Campbell Sr., born 1715 in Scotland, came in 1755 and lived in Chester County, Pennsylvania. A son, Thomas Jr., was born 1738, lived in New London Township and married Susan Brown of Lancaster, Pa. He served in the Revolutionary War, Company of Captain John McKee. He moved to Virginia following the war as late as 1792. This union had four children: John (B 1760, D 1820), James (B 1762, D 1832), Samuel (B 1764, D 1852), and Alexander Campbell, born 1767 in Cecil County, Maryland and died in 1845 in Highland County, Va.

Alexander married Margaret Brown (B 1769, D 1823) and moved to Missouri. They had the following children: James (B

1797, D 1852), Thomas (B 1800, D 1876), John (B 1802, D 1882), Samuel B. (B 1806, D 1883) whose family will be followed, Benjamine B. (B 1808, D 1882), William M. (B 1811, D 1881), Alexander Hanson (B 1815, D 1889) and Edgar Campbell (B 1818, D 1886). After the first wife and mother of the above children died, Alexander Campbell married Polly Moore of North Carolina and lived in Hightown, Highland County, Va.

The fourth generation, Samuel B. Campbell, born 1806, married Jane Woods in 1828. She died in 1849. This union had eight children. In 1855, Samuel B. married Isabelle Woods, the niece of Jane Woods. Their children were Mary Ann, Alexander (1830–1918), Rollin B. (1832–1890), Rachael R. (1834–1916), Vernon (1836–1900), Annanis (1838–1861), Caleb (1840–1925) and Margaret Jane (___–1825).

The fifth generation, Alexander Campbell (1830-1918), son of Samuel B. and Jane Woods Campbell, married Susan E. Matheney in 1856 in Highland County, Virginia. This union had two children, William Henry (Dec. 3, 1857–1947) and Margaret Jean Campbell (1867–1897) who married Fredrick Hoover. They had two daughters, Ann and Susan Hoover. After the death of the first wife, Susan Matheney Campbell, Alexander married Margaret Hoover, the sister of Frederick Hoover. This union had two children, Minnie (1879–1952) who married Tupper N. Shreve and Mary Sue (1882–1927) who married S. T. Fletcher.

Alexander and Susan Matheney Campbell moved to Burnsville, W.Va., about 1867 where Susan died April 8, 1874. He later married Margaret Hoover. They continued to live in Burnsville where all three area at rest in the Feeney Cemetery which is on the hill across the road from the Campbell house.

The sixth generation, William Henry Campbell, son of Alexander and Susan Matheney Campbell was born Dec. 3, 1857 in Highland County, Va., a rural farming community formed from Bath and Pendleton counties. William Henry was about 10 years old when his parents moved to Burnsville, Braxton County. It isn't known what brought Alexander to Burnsville, except timbering was in big demand and Alexander was a planer or carpenter by trade. Son, William Henry, and father, Alexander, were ahead of their time in building a pre-cut house and assembling it on site. The house still stands in Burnsville on the Burnsville Lake Road. Alexander and son also built a church in Burnsville. The Campbell house is presently owned by descendants of the Campbell family. The original house faced the river but was turned later to face the road.

The challenges that faced William Henry Campbell will be addressed in the next article.

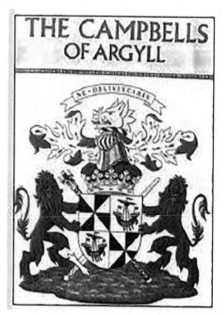

The Campbell Coat of Arms is the Arms of the Dukes of Argyll who are the chieftains of the Campbell clan.

The Campbell house in Burnsville is presently
owned by descendants of the Campbell family.

12

WILLIAM HENRY CAMPBELL AND FAMILY MOVE TO THE STARBUCK PROPERTY

In failing health, Oliver P. Starbuck invited daughter, Florence, and her husband, William Henry Campbell, to move from Burnsville to Summersville to assist with the Starbuck Mills and carding machine business. The Campbell family with four young sons arrived to live with Oliver P. at the Starbuck residence on Mumble-the- Peg Creek in late 1896. The next year, 1897, a daughter, Lottie Jean was born on Dec. 27. A second daughter, Anna Elizabeth was born Oct. 20, 1900. William Henry Campbell worked with his father-in-law, Oliver P. Starbuck, learned the business and operated the mills, including grist, lumber and carding machines.

In a letter of Jan. 3, 1897, to William Henry's sister, Margaret Campbell Hoover of Braxton County, he displayed in words the tenderness and kindness toward family when Margaret's baby died. He also yearned to return to Burnsville but knew he was needed at the Starbuck Mills. Shortly after taking charge of the mills, William Henry Campbell increased its service to the community by purchasing a sawmill unit and harnessing it to the water wheel. This gave him a new outlet for his energies during seasonal times when the demands were not heavy for grist grinding and wool carding. The appreciated increase in his business were the results of adding the new community service to his enterprise. Steadily, the patronage in each of the three departments of his mill continued to expand.

By the turn of the century, the business was efficient and satisfactory that the demand of William Henry's daily time began to exceed the daylight hours and it was necessary for the frequent use of the mills during night hours. Due to inefficient illumination that was furnished by crude and primitive oil burning lamps and lanterns, he found it difficult to do good work and maintain his production schedule at night.

The Starbuck Mill on Mumble-the-Peg Creek (Muddlety Creek) was becoming the "hub" of Summersville with increased activity at the mills. About the same time, Oliver P. Starbuck died Jan. 16, 1900, leaving his widow, Susan Ellen Herold Starbuck, to be cared for by her daughter, Florence, and husband William Henry Campbell.

More information will follow on William Henry Campbell's search for better lighting and improvements at the Starbuck Mill.

End of Starbuck Mill on Mumble-the-Peg Creek
Wagon Bridge cross creek circa 1880s

13

WILLIAM HENRY CAMPBELL

After William Henry and Florence Starbuck Campbell moved to the Oliver P. Starbuck property and took charge of the Starbuck Mills, William Henry, being a quiet and "thinking" man, wanted to find a better way to light the mill since the demand had increased to operation into the night. The oil lamps and oil burning lanterns were inefficient for the dark days and night hours. So he began seeking ways and means of overcoming this handicap. Vaguely, a daydream of lighting his mill with electric lights occurred to him. This dream rapidly grew into ambition. There was nothing impossible or unreasonable about the thought reasoned William Henry. He had been an avid reader of books and knew that electric lights were being used in larger towns and cities. "If others could make them burn, so could he." Such was the faith that William Henry had in himself.

This was a big task as much had to be done before there could be electric lights burning in the mill. First of all, an electric dynamo must be provided to generate the electricity. There were few in the country at that time where such contraptions could be bought as a unit. Also, William Henry Campbell's funds were limited, and the cost of dynamos was so expensive that he couldn't have bought one if they had been plentiful. The next best thing that occurred to him was to make a dynamo. How could he do this? This was a complicated undertaking. William Henry Campbell had always been interested in the electrical experiments of Benjamin Franklin. He had never even seen an electric dynamo in practical use. He had no technical training whatsoever and his academic education was limited to only a few years in primitive country schools. These limitations were serious handicaps, but William Henry was determined to learn how to build a dynamo.

The first thing he did was order a set of 12 volumes of Terrell Crofts handbooks from a mail order house. When these books arrived on Mumble-the-Peg Creek, William Henry Campbell became so absorbed in studying the books that seemingly little else concerned him, according to his wife, Florence Starbuck Campbell. She said that many was the time she had to threaten him with dire treatment to get him to leave his books and experiments long enough to eat his meals. She was frequently "irked" because William Henry stubbornly refused to explain to her or the neighbors what he was trying to do.

After obtaining sufficient information from the mail order books, he proceeded to whittle out wooden patterns for castings for a frame for his dynamo. When these patterns were completed, he sent them to a small foundry operated by John Shuttlesworth at Sutton, WV to have iron castings made. Upon competition of these iron castings, they were shipped to Camden on Gauley, WV, which was the nearest railway station to Summersville, WV. William Henry Campbell rode his horse to the Camden on Gauley Station to get his castings. He was so excited to make that long trip and the thoughts of the next part of his dream on his mind.

The building of the dynamo will follow in the next story.

William Henry and Florence Starbuck Campbell

14

THE BUILDING OF A DYNAMO

When William Henry Campbell returned from Camden on Gauley Railway Station with the castings he was a happy man. Due to limited machine shops equipment, it was necessary for him to machine and fit these castings by hand. This required many hours of tedious toil, but William Henry enjoyed the challenge. Building of the cast iron was a simple task compared to the complications of making the armature and shaft and the communtator and brush holders. Much more complicated was the winding of the armature and field coils. In doing these jobs many things had to be considered. For instance, the size of wire, the number of turns of it around each coil to provide certain generating capacities without permitting the machine to "run hot" had to be predetermined. Also, adequate insulation had to be provided to prevent the machine from "burning out" in operation. With all these interesting things to be done along with the simultaneous operation of his mills, it is not surprising that William Henry Campbell found little time for eating his meals and explaining things to his neighbors of Mumble-the-Peg Creek (Muddlety).

With the assistance of his eldest son, Howard B. Campbell, by whom a considerable amount of the complicated work including the winding of the coils was done, the job of making the "dynamo" was completed. The coils were wound upon four horizontal cores that resemble large cylinder shafts across the top and bottom of the machine. Technically known as a bi-polar direct current, electrical generator, this dynamo generated sufficient electricity at 45 volts to keep the equivalent of approximately eight modern 20-watt madza bulbs burning when driven by a belt connected to a line shaft, which in turn was operated by the water wheel at the mill.

This dynamo was put into service in 1901, which caused much excitement and skeptics, who shook their heads in sincere doubt when they heard the gossip that William Henry Campbell was making the machine, came and observed the electric lights at the Campbell Mill.

With this job accomplished, William Henry Campbell turned his chief concern to the operation of the mills, the night efficiency of which was considerably increased by the improved illumination by electric lights. By this time, the four Campbell sons were growing into young boys who were curious about their father's creation of electricity for the mills. They were also helping with chores and spent some time fishing in Muddlety Creek.

Florence Starbuck Campbell was busy caring for two young daughters, cooking for her growing family and raising a vegetable garden. She saw little of her husband, William Henry, since the mills were in operation days into the night hours with the new electric lights. People were coming from all around the area with grain or wool to be processed at the Campbell Mills and to see the lights.

The next story will address the demands of extending electricity to the town of Summersville.

William Henry Campbell

The "Dynamo"

15

WILLIAM HENRY CAMPBELL'S
ELECTRICAL VENTURES

William Henry Campbell's ventures were limited to the lighting of his own properties until 1910 when he began thinking seriously of extending electrical service to the town of Summersville. The town people were eager to have the electricity, but many challenged his contentions that the demand could be established for commercial purposes.

To make that possible, it was necessary for him to build a transmission line from Muddlety Holler to Summersville, which was about two miles away. Also, more generating capacity was needed, as the small dynamo was not capable of generating any more than enough electricity to light his mill and home. Another generator was purchased by William Henry, one that was 25 kilowatt, alternating current, 2300-volt machine.

The Starbuck heirs deeded their four-fifths interest of the land to William Henry Campbell, which included 20 acres more or less on both sides of Mumble-the-Peg Creek in Summersville, Nicholas County, W.Va.

A franchise was granted to W. H. Campbell by the County Clerk of Nicholas County on Nov. 14, 1910, and of record in the Clerk's office of said county clerk in Order Book Number 6, at page 474. It granted to said W. H. Campbell, his successors and assigns for the term of 20 years with the right to enter upon and along the public roads, bridges and ways from a point near the residence of W. H. Campbell in Summersville District in said county, to the town of Summersville to construct, maintain and operate an electric lighting and distribution system.

Much work remained to be achieved with getting the poles cut and set along the two or more miles into the town of Summersville. William Dotson was hired to furnish and set the poles for the sum of one dollar ($1.00) each.

There was the financial problem for additional equipment, which faced William Henry Campbell. The small dynamo, which supplied electric current for his mill and house for the first 10 years, would need to be replaced. He was promised financial aid when he purchased the equipment and had it shipped to Camden on Gauley, but it lay there for some time when the promise of financial aid fizzled. Mr. Campbell could not even coax teamsters to haul the equipment to Summersville in exchange for a promise of electric current for their pay.

The second generator was a factory job, built by North Electric Machinery Company of St. Paul, Minnesota. It required 30 horsepower to turn the armature and the water came from the three water wheels. That was about 1910. By saving and scraping, Mr. Campbell was able to get the new equipment to the site and assembled his new plant with the 25-kilowatt, alternating current 2300-volt machine. The hand built dynamo by William Henry Campbell was retired after 10 years of service.

The dam, which O.P. Starbuck had built with the raceway to the mill to harness the waterpower from Muddlety Creek, was no longer adequate. A larger dam was built upstream of the creek so as to have more waterpower to run the turbine at the mill.

So coming down along Muddlety, there was a large rock cliff area. To get through in that area they built a 36-inch pipeline from wood. It was held together by metal bands. The concrete abutments that held the pipe are still along the Muddlety Creek. Water came down a steep hill and hit the turbine that turned the generator and ran through another channel and back to Muddlety.

After installation and completion of the electrical line to town, William Henry was ready to lead Summersville from darkness to light.

The next story will be the "First Light" in the town of Summersville.

Robert (Bob) Campbell stands on part of the cement raceway at Campbell Power Plant built by his grandfather, William Henry Campbell.

The dam on Muddlety Creek for the Campbell Power Plant, circa 1910

16

THE FIRST ELECTRIC LIGHT IN THE TOWN OF SUMMERSVILLE

After having electricity at the Campbell Mill and residence located on Muddlety Creek for about 10 years, two miles from Summersville, the franchise was in place with the county. Poles were set and lines ready to carry the electrical current to the town.

The first Nicholas County Bank, organized in 1900, rented a building on Main Street for the sum of $72 per year. In 1904, the staff decided to build, after acquiring land on the corner of Church and Main Street for $450 from owner, John A. Grose. A contract was awarded to erect a concrete block building. There was no electricity in the town, so lamps lighted the building. The directors heard about the electric lights at the Campbell Mills and wanted William Henry Campbell to furnish electricity for the Nicholas County Bank.

In 1911, Mr. Campbell was ready to install the light located on the front wall of the bank building. Plenty of debate and skepticism about whether it would burn or not was evidenced by the crowd that gathered to witness the feat of turning it on. It was nearly dark, Mr. Campbell was very tired but believed it would work and telephoned over the grounded wire party line, which ran to his mill on Muddlety and told them at the electrical plant to turn on the current. Soon afterward, the light flashed, and everyone seemed to jump back in surprise to view the first light.

After all the hard work, expense and time spent in this accomplishment, William Henry Campbell said, "I felt this was one of the big days of my life." The lines had been completed despite the many hitches and the sign, CAMPBELL ELECTRIC COMPANY, went up on the Muddlety Creek Mill.

The first light in the town of Summersville at the Nicholas County Bank building got much attention from the citizens entering the bank. They, too, wanted to have electricity in their homes and businesses.

The number of light bulbs in the building determined the customer's bill.

William Henry Campbell and his growing four sons were very busy meeting the demand, keeping the lumber, gristmills and wood carding machines in operation.

The first Nicholas County Bank building was used for about 15 years, until it was moved back from the corner to make room for a larger stone bank building. After the first bank building was moved, it was used as a grocer and feed store for many years. It is now owned and used as attorney at law offices on Church Street.

Following the four Campbell sons will be the next story.

Taken in 1906 or 1907 this picture of the old Nicholas County
Bank Building features the following: Lee Fitzwater, Oscar
Fitzwater, Drew Barrett, Harry Pettigrew, Pat Horan, Hugh
Mearns, Joseph A. Alderson, Allen Rader, Paris Herold and
Okey Mearns. The building was the site of the first electric light
in Summersville in 1911. Lee Fitzwater furnished the photo.

17

THE CAMPBELL BROTHERS

The sons of William Henry and Florence Starbuck Campbell, Howard B. and Herbert M., were young men in 1916. They were interested in establishing a business of their own in Summersville. During their youth, they had worked with their parents at the Campbell Mills and learned many valuable lessons. They were eager to pursue other interests, mainly automobiles.

In the fall of 1916, Howard B. and Herbert M. purchased the former H.C. Brock Building on Main Street. A garage was started. They sold the "Regal" the first make of a car for a short time, before taking on the Ford Agency.

When Howard B. went to the U.S. Army during World War I in August 1917 and brother, Herbert M., was also in the Army, they had their Uncle Fielding Starbuck operate the garage. Both brothers paid for the garage with their pay from serving in the Army.

The Campbell Brothers Garage, as it was known, sold the Ford car through the Yew Pine Inn Agency in Richwood for French Herold from 1910 to 1924, at which time they acquired the Ford Franchise for themselves.

The four Campbell brothers, Howard B., Herbert M., Russell H., and Eugene L. all served in the Army during World War I. Howard and Eugene both served in France, while Herbert and Russell remained in the United States.

Eugene L., the younger brother, could drive a car, so he had the position of driver for his commanding officer while in France. On one occasion, Eugene and the officer traveled to a destination on a road that forked. Neither knew which road to take but chose the road they thought would take them to the destination. It was a wise choice, as an explosion happened on the road not chosen. They considered themselves very fortunate.

The four brothers were honorably discharged and returned to Nicholas County when the World War I was over in 1918. Howard B. and Herbert M. resumed the management of the Campbell Brothers Garage. Not many cars were in use, or could many people afford to own a car at that time. Main Street was a dirt road, very muddy in the wintertime. The town used much broken stone on the street, which in the summertime was very rough. Since brick was locally made and there were some brick side walks, but mostly large flat stones that were hauled from the river and placed in front of businesses like Campbell Brothers Garage. In 1923, the State Road Commission let a contract to hard surface Main Street from the west corporate limits to the east corporate limits.

Eugene L. Campbell and Okey Ward served in the Army. Upon their return home in Nicholas County, they established the first "silent movie" theater, CASINO THEATER, located upstairs in a building (about where the Radio Station is located) on Main Street. According to a 1919 Chronicle, they installed a "new engine" to give their patrons a live, clean show. Grace Lee Evans was the piano player for the silent films. Some of the movies of that period shown in the Casino Theater were: The Games Up, Winner Takes All, The Lion Man, A Tough Tenderfoot (Western) and One-Reel Comedies. The Diamond Queen, Saddle King and Tick, Tick Man were shown on December 7, 1921. Eugene L. Campbell sold his interest to Okey V. Ward who continued in the theater business as the Ward Theater.

Eugene L. Campbell attended Marshall for a short period before he helped his father, William Henry Campbell operate and expand Campbell Electric Company Hydro-Electric Plant on Muddlety Creek. The demand to serve many more customers with electricity had increased rapidly.

Pfc. Eugene L. Campbell Hq. Co. 313 Field Artillery World War I, circa 1917-18

Sgt. Howard B. Campbell 1917-18 World War I

18

FLOODING OF MUDDLETY CREEK

In 1918, Muddlety Creek was the highest as it had been known, with two bridges swept away, the Jones Bridge on the Webster side and the bridge at William Henry Campbell's Mill. The destruction of these bridges cut off mail and other travel between Summersville and Camden-on-Gauley, except by way of the bridges across Muddlety at H.W. Herold's and the "twin churches." A number of other bridges across smaller streams in the county were destroyed.

According to the Nicholas Chronicle, the damage done to the roads, bridges and public and private property was estimated at a conservative figure of $1 million. The effects of the flood were felt for many months. No papers or parcel post reached Summersville from the C and O Railroad; very little first-class mail arrived from Camden-on-Gauley Route daily. The carrier went by the way of Mr. William Henry Campbell's place, where they crossed Muddlety Creek in a small skiff, which Mr. Campbell constructed. The county road between Swiss and Belva in the lower end of the county was practically demolished. Putting the road in shape with gravel was rushed for travel in that direction. The C and O train was unable to complete the run.

A new bridge across Muddlety at William Henry Campbell's Mill was later completed. The bridge is about two feet higher than the old bridge, which washed away in the flood. Jones Bridge was rebuilt later. Richwood was also flooded with the railroad bridges washed out.

Muddlety Valley and Muddlety Creek had a long history of flooding, but the flood of 1918 affected much of Nicholas County.

A flood swollen Muddlety Creek rushes under Jones Bridge on June 11, 1922. Standing on the bridge are the Campbell brothers.

The Campbell brothers watch as high water rushes under the bridge over Muddlety Creek at Campbell Mill and Power Plant on June 11, 1922.

19

CAMPBELL ELECTRIC COMPANY INSTALLS NEW POWER PLANT – 1923

(The following appeared on the front page of The Nicholas Chronicle, June 7, 1923)

Believing it to be of great interest not only to the people of Summersville but to the County generally, we interviewed the Campbell Electric Company as the new electric plant which they are preparing to install in order to furnish ample power and light to this town and its vicinity.

Upon making investigation, we were surprised at the magnitude of this enterprise and most certainly congratulate Mr. W. H. Campbell and son, Eugene L., who compose the Campbell Electric Company, for their progressiveness and farsightedness and at the same time, feel we must congratulate the people of Summersville in getting an up to date electric plant, which would do credit to many towns of several thousand population.

The new plant, which will cost from $12,000 to $15,000, has been contracted for, and the preliminary work will commence next week and the entire plant will be installed and in operation about December 1st, if possible, so as to have the new service available during the coming winter.

The turbine is one of the most modern pieces of machinery for the utilization of waterpower and is known as a horizontal turbine. It is to be built and installed by the James Leiffiel and Company of Springfield, Ohio, who are probably the largest builders of turbine wheels in the United States. It is a steel turbine encased in steel and will operate under 36 foot head of water through a 32-inch pipe. The new turbine will develop power to generate more than three times the amount of electricity now being generated by the present plant, and it will, therefore, be seen that the Company has confidence in the growth of Summersville and in the development of the County as they are preparing to install a plant which will take care of the electrical needs of a town of 2,500 people or more as this installation is being made in such a way that an additional unit can be installed without undue expense when conditions demand it.

Water for running the plant will be stored in a dam in Muddlety Creek, a short distance below Jones' Bridge on the Webster Road and from the dam will be carried partly in an open mill race and partly through a large wood pipe three feet in diameter, to a point above the turbine wheel. The total distance from the dam to the powerhouse will be approximately one-half mile.

The Campbell Electric Company will be of modern design. The turbine and generator will be placed on large steel beams and on a concrete foundation, so as to have the utmost stability and freeness from vibration.

The new plant although generating over three times as much electricity as the present plant, will use about the same amount of water and with added storage facilities for water, it is not anticipated that there will be any interruption of service on account of dry weather, but even the possibility of interruption has been provided against as they have also arranged to install auxiliary power in the form of a large engine to be used in case the water at any time should be too low to operate the new plant.

It is needless to say that the present business alone would not justify this large expenditure but looking to the future and realizing the possibility of expansion in the use of electric current, the Campbells feel that they are fully justified in increasing this large expense at this time and as they are sound business men and conservative, we have confidence that their view is correct.

We are also informed that immediately upon the installation of the new plant, the hours of service will be extended to the entire 24 hours.

It is anticipated at first, however, the service will be furnished from about four o'clock a.m. to 12 midnight without interruption and in sufficient quantity to allow the use of motors and electric power, as well as lighting facilities.

The use of electric washing machines, vacuum cleaners, electric stoves, irons and many other household devices has grown enormously in the last few years and such use will of course, grow here when the current is available.

The installation of the new plant will also open the way for light manufacturing and the use of the current in many ways not now anticipated, and therefore, with the growth of the town, and we have confidence that it will grow rapidly as we believe that Summersville is entering upon a new era, there will, no doubt, be established many new enterprises, which are not now anticipated.

The uses of electricity are so numerous that it would be almost impossible to name all of them. A small electric motor in many instances is not larger than the fist of an average person, will run many kinds of light machines and larger motors are capable of running the largest and most complicated machinery. In this modern day, amongst the uses of electricity, we might mention that nearly all commercial ice cream is frozen in freezers operated by electricity; laundries are largely operated in the same manner, and even shoe repairing machines are used in many places, the most intricate repairs are made, "while you wait." Planers, lathes, drills and other machines used in working in both wood and metal are now almost universally operated by individual motors. The household labor saving devices as operated are legion and range from small electric hair curling iron, so essential to the modern girl, up to the most complicated electric range capable, of boiling, baking and frying and other forms of cooking, all at the same time. Even modern bakeries are using electricity and electric baking systems, are seen in various parts of our larger cities. The new plant will make all these modern forms available, and we hope that the enterprise of the Campbells will be appreciated by the people taking advantage of the current to save labor and increase their efficiency both in the house and in business whereever possible.

To show we have faith in all that way, we will conclude by saying that this paper will arrange to operate all of its machinery by electric current as soon as it is available for us.

Wood and metal wheels that were used at the Campbell's Hydro-electric Power Plant

20

CAMPBELL – GROVES MARRIAGE

July 20, 1923 Eugene Leslie Campbell, son of William Henry and Florence Starbuck Campbell, married Edna Hall Groves, daughter of M. R. and Rebecca Bays Groves. The wedding took place in Huntington, W.Va., at the home of Dr. Robert and Etta Starbuck Petty.

The couple established their home in two rooms on the right side of the Campbell Electric Power Plant on Muddlety Creek near Summersville. Electricity was generated on the other side of the building. There was constant noise of wheels turning to generate electricity. One of the two rooms was a kitchen and the other room was a combination bedroom-living room.

Eugene remained close by at all times to check on the controls and the generator to make sure all was in operation. Electrical power was furnished from 4 a.m. to 10 p.m. When the power generating was stopped about 15 minutes before 10 p.m., there would be two or three flickers of the lights to warn the customers that power would be cut off for the night.

As time permitted from the operation of Campbell Electric Company, Eugene L. Campbell wired and installed electrical systems to homes and businesses.

With no conveniences other than electricity, Edna Campbell kept their apartment as good as possible in the two rooms. On April 18, 1924, a son, William Eugene Campbell was born in the small apartment at the Electric Power Plant. Dr. F. H. Brown Sr. was the attending physician.

About two years later, another son, Robert Burns Campbell, was born on Feb. 16, 1926, with the same attending physician, Dr. Brown.

The first radio enjoyed by the Campbell family was a 1923 Atwater-Kent Model 10 C Breadboard Radio (Open Set).

Mrs. Campbell was busy keeping house and caring for the two young sons, making sure that Billy didn't go near Muddlety Creek.

Eugene and his father, William Henry Campbell, were very involved with the expansion and the operation of the new and larger hydroelectric plant.

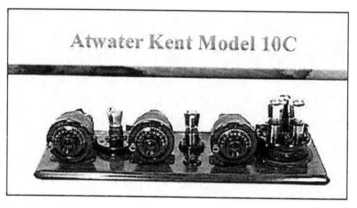

The first radio enjoyed by the Campbell family was a 1923 Atwater-Kent Model 10 C Breadboard Radio (Open Set).

Eugene L. Campbell II, part owner of
Campbell Hydroelectric Company

Edna H. Groves Campbell married July
20, 1923, to Eugene L. Campbell

21

HOWARD BLACKBURN CAMPBELL

After returning from serving in World War I, Howard and brother, Herbert, resumed operation of the Campbell Brothers' Garage on Main Street, Summersville. Their uncle, Fielding Starbuck, managed the garage while they were in the army until 1918. The garage was known in 1920 as the Summersville Garage. In their newspaper ad, they claimed, "Campbells can fix it" on any repair work.

In January 1922, the town basketball team met the Nicholas High School team at the Summersville Garage for a basketball game to entertain a large number of fans. Eugene L. Campbell, brother of Howard, was the star of the afternoon game. Others on the town team were F. Bell, W. Dorsey, J. Burr, R. White, S. Groves and R. Wiseman.

Howard B. Campbell, son of William Henry and Florence Starbuck Campbell, married Catherine Rebecca Damron (born 8-21-1892), daughter of Robert O. and Mary Jane Gordon Damron of Kentucky. They moved into the S. F. Dixson building on Main Street in 1924. Later, Howard and Catherine Campbell moved into the former Skaggs Hotel building on Main Street. They rented rooms but didn't operate hotel services.

Howard Campbell established an electrical and sales business in the front part of the building on Main Street. He only needed to hear "It can't be fixed." With determination, he could repair or fix any appliance. Many customers brought radios to his shop to have tubes tested or replaced.

In 1930, Howard B. Campbell served as mayor of Summersville and served as recorder from 1934–1939. He was an active member of the Methodist Church, a Sunday school teacher, member and past grand master of the Masonic Lodge and Order of Eastern Star. He served as president of Nicholas County Court, taught in the trade school at Richwood and Nicholas County High Schools. Howard and brother, Herbert, continued with the garage business until Herbert died in 1954. Howard continued with the Ford and Mercury business. Howard's favorite pastime activity was to operate the wrecker service. The challenge gave him much satisfaction. In his late years, Howard liked to retrieve lost golf balls from the golf course pond at Memorial Park.

Howard and Catherine Campbell were the parents of three children: Joan (born March 26, 1925), married David Lewis of Indianapolis, Ind.; Mary Elizabeth (born Oct. 16, 1926) married William Adams; and James Howard Campbell (born May 5, 1929 and died April 21, 1999). They also have three grandchildren: Beverly Diane (born Oct. 12, 1951), David Allen Campbell (born June 24, 1954), and Christopher Adams (born April 25, 1969).

Catherine Damron Campbell was known about Summersville for growing pretty flowers and wearing lovely hats. She was a charming lady, active in the United Methodist Church, Order of the Eastern Star, Mt. Azalea Garden club and the D.A.R.

Howard died July 5, 1970 and Catherine Campbell passed away at the age of 91 on April 4, 1983. Both are resting in the Walker Memorial Park Cemetery.

Howard Blackburn Campbell 9-23-1890 – 7-5-1970

Herold Home 1917-18 Pictured, from the left: Etta Starbuck, Ellen Herold Starbuck, Howard B. Campbell, Henry Herold, Florence Starbuck Campbell, and Mrs. Henry Herold

1963 WV Centennial Parade Summersville Pictured in the background are Martha Campbell, R.B. Campbell Sr., Bobby Campbell, and Harry Taka. Riding in the 1911 Ford, owned by Howard Campbell, front row, Judy Epling, Howard B. Campbell; back row, Catherine Campbell and Gladys Vaught, representing the D.A.R.

22
CAMPBELL ELECTRIC FRANCHISES

William Henry Campbell was granted a franchise by the county court of Nicholas County on Nov. 14, 1910, recorded in the clerk's office of said county, Order Book No. 6, page 474. It granted W. H. Campbell, his successors and assigns, for the term of 20 years, with the right to enter upon and along the public roads, bridges and ways from a point near the residence of said W. H. Campbell in Summersville District in said County, to the Town of Summersville to construct, maintain and to operate an electric lighting and distribution system.

That certain franchise granted to Campbell Electric Company by the County Court of said Nicholas County on May 16, 1927, and of record in said County Clerk's office in Order Book No. 12, page 252, to construct, maintain and operate an electric lighting and distribution system upon and over all the county roads in Summersville District of said County.

That certain franchise granted said Campbell Electric Company by the County Court of Nicholas County on the 5th day of May, 1930, for the term of 50 years, granting the right and privilege to construct, maintain and operate an electric lighting and distribution system, upon, over and along the public roads and highways in said County under the jurisdiction and control of said Court.

All that certain electric light and power plant generating current for the said Town of Summersville and territory adjacent thereto and surrounding the same, and all structures, dams, water races, engines, boilers, wires, fixtures, appliances, appurtenances, and equipment, there unto belonging, located in and adjacent to said Town of Summersville, and all those certain transmission systems, consisting of poles, wires, cross-arms, and fixtures owned by the party of first part, and located and maintained in said Nicholas County, and more particularly located in said Town of Summersville and in the territory immediately adjacent thereto, together with the electric distribution system owned by the party of the first part and located in said Town of Summersville, including all transformers, switch board, towers, poles, wires, insulators, conduits, connections, materials, service connections, appliances, and all other property forming a part of or appertaining to or used in the street lighting system and owned by the Town of Summersville together with all rights-of-way, easements, tunnels, permits, privileges, franchises, contracts, agreements, and rights for the construction, maintenance or operation thereof, and generally any and all other equipment of any kind whatsoever installed, used or intended to be used, or being a part of the aforesaid lighting and distribution system including the rights of the first party in and to all contracts with consumers for electric power or electric current and likewise including all office furniture and fixtures, and all leases upon or leasehold estates in any building or buildings or other property held by the party of the first part and located in or near the Town of Summersville.

The greater part of the aforesaid properties was granted to the first party by William H. Campbell and others, by deed bearing date March 31, 1930, and of record in Clerk's office of the County Court of said Nicholas County.

The dreams of producing electricity with a handmade dynamo, later updated with larger generator to meet the public demand for electricity and securing franchises to bring electric current to the Town of Summersville were challenging for William Henry Campbell who had a limited education but made a dream a reality.

Starbuck-Campbell House on Muddlety Creek
and early power plant buildings

23

HERBERT MATHENEY CAMPBELL

About 1920 when Anthony Rader was mayor of Summersville and electric lights were installed in the kitchen and hallways of Nicholas High School, the Summersville Garage, operated by brothers Howard and Herbert Campbell, was receiving attention. After World War I ended in 1918, the automobile was being used by those who could afford the horseless carriage. The roads were very rough and the cars needed repairs at a garage.

Herbert Matheney Campbell, born May 30, 1892, son of William Henry and Florence Starbuck Campbell, was interested in automobiles, unlike his brother, Eugene, who followed his father, William Henry Campbell's interest in electricity.

Howard B. and Herbert M. Campbell bought the property in partnership from C. H. Brock with their World War I Army pay. The first make of car sold was "Regal" before taking on the Ford dealership. The original building, built in 1914, was changed in appearance several times.

The Ford garage was at its peak about 1948-49 when more than 20 people were employed. After World War II, automobiles were in demand and in short supply. There was a waiting list of customers for a new car.

Herbert M. Campbell, being civic minded, supported the Lions' Club and the Nicholas County High School Band. Whenever a new model was available, the Campbell Brothers

Garage employed the NCHS Band to lead a big parade on Main Street, Summersville. It always brought out large crowds of people to view the new cars.

Herbert, a courteous gentleman, tipped his hat to the ladies while puffing on a cigar. He was known by the local citizens as Hub Campbell and his nieces and nephews called him Uncle Hub.

As a Summersville town councilman in 1923, Herbert continued to support the city in many generous ways. A member of Memorial United Methodist Church, Herbert served on the building committee for the church from 1948 until 1950. The red brick church on Webster Road is still an attractive building with an active congregation.

Herbert Matheney Campbell died at 62 in a Charleston hospital of renal failure, Dec. 1, 1954. He rests at the Walker Memorial Cemetery, Summersville with a World War I military marker.

Howard B. Campbell continued to operate the Ford-Mercury dealership and garage for several years.

Circa 1918-20 Campbell Brothers Garage Summersville Garage, Lincoln — Ford — Fordson Tractors

Herbert M. Campbell, 1940 — Campbell Brothers Garage

1920 — Campbell Brothers Garage, Main Street, Summersville

Herbert M. Campbell May 30, 1892 – Dec. 1, 1954

24

THE CAMPBELL SISTERS

After having four sons (Howard, Herbert, Russell, and Eugene) William Henry and Florence Starbuck Campbell welcomed a daughter, Lottie Jean, born Dec. 27, 1897 at the residence near the Campbell Electric Power Plant on Muddlety near Summersville, W.Va.

When Lottie Jean was almost 3 years old, a sister, Anna Elizabeth, was born on Oct. 20, 1900.

The daughters were taught the social graces by their mother, Florence, as they grew and developed into young ladies. They attended public schools and were active in girls' basketball when they attended Nicholas County High School in 1917-1918.

Lottie Jean attended schools in Summersville, Charleston, and Huntington, West Virginia and Colorado College in Colorado Springs. She married Carl Herman Fletcher on June 26, 1940 in Asheville, N.C. They lived in Chelsea, Mich., where Carl was employed by the A & P Company. Later, they moved to Asheville to be close to Lottie Jean's parents. Carl and Lottie Jean enjoyed fishing and spent the winter months near St. Petersburg, Fla. They had no children. Carl and Lottie Jean delighted in visiting relatives in Summersville. Carl liked to play Santa Claus at Christmastime for Lottie Jean's great-nieces and great-nephews.

Lottie Jean Campbell Fletcher died in Asheville on Jan. 21, 1989. The burial was in Lewis Memorial Park, Asheville.

Anna Elizabeth Campbell attended college, became a teacher, and taught in Virginia where she met and married her husband, Ray McClure. They had a son, Douglas McClure, born Feb. 14, 1939. He was a bright little boy who enjoyed spending some time in the summer with relatives in Summersville. When Douglas was about 6 years old, on Oct. 17, 1945, his life ended when he was hit by a car. Mother, Elizabeth, was devastated by the loss of her only child. After the divorce from McClure, she continued to reside in Asheville and taught school. Later, Elizabeth went to Spokane, Wash., to be near her brother, Russell. She met her second husband, Wendall Gage. They adopted a pretty baby girl named Jean Elizabeth. They spent time in Spokane and later moved to Asheville where Elizabeth taught elementary school, raised her daughter, Jeannie, who married Rick Fleming and they gave Elizabeth three grandchildren. Elizabeth died Nov. 3, 1990, in Asheville where she rests at Lewis Memorial Park.

Lottie Jean Campbell (Dec. 27, 1897 – Jan. 21, 1989) married Carl Fletcher

**Elizabeth Campbell Gage (Oct. 20, 1900 – Nov. 3, 1990)
with son Douglas McClure (Feb. 14, 1939 – Oct. 17, 1945)**

25

CAMPBELL GRANDSONS BORN AT CAMPBELL ELECTRIC POWER PLANT

In the two-room apartment at the Campbell Hydro-Electric plant building, on April 18, 1924, a son, William Eugene Campbell, was born to Edna Groves and Eugene Leslie Campbell. The baby was delivered by Dr. F. H. Brown Sr. The grandparents were William Henry and Florence Starbuck Campbell who also resided in a house near the Electric Power Plant. The maternal grandparents were M.R. and Rebecca Bays Groves who resided on a farm near Nettie.

Almost two years later, another son, Robert Burns Campbell, was born in the small two-room apartment on Feb. 16, 1926, and was also delivered at home by Dr. F.H. Brown, Sr.

With the generators running most of the time, there was always noise being heard in the small apartment. The young boys must have gotten accustomed to the turning of wheels and learned to sleep with all the activity about the Power Plant. Eugene was busy making sure all ran smoothly so as to produce enough electricity to meet the growing demand.

Early settlers knew the importance of locating near water. So was the case with the Starbucks and Campbells who located on the banks of Muddlety. The stream was plentiful enough for the mills and clean and pure for the families' laundry.

William Henry, a quiet, thinking man, liked to play pranks on his wife, Florence. On washday, Florence dipped buckets of water from the cool stream of water to fill a washtub, situated over a fire of small logs to heat the water. She used a washboard to scrub the clothes in the warm water. After lathering the soiled garments with homemade lye soap, Florence started to rub down the washboard to the water. She felt a tingle in her hands and jumped away from the tub. Again, she assumed the scrubbing position and another tingle appeared. As she looked toward the mill, she saw her husband, William Henry, chuckle to himself. The she knew he had wired the washtub with an electric current produced by a magneto.

Edna Campbell also did the Campbell laundry by the same method, but no pranks were played on her during washday.

As the Campbell boys, Billy and Bobby, grew, they played about in the yard with a petal car made by their father, Eugene. Billy and Bobby had a wagon to pull and ride in. They liked to play on the big flat rocks near Muddlety Creek. They were warned and carefully watched to keep away from the water.

While living at the Hydro- Electric Plant apartment, it was a treat to go a couple miles to downtown Summersville to visit their cousins, Joan and Mary Elizabeth Campbell, children of Howard B. and Catherine Campbell. On this day, as they were getting ready to return home, Bobby ran across the street to the car when called and was hit by moving automobile driven by Mr. Leo Vogel from Pittsburgh, Pa. who was passing through town. Uncle Howard Campbell ran to Bobby and carried him to Dr. F.H. Brown's office, located upstairs of the Nicholas County Bank. Eugene Campbell followed closely behind his injured son to the doctor. The head injury was stitched and bandaged so the family could return to their apartment on Muddlety.

Bobby felt much pain, but soon fell asleep in his bed. He recovered, but to this day, displays a large scar on the top of his head. Mr. Vogel kept vigil until he knew the injured little boy would be okay. For many years following the accident, Mr. Vogel sent gifts and cards to Bobby. He continued to keep in touch by phone until he passed away. He, too, felt the pain of the accident of 1930 in Summersville.

Bobby Campbell in his pedal car and Billy Campbell in his wagon near Muddlety Creek, circa 1929-30

1930, Billy, Joan, Mary E., and Bobby Campbell: This photo was taken before Bobby was hit by a car. The St. Nicholas Hotel is in the background.

1930, Billy and Bobby Campbell on a rock near the Campbell Hydro-electric Plant on the banks of Muddlety Creek

26

CAMPBELL ELECTRIC COMPANY SOLD TO WEST VIRGINIA PUBLIC SERVICE CO.

The "torchbearers" as Campbell Electric Company was referred to, for bringing electricity to the town of Summersville, was well established by 1930, with a 50-year franchise in place. The founder and creator of the Electric Power Plant, William Henry Campbell, was getting older and depended more on his partner and son, Eugene L. Campbell, to take charge of the Company.

In 1927, a Fairbanks Morse, 100 horse-power fuel oil burning engine was purchased and installed to the Electric Power Plant to function as an auxiliary to the water driven equipment during peak load intervals, low water periods and when it was necessary to take the water driven equipment out of service for repairs. The demand for electricity continued to grow in Summersville, as customers could purchase small appliances.

Monongahela Power Company was expanding close to the area. An offer was made to purchase the Campbell Electric Company Hydro-Electric Plant.

William Henry and son Eugene L. Campbell, parties of the first part, agreed to sell to West Virginia Service Company on the 31st day of March 1930, the party of the second part.

The parties of the first part did grant, convey, sell, assign, transfer, release, set over and confirm unto the party of the second part, and its successors and assigns forever all and every singular properties, real, personal and mixed assessments, franchises and other rights, which the parties of the first part in the conduct of The Campbell Electric Company now owned.

The parties of the first part (Campbell Electric Company) hereby agree to execute such further assurances of and for said properties and appurtenances as may be requisite to make the title thereto of the party of the second part, its successors and assigns, sure and complete forever.

William H. Campbell (seal)

Florence E. Campbell (seal)

Eugene L. Campbell (seal)

Edna Campbell (seal)

Mr. A. N. Breckinridge, Notary Public and Attorney of Nicholas County, witnessed the signatures on the 31st of March 1930.

William Henry and Florence Campbell moved that year to Staunton, Va., to enjoy much earned retirement.

Eugene L. Campbell continued to work for Monongahela Power Company for a while longer at the former Campbell Electric Power Plant. Eugene and Edna Campbell moved their family of two sons to a newly purchased home on Webster Road in Summersville.

The main building of the Summersville Power Plant, housing the oil engine, furnished most of the operating power.

**Florence and William Henry Campbell at their Staunton, Va.,
home in the 1930s after their retirement from the Power Plant**

27

THE ELECTRICAL PIONEER DIED

Florence and William Henry Campbell spent the winter months in Florida and returned to their residence in Staunton, Va., during the summer for a few years,
They sold the Staunton property and moved to Asheville, N.C. where they resided on Normandy Road until William Henry Campbell died Sept. 26, 1947 at the age of 89.

William Henry Campbell was a member of Summersville Lodge No. 76 and the First Presbyterian Church of Asheville. Survivors included his wife, Florence Starbuck Campbell; four sons, Howard, Herbert and Eugene L. Campbell of Summersville, Russell Campbell of Spokane, Wash.; two daughters, Lottie Jean Fletcher and Elizabeth McClure Gage of Asheville, N.C.; a sister, Minnie Shreve of Burnsville, W.Va., and six grandchildren and one great-grandchild; nieces and nephews. The service was conducted at First Presbyterian Church and interment was made in Lewis Memorial Park, Asheville.

Florence Elizabeth Starbuck Campbell was active in the Methodist Episcopal Church, South when she and husband, William Henry lived in Summersville. The pulpit chairs presently used in Memorial United Methodist Church were purchased by Florence Campbell circa 1898. She was a member and Past Worthy Matron of Wakoma Chapter #2 Order of the Eastern Star in Summersville.

After the death of her husband, William Henry, Florence resided with daughter, Elizabeth Gage of Spokane, Wash., where she died July 3, 1954, at the age of 90. Services were held in Asheville. She was survived by her children, Lottie Jean Fletcher, Elizabeth Gage, Howard B., Herbert M., Eugene L. and Russell Campbell; two sisters, Etta Starbuck Houston and Virginia Starbuck Cotton; seven grandchildren and six greatgrandchildren. Florence and William Henry Campbell were interned at Lewis Memorial Park, Asheville.

The creator of the original Power Plant and his wife contributed much to Nicholas County by the way of their grist and lumber mills, carding machines and most of all the electricity to the people of Summersville.

The name of William Henry Campbell is recorded in the History of Nicholas County by W.S. Brown. The Richwood Publishing Company printed an impressive story on Nicholas County Pioneers in December 1937, named W.H. CAMPBELL: ELECTRICIAN and J.A. MEARNS: EARLY MERCHANT. There were numerous stories printed in newspapers during the 1930s and 1940s about William Henry Campbell's accomplishments in bringing electricity to the area.

A reader of the Passage of Time stated that the people of Nicholas County and Summersville, "owe a lot to the Starbucks and Campbells," the pioneers who led the way to advancement in Nicholas County from the banks of Mumble-the-Peg (Muddlety). After serving as a "hub" of activity, Muddlety has returned to nature with pristine beauty of water, rocks, and trees with the quiet sounds of nature all about the walking trails that were established in 2001.

Like those who lived, worked, invented, and spent most of their life on the Banks of Muddlety, they, too are at rest.

After serving as a "hub" of activity, Muddlety has
returned to nature with pristine beauty of water, rocks,
and trees with the quiet sounds of nature all about
the walking trails that were established in 2001.

28

NEW HOME – NEW BABY – NEW SCHOOL

After the sale of Campbell Hydro-Electric Business and property, Eugene L. Campbell, co-owner of the Power Plant with his father, William Henry Campbell, moved his family to newly purchased property on Webster Road. Eugene and wife, Edna, were happy to be in their first house away from the noise and activity in the two-room apartment within the Power Plant. The house was a small two-bedroom house, no indoor plumbing but with some remodeling and new furnishings. It was a comfortable home. The heat was supplied by a coal-burning stove, as was the source of heat for most homes in Summersville in the 1930s.

A well-known man by the name of Thomas O. "The Farmer" Reynolds was a dinner guest of Eugene and Edna Campbell in their home on Webster Road. While sitting on the front porch, Farmer Reynolds, a great naturalist, said to Mr. Campbell, "Law me, neighbor, you wouldn't put a price on that tree." The large three-trunk oak tree, unusual in appearance, stood in the front yard.

Eugene continued to assist the new owners of the Power Plant for a year or two. A few months after moving into their new home, a daughter, Carolyn Sue Campbell, was born on Dec. 9, 1930. Her brothers were 6-year-old Bill and 4-year-old Bobby.

Carolyn Sue was delivered by the same physician as her brothers, Dr. F. H. Brown of Summersville.

A desire to further his education in electrical engineering, Eugene moved his family to an apartment near Takoma Park, Washington D.C. where he enrolled in Bliss Electrical School in the fall of 1933. The sons, Billy and Bobby, enrolled in elementary school in Takoma Park. Billy went to third grade while Bobby was a second grader. They walked from home to the school.

The father, Eugene L. Campbell, worked and studied to learn as much as possible in the intense courses while at Bliss Electrical School, which was highly recognized in the field of electricity.

In the spring of 1934, the Campbell family was anticipating graduation for Eugene in June. The young boys had quite an experience in the large Takoma Park School.

June 5, 1934, Bliss Electrical School graduation, was a day happily celebrated by the Campbells. Billy, Bobby and mother, Edna, attended the ceremony. The young sons were concerned when their father, Eugene, didn't appear with the other graduates. Billy told Bobby, "Dad must have failed! He isn't here." Later, a small group of men took their place on stage and Eugene was among the group of men. These men were recognized as the Honor Students. Eugene L. Campbell received the honor as the "Best with Electrical Wiring."

With school and graduation behind them, the Campbell family returned to Nicholas County, West Virginia, to a great disappointment.

Bobby Campbell

Billy Campbell

29

FIRST HOME RAZED BY FIRE

While Eugene L. and Edna Campbell were away for a year in Takoma Park, Washington, D.C., they rented their home in Summersville to an employee of West Penn Power Plant, formerly the Campbell Hydro-Electric Company.

A passerby noticed fire or smoke from the back of the house. The man stopped, broke out a window, pulled on a rug and was able to get a reed rocking chair, a bookcase, floor lamp and a telephone table through the broken window, set the items away from the burning house and drove away. His name was never known.

It wasn't known how the volunteer firemen learned of the fire, but they pulled the water tank on wooden, five feet in diameter wheels from near the center of town for about one mile to the location of the burning house. The wooden wheel cart had a steel tongue by which it was guided and pulled. A large rope was tied to the tongue for the firemen to pull by. The cart had a large drum or reel upon which the hose was carried.

The inadequate water supply necessitated a bucket brigade from across the road. Before moving to Takoma Park, Billy and Bobby Campbell built a small dam in the creek across the road from the house. The dam of water supplied buckets of water to save the nearby garage, but the house was a total loss. The fire occurred on February 5th, 1934, while the Campbell Family lived in Takoma Park.

After Eugene Campbell's Graduation from Bliss Electrical School, the family returned to Nicholas County to live with Edna Groves Campbell's parents, M.R. and Rebecca Bays Groves, in their farmhouse on O'Dell Town Road near Nettie. It was starting over and a very difficult time for the family as their first home and contents were lost in the house fire on Webster Rd

Bobby and Billy Campbell walked about two miles to a one-room school. This was quite a contrast from attending a big city elementary school the previous year in Takoma Park, Washington, D.C. The young boys learned a lot from the older boys, some good and also not-so-good things.

Little sister, Carolyn, stayed at home with her mother and grandmother, as she wasn't old enough to attend school, only as a guest of her brothers on a special occasion.

Eugene L. Campbell started to get things in place to build a new house as soon as the fire insurance claim was settled. As work progressed with the new house, Eugene stayed through the week in the garage, which had been spared from the fire. Elzie Boso and son, Ted Boso were employed to do much of the building. Eugene wanted to build a new house that would not burn down, so he chose to use metal lathe and less wood in the main construction of the house.

While at the Grandparents farm, Billy and Bobby learned to help with the farm chores in caring for the animals and to help with a vegetable garden.

For two years while the new house was under construction, the Campbell Family resided at the farm. The winters were very cold, and the snow got deep for the walk to the one-room school, but the young boys cherished the experience.

30

THE MOVE HOME AND TO MILITARY SCHOOL

The new house was finished for the Campbell Family to move into about 1936. Since all previous furnishings were destroyed in the fire of the first home, all furniture and appliances were purchased to fit the new house. It was an exciting time for the three young children to move from the Grandparent's farmhouse to a new house in town and to have their own room. A bathroom was a welcomed treat after two years without running water and inside plumbing.

Eugene and Edna Campbell were busy with smaller details in making the new house a home for the family. Eugene started working shiftwork for the Electric-Hydro Power Plant near Hawks Nest on Route 60.

The three children attended Arbuckle Grade School in Summersville. The school bus didn't transport the in-town students, so the walk to the school for the Campbell children was more than a mile each way. Before going to school, Billy and Bobby had a morning paper route, which required getting up early to pass the papers, return home for breakfast and clean up for school. Edna packed lunches for the children as well as for her husband, Eugene. In the evening after school, there were chores to do at home.

In the 1930's and 40's, most families who lived in the town of Summersville raised a garden and kept chickens for the eggs and to eat for Sunday Dinner. Also, most everyone kept a cow either on their property or rented pasture from someone close by. Those who had neither cows nor chickens would buy milk, butter and eggs from those who had them to sell. There were no refrigerated trucks for home deliveries in Summersville. It was a common practice for each house to also keep a pig or hog in a pen in the back yard. Butchering day was usually in November.

Eugene planted an apple orchard, which he was proud to watch grow into producing apple trees. Bobby and Billy delivered apples in the pull-wagon to the customers upon request for a few cents. They also had a pony to help with plowing and hauling hay from the field to the barn. There were only push lawn mowers and no garden tractors. Those chores required both animal and manpower.

Carolyn attended Arbuckle Grade School, played in the Toy Band and served as Drum Major under the leadership of the teacher, Blanch McCoy Summers. Arbuckle School was closed in 1939 and the students attended the Summersville Grade School, a red brick building near the high school.

After attending Arbuckle School, Bob attended the eighth grade at the new Summersville Grade School in 1939-40. Billy went to the Greenbrier Military School in Lewisburg in 1939 for four years of high school.

Billy graduated from Greenbrier Military School with honors in 1943. Bobby attended Greenbrier Military School from 1940-44, and graduated with honors. Both Campbell boys were servers in the mess hall and were active on the Rifle Team. At first they were homesick but realized going to military school offered them many advantages.

It was a special day when a package of their Mother's cookies and candy arrived at the school. They were usually shared with the other boys.

Parents could visit on special occasions, mostly on Sunday for the drills and dress parades. A well-stuffed picnic basket brought by parents was a delight for the growing boys.

Bill and Bob were accustomed to drills, military discipline and wearing a uniform, as they knew what faced them upon graduation. They also knew that a continuing education would be on hold for some time in their future.

Greenbrier Military School — 1943
Pictured left to right: Robert B. Campbell Sr., Edna G. Campbell,
Eugene L. Campbell (Parents) and William E. Campbell

31

CAMPBELL BROTHERS
WORLD WAR II SERVICE

The War had escaladed in Europe and also in the Pacific Theater by Dec. 7, 1941. Every healthy young man at the age of 18 was drafted to serve in the military. Those who wanted to serve in the Navy, Air Corps or Marines volunteered before the draft board called them to report.

When the Japanese bombed Pearl Harbor, President Franklin D. Roosevelt declared war to end the aggression. The country went into defense mode, serving in any patriotic way. There were practice blackouts for any unwelcome air raids, rationing of most supplies and essentials.

Families knew that sons would have to serve and young husbands, too. In some families, all sons, if able, served in the military, perhaps five or more from large families. Some women volunteered in WACS, WAVES, Marines as nurses, clerks, or where needed.

William Eugene Campbell, upon Greenbrier Military School Graduation went to the Army as a sergeant and received training in Ft. Knox, Kentucky in 1943. After further training at the University of Missouri, he was a section leader in Company L, 254th Regiment, 63rd Infantry Division and served in Europe, where he was captured by the Germans, kept as a prisoner for about six weeks.

William Eugene was reported MISSING IN ACTION since March 19,1945. Three soldiers were captured by the Germans who put them in a prisoner of war camp that was being evacuated. They were among many American soldiers, British Flyers, Indian and Russian troops who were ordered on the march. They endured miserable treatment and food shortages. The soldiers were not sure what the next day offered,

Sergeant Campbell, T-5 Howland and Pfc. Weaver, escaped and traveled by foot at night, ate what they could find with some narrow escapes from the enemy. They were finally picked up by an American half-track patrolling on the South side of the Danube. The three soldiers were dog-tired and weak from the days of starvation. Sgt. Campbell kept a diary of his prisoner of war experience.

Robert Burns Campbell was drafted into the U.S Navy upon Graduation from Greenbrier Military School in June 6, 1944. Seaman Second Class Campbell underwent training at the Great Lakes Naval Training Station at Great Lakes, Illinois, and served in the Pacific War Area on the Communication Ship the USS TETON, AGC 14.

The mail was censored during the war, so Robert had no knowledge of brother "Bill" Campbell missing in action until he received a telegram stating, "Bill is okay." from Mother Edna Campbell.

A Navy Buddy from Beckley, W.Va., on the USS TETON Ship received a sports page from his home, and on the back of the newspaper was a picture of Bob and Bill Campbell with the information about William Campbell missing and freed in Germany. Now Robert understood the telegram from his Mother.

After both Campbell brothers were honorably discharged, they returned to West Virginia where they enrolled at West Virginia University.

William E. married Alice Anne Meckes and moved to Nevada for a while before locating in Summersville where William E. and Father Eugene L. Campbell started Campbell Tractor and

Equipment Company. The business grew successfully and moved from Main Street to a larger facility on Broad Street.

Three children were born, Susan Anne (4-13-1947) who married Bill Auxier, Eugene Leslie II (4-21-1949) who married Margaret Bracken, and Mary Catherine (10-24-1951 who married Ellis Frame IV. After 48 years in the business, William E. "Bill" Campbell retired in 1996. He died June 26, 1998, at the age of 74.

Robert Burns Campbell graduated from West Virginia University with a degree in business. He married Anna Lee Murphy on Sept. 15, 1950, and lived in Summersville where he worked for Peters Creek Coal Company, which later became Peerless Eagle Coal Company. He was an active member of Summersville City Council, Region IV Council, Nicholas County Commission and other civic organizations. The Campbells are the parents of Martha Jane Campbell (12-24-1952) who married G. Richard Larkin and Robert B. Campbell Jr. (6-29-1957).

After 35 years with Peerless Eagle Coal Company, where Robert served as Accountant, Secretary-Treasurer, Vice-president. President and Chairman of the Board, he retired in February 1988.

After retirement, Robert remains active in Memorial United Methodist Church and the community. He is interested in history and preservation for future generations.

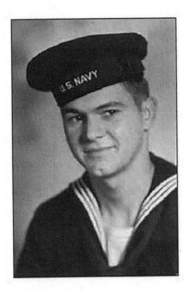

Robert B. Campbell — served in the U.S. Navy 1944-46

William Eugene "Bill" Campbell — Greenbrier Military
School graduate 1943; served in the U.S. Army 1943-45

32

A SISTER FOR THE CAMPBELL BROTHERS

After two sons, a daughter, Carolyn Sue Campbell, was born December 19, 1930, to Eugene L. and Edna Groves Campbell in Summersville. As the sister to "Bob and Bill" grew, she liked to do things that the brothers could, but they liked to tease little sister, Carolyn. A favorite tease was to keep or hide the Sears, Roebuck Catalog from her. Most children enjoyed looking at each seasonal catalog when it arrived in the mail.

During those years, little girls liked playing with paper dolls and the Shirley Temple Doll. There were Shirley Temple- Look-Alike contests, which were popular among little girls. Carolyn treasured her Shirley Temple Doll, which is still a favorite possession.

Carolyn attended Summersville Elementary "Arbuckle School" in the first and second grades where she served as Drum Major for the Toy Band. When the Summersville Grade School was completed in 1939, Carolyn attended there through the eighth grade. In 1945 she started attending Nicholas County High School. She was active in NCHS Marching Band, played with a small group known as "Three Hits and A Miss" and was active in many school organizations.

After graduation from Nicholas County High School, Carolyn attended Duke University.

The Campbell Family was active in the Methodist Church. Carolyn took an active part in MYF and attended church camps and meetings. She met Theodore S. Hoffmann at a Methodist event, and he later became her husband on August 30, 1952 at Memorial Methodist Church in Summersville. They both attended Duke University and after her graduation from Duke and he from Duke Seminary, they stayed in North Carolina, where the Rev. Hoffmann served as a Methodist Minister. Later they moved to Columbus, Ohio, where a baby boy named Brian became part of the family. After a few years, the Hoffmann family moved back to Charlotte, North Carolina, and a baby girl named Lorie joined the family. The children brought much happiness to them.

As the children grew and started to school, Carolyn took classes in preparation of teaching Kindergarten and the early grades. She taught in Charlotte- Mecklenburg, North Carolina Schools for 15 years.

The Rev. Hoffmann was Chaplain of the Methodist Home, Charlotte, for many years. They are both retired in Mooresville, N.C., where they enjoy their family and two grandchildren.

Eugene L. and Edna Groves Campbell spent the winter months in Florida and the summers at their home in Summersville. They visited with the two sons and their grandchildren in Summersville. Edna G. Campbell died July 27, 1961, age 59, from cancer.

Eugene L. later married Blanch Walker and they had about 10 years together before he died on May 7, 1972, of a heart attack. Eugene and Edna Campbell are buried in the Groves Cemetery, now known as Walker Memorial Park, Summersville.

This concludes stories of the Starbuck and Campbell Generations, for which we are grateful for the heritage and have deep appreciation for their struggles and many contributions. The present generation has yet to live and make their life story.

The kind words, letters and phone calls on behalf of the Passage of Time stories are appreciated. We shall continue writing stories of pioneer families, early Summersville, schools, churches and businesses.

As the sister to "Bob and Bill" grew, Carolyn
liked to do things that the brothers could.

Carolyn Sue Campbell Hoffman

33

SUMMERSVILLE GRADE SCHOOL "ARBUCKLE SCHOOL"

The Summersville Elementary School, "Arbuckle School" located on the Wilderness Road, Summersville, was used to school children first through eighth grade. There was no indoor plumbing in the building, only outside toilets and crock water coolers were used. Each child furnished his or her drinking cup, which was metal or aluminum.

The Principal at "Arbuckle School" was Ernest "Buck" Mearns who used the paddle to discipline the students if needed. At noon or recess periods, the playground equipment consisted of swings, slide and seesaw. The boys played marbles on the ground. Those who couldn't go home for lunch at noon, brought a lunch in a lunch or lard bucket or in a paper bag. There was no lunchroom.

The last year that "Arbuckle School" was used as a school was 1938-39. The legal records refer to "Arbuckle School" as Summersville Elementary School, but those who attended knew the name as "Arbuckle School".

After closing the building as a school, the Nicholas County Board of Education used the building as offices for many years before moving to the former High School property.

Blanch McCoy Summers, first-grade teacher, organized the "Toy Band" for the first- and second-graders. The instruments played were drums, tambourines, metal triangles, sticks, symbols and whistles. The students wore blue and white capes and hats as the uniform for the band. The drum majors, Carolyn Campbell and Marsh Dietz, wore all white attire to lead the band. They played for special events at the school.

There was another Summersville Elementary School on Arbuckle Road prior to the above-mentioned school in 1902 and later. (Located near where the present Summersville Fire Department is located.) The school was moved to the red brick building in 1939, which was very modern at that time with a lunchroom, bathrooms, teachers' lounge and big classrooms. That building later was used as the Junior High School.

After the Nicholas County Board of Education was moved the "Arbuckle School "property was sold to Heater Oil Company. On Sept. 2, 2008, the building was torn down after being unoccupied for several years.

Summersville Elementary "Arbuckle School" Toy Band — 1938-39

34

SUMMERSVILLE ELEMENTARY (ARBUCKLE) SCHOOL 1938-39

E arly records were not required under the school law. Teacher's reports to the Secretary of Board of Education were not preserved. The secretary's report to County Superintendents was not recorded and saved, and the County Superintendent left no record of his office. W.G. Brown addresses much of the early information on the early schools in the "History Of Nicholas County."

However, there is nothing, to our knowledge, in print that describes the Summersville Elementary "Arbuckle" School, which was located on Wilderness Road. It has been reported that records of Nicholas County Schools were not kept until 1932-33.

The following list of students, taught by Ernest Mearns, were the last seventh-grade class to attend Arbuckle School. The eighth grade was included at Nicholas County High School. The "Arbuckle School" was closed at the end of school in 1939, and the Board of Education of Nicholas County moved their offices into the building. The new red brick building housed the Summersville Grade School starting in the fall of 1939. The eighth grade was included in the school at this time.

Row one, left to right: Mary Elizabeth Campbell, Anne
Smith, Marie Nelson, Frances Dooley, Elizabeth Jane King,
Emogene Brock, Braidy Perkins, Paris Brown, Paul Cutlip;
row two, Earl Brewer, Ed McCutcheon, Charles Brown,
Harold Lee Burr, Joe Spinks, Alberta Bailes, Barbara Herold,
Scotty (Babe) Trent, John Rich; row three, Ed Bailes, Junior
Gray, Howard Fitzwater, Ruth Lee Herold, Vivian Herold,
Fred Perkins, Bob Herold, Robert Campbell; row four, Anna
Mae Hughes, Dana Watt Groves, Jim Crites, Cora Sawyers,
Reva Lou Bailes, Jim McCombs and Glen Wiseman

35

ARBUCKLE SCHOOL
(SUMMERSVILLE GRADE SCHOOL)

Since early Board of Education records were not available until 1933, only teachers attendance and grade books were kept at the Board Office, and from those earlier records, the following teachers were listed: 1924-25 Lena Ransberger; 1924-25 Egbert Jones; 1925-26 Eva Hamilton; 1927-28 Cloe McMillion, E. P. Williams and Mary Bell Brown; 1930-31 Ernie Hicks and Roy Cartwright; and 1933-34 Ernest Houghton and Loretta Bell. The above teachers taught other years. The dates given were from their reports.

The last year that students attended Arbuckle School before moving to a new school (red brick) Summersville Grade School located near the Nicholas County High School was 1938-39. The principal and teachers Ernest "Buck" Mearns, Blanch Peck, Runa Summers, Corile Hill, Gladys Chapman, Cleoris O'Dell and Blanch McCoy Summers taught that year at Arbuckle.

Most Nicholas County schools heated with stoves and furnaces that used coal. The Board of Education asked for bids, per ton of coal, to be furnished from local coalmines. In 1937, the bids for a ton of coal delivered ranged from $2.00 and up in cost.

The Nicholas County superintendent of schools during the planning of a new school and the closing of the Arbuckle Summersville Grade School was L. O. Bobbitt, 1935-1939.

The local students walked to school. Many also went home for lunch or took their lunch to Arbuckle, as there were no provisions made for a lunch program. The lunch program for Summersville Grade students started in 1939-40 school year in the Red Brick School.

The name of Arbuckle School was changed to Summersville Grade School in 1925.

Those who attended first grade in 1938-39 at the Arbuckle (Summersville Grade School) were: Row 1: Betty McElwee, ??, Esther Simms, Robert Coleman, ??, Nancy Stump and Evelyn Morrison. Row 2: Tom Dooley, Mary Sebert, Anna Lee Murphy, ??, Barbara Wallace, Marsh Deitz. Row 3: ??, Eloise Lambert, Josephine McClung, Oleta Propps, Lou Ann Rader, Paul Stump, ??, and David Champe. (Not pictured – teacher, Blanch McCoy Summers).

36

SUMMERSVILLE NORMAL SCHOOL 1893-1914

William G. Brown, son of William H. Brown and Arminta Hypes Brown, was born at Harrisonville, Ohio, in 1864 while his father was a scout in the Twenty-second Ohio Regiment. He began his education in Ohio. After his parents returned to their farm in Nicholas County in 1873, he attended free schools of Nicholas County. He taught his first school at Rocky Point at the age of 17. Finishing a school in the latter part of 1887, he entered the National Normal University at Lebanon, Ohio. Professor Brown had studied Latin and some higher mathematics. With this start, doing special work during the summer and vacation periods, he earned his degree in three years. He had a vision to make a better higher education available to the young people of Nicholas County. That was the time of a general countrywide movement toward higher education.

Professor Brown started his Normal or Teacher Training School at the Oak Grove School House, Kesler's Cross Lanes in 1889. The first year there were 60 students, whom he taught without assistance. In 1890, the school was moved to the old Temperance Hall on land of Arthur Vaughn. The second year, Homer Groves and Luther Gibson were added to the faculty.

A joint stock company of more than 40 of the most influential business and professional men of Nicholas County was formed. The north end of the hill on the east end of Summersville, comprised of four acres, was purchased from Mrs. Sallie Duffy. Upon the summit of the knoll a two-story frame building was constructed in 1892. This building was almost a square with a pyramidal roof reaching an apex in a belfry. There was a front door and a back door on the first floor. There was an auditorium for recitals and educational entertainment.

Spring Term, regular business course for 15 weeks cost $12; Fall Term, for 10 weeks cost $8. Piano, organ or singing, once a week for 15 weeks cost $9. Teacher's Course, Spring Term for 15 weeks cost $10, and the Collegiate Course, Spring Term for 15 weeks cost $12.

Ladies rooms furnished and cared for daily cost $8 per month. Gentlemen paid $9 and board in private family homes cost $6 to $8. Many students stayed at the Fitzwater Hotel and the Brock Hotel in Summersville.

The Searchlight was the school newspaper published by the Normal School Students. The monthly publication contained essays, compositions, work of the students, lists of students and faculty editorials.

Other teachers at the Normal School during the first term, Spring 1893, other than W. G. Brown, Principal, who taught Latin, mathematics and normal training, were: B.H. White, Principal to Business Department who taught typing and book-keeping; Miss Lillie McAdams taught piano and organ, and H.C. Robertson taught Primary. During that year there were 251 students from eight counties in attendance. James A. White joined the faculty for Fall Term 1893.

It is not any wonder that so many pupils later became successful in engineering, law, medicine, ministry and teaching, when you consider the subjects in the Collegiate Course, which were Algebra, Geometry, Geology, Astronomy, Zoology, Caesar, Ovid, Virgil and Latin Composition, English and American Literature, History, Debating, Essays, and Orations.

Students were also required to attend Chapel Services each morning from 8:30 to 9 a.m. at the Normal School.

Summersville Normal School

37

SUMMERSVILLE NORMAL SCHOOL – PART TWO

E dward W. Skaggs, who had been working at lumbering and mining, entered the Cross Lanes Normal School in the Spring of 1891. He not only later entered the teaching profession, but was associated with Professor W.G. Brown on the Faculty of Summersville Normal in 1897 and 1898. From 1902 until 1924, the Normal School was under his principalship and he, too, became known to pupils and friends as Professor Skaggs.

The Craig family was one of the promoters of the Summersville Normal, especially James S. Craig. The family was also interested in its success. A.L. (Bruddy), Sterling, Lilly, Dainty, Camilla and Bonnie Craig all attended and completed one or more of its courses of study.

The first Board of Directors were James S. Craig, President, James A, Mearns, Vice President, A. J. Horan, Treasurer, B.H. White, Secretary, W.G. Brown, W.G. Graves, James A. White, Alien Rader, H.W. Herold, George H. Alderson and Daniel Brock. Professor Brown's last year as principal of the Normal School was 1898. Professor Skaggs resigned that year to volunteer for the Spanish American War.

Associated with Professors Brown and Skaggs in 1898 were R.M. Cavendish, J. E. Brown, and Miss Edith Sexton.

R.M. Cavendish became both a civil engineer and an attorney and was also a valuable counselor in both capacities to the Pardee and Curtin Lumber Company.

Spring 1899, Professor Brown and H.C. Robertson took charge of the Fayetteville Academy where he remained until 1901. He then went to Oklahoma and was elected Superintendent of Day County Schools in 1902 and 1903 served as Superintendent of Gage City Schools. In 1904, he quit the teaching profession for that of law. It was stated, "when Mr. Brown quit teaching school, he made a mistake in so doing and the school system of our state (West Virginia) sustained thereby a distinct loss."

No worthy youngster was kept from attendance at the Normal School for lack of books. Professor Brown helped a number of boys buy books, and not a single account for books was ever unpaid.

J.L. Stewart, Thomas L. Bryan and Lucy Kincade taught in 1899 at Normal. Pat. H. Murphy and J. L. Stewart rented the Normal Building for a year at the cost of $150. Money was an issue, so they had to execute a note for the full amount of the rent from John McCue on Muddlety. He was later, a year from the date, paid with earnings acquired in operating the Webster Echo, which J. L. Stewart took over Sept. 13, 1901.

Professor Skaggs returned to Summersville to take charge of Normal in 1902. In the spring of 1907, Professor Skaggs and Homer D. Groves rented the building and were partners in the conduct of the Normal School from 1907 to 1911.

Professor Skaggs met Mrs. Skaggs, Lydia Goodridge Spinks, when she was a student at the Normal. The Normal School was active and continued under Professor Skaggs until 1914 when the Nicholas County High School was established.

Edward W. Skaggs also operated the Skaggs Hotel, Main Street, Summersville. Later, the building was owned and was the residence of Howard B. and Catherine Campbell. A part of the building was used for the Campbell Electric Business.

Miss Hattie Murphy attended Normal School in 1910

Professor W.G. Brown Founder and Principal 1864–1957

Miss Hattie Murphy's grade report for the Spring Term 1910

38

NICHOLAS COUNTY HIGH SCHOOL

I n 1911 the state legislature passed a bill creating the Nicholas County High School provided that the voters of the county wanted it. The campaign among the voters was bitter and hard fought, and the legality of the steps taken to secure the school was decided in the courts, but the school was saved to the people of the county, and it has demonstrated its worth.

Fifteen acres of land was obtained from the old "Alderson Homestead" and paid for by donations and turned over to the Board of Education.

The sum of $1, 500 was paid for the land. The building was built with native stone, mostly sandstone quarried back on the mountain not far from the building site. (Known as Lone Tree Mountain)

After considering a number of bids, it was decided the P.Q. Schrake and Son would build the school for $33,000. As it turned out, there was so much delay and unsatisfactory work done on the high school building. A settlement was made with Schrake, and M. H. Brock completed the project.

July 4, 1913, the cornerstone for the building was laid by the Masonic Fraternity. It is said that the largest number of people ever in Summersville at one time were here on that day. The Board of Directors took over the contract for the completion of the portion of the building that was used for the fall 1914 opening.

Principal C.E. Myers arrived in August in preparation of the opening on September 14, 1914 with an enrollment of 65 students and four teachers. The first teachers were: C.E. Myers, Principal; F.A. Mudd, County Agent; Gayle Threlkeld, Home Economics, and Maude Yoak, English.

December 1914, F.A. Mudd was forced to resign due to ill health, and Will D. Click was secured to take his place.

The state legislature amended the bill creating the school so that the Richwood Independent School District was relieved from paying tax for the support of Nicholas County School and changed the Board of Directors to three members. Harrison Groves received an appointment from the State Superintendent to serve on the Board.

The first year of regular high school work closed on June 8, 1915 Ida Lee Alderson and John Yoak graduated as exercises were conducted in the Baptist Church with the Rev. Helen Hill of Richwood as the speaker.

The school building, situated on a hilltop overlooking Summersville, was a structure 120-feet, six inches long by 42-feet, six inches wide and an auditorium 67-feet by 55-feet. The main portion of the building contained seven classrooms, four laboratory rooms, library room, two cloakrooms and two toilet rooms. The furnace, coal room and pneumatic water tank were located under the auditorium. The auditorium had a seating capacity of 700 people.

The Domestic Science Laboratory contained seven sanisteel maple-top tables and all the cooking utensils and appliances needed for 14 girls working at one time. Two-burner oil stoves and ovens for the same served as a satisfactory cooking arrangement. The Manual Training Shop contained 12 individual sets of tools besides a number of larger and less used tools for general use. Lumber was purchased for furniture making. The school also owned three microscopes, 18 magnifying glasses and a supply of test tubes, flasks, rules, scales, and other items for the General Science, Biology and Agriculture.

Students were encouraged to attend church services and for 20 minutes daily, they assembled in the auditorium for devotional exercises, song and short talks. Each student enrolled was assigned to a Literary Society.

First electric lights were installed April 1920 and the building was used until August 1978 when NCHS moved to new location on Route 19.

Nicholas County High School — Circa 1920s

39

NICHOLAS COUNTY HIGH SCHOOL AND SPORTS

Athletics was encouraged in the extra activities. Every student, boy or girl should take interest in some form of Athletics, or else take some systematic and regular exercise. Class teams were organized and a regular schedule of games arranged so the teams could play for the Championship of the school. When it was possible, the best players from class teams were selected to represent the school.

The first Varsity Basketball Team was coached by Principal C.E. Myers. The team players were D. Manning Dorsey, Michael Murphy, Joe Hamilton, Haymond Rader, Mr. Davis, and Eugene L. Campbell. In 1917 the team was also coached by Principal Myers, team players were Joe Hamilton, Ruskin Wiseman, Shando Huffmann, Sterling Groves, Guy McMillion, Cecil Groves and Michael Murphy. This team scheduled five games and won only one game with NCHS making 18 points and Gassaway making 13 points.

By this time, the Girl's Basketball Teams Reds and Blues were becoming popular. Sisters Lottie Campbell played on the Red Team and Elizabeth Campbell played on the Blue Team.

Basketball and Baseball were the two sports with the "Clean Play" as the watchwords for physical development, effective methods of developing honesty and self-control.

The Teachers Short Course started in 1915 was well attended and repeated in succeeding years. It was designed for students who expected to teach, or wished to further their teaching skills or receive credit toward graduation from high school. In 1917, 40 students enrolled in the Short Course Program. The subjects were: the Common Branches, Drawing and Music, Agriculture, Home Economics, English, Algebra and Manual Training.

In 1918, Nicholas County High School had 80 students enrolled. March 1920, the High School closed for an indefinite time due to flu among the teachers and students. James Carl Cox was the Principal at that time.

By 1924, Nicholas County High School had a great football team, and wasn't scored upon the entire season. The score of the NCHS-Webster Game was 92 to 0 in favor of Nicholas County High School.

A gymnasium was completed in 1926. This building was built at the bottom of the hill below the High School.

Jennings Wayne Black, came to coach in 1923 at NCHS and had an outstanding record. During three years his football teams lost only two games. He came from Penn State and left in the 1926-27 year.

James Carl Cox, served as Principal at NCHS from 1920 and had been there six years in 1926-27. The teachers that year were: Lee Otis Bobbitt, Jennings Wayne Black, Hester Burr, Estelle Dunbar, E.S. Dunbar, Nelle Harris, James Kane, Iris McCue and Margaret Nicols.

NCHS Gym 1926

40

NCHS — THE PATH TO THE FUTURE

Volumes could be written about the students, teachers and activities at Nicholas County High School. After the stately stone building and a gymnasium were in full use, sports increased as well as student enrollment.

It was difficult for students to attend high school regularly from the outlying areas, so boarding houses were established in and around Summersville.

The roads weren't paved from Nallen to Summersville, only wagon roads.

In 1933 the first school bus was purchased by the county, a 1933 International Bus with the first driver, Filmon Mullens.

There were some difficult times during the Depression and the Stock Market Crash of 1929 during the Herbert Hoover Administration. Banks closed and many lost their savings, as there was no F.D.I.C. to cover the losses of depositors. Food and jobs were scarce, but schools remained open for those who could attend. It was a very difficult time for everyone. Those who managed to hold on and live frugally learned lessons of skimping, saving, and hard work to survive. Some people were not paid in wages but with "bean orders," which were orders for dried beans from a store.

As the recovery in the 1930's under President Franklin D. Roosevelt with the new government sponsored programs in place, roads were built and paved, which helped the student transportation to schools. More buses were obtained, which provided transportation for students in the rural areas.

With only two high schools in Nicholas County the majority of students were transported to both Nicholas County High School and Richwood High School.

The Second World War in the 1940's took many young students from high school to serve in the Military Service. Some lost their life in battle, while others returned after the War ended in 1945 to continue their education. Educational opportunities were made available to all who served in the Military Service with the G.I. Bill of Rights. Great numbers of men and women furthered their education who might not have done so otherwise.

In the late 1940s and early 1950's, the Korean War took many men to battle and away from high school and college.

There were many changes of school personnel after World War II, some moved on to better jobs or a new career. From 1946 to 1950, three principals and one acting principal served Nicholas County High School. Lyle D. Herod served as Principal from 1942 to 1947, Harry Straley served as Principal from 1947 to 1949 to become Nicholas County Superintendent.

Hoyt Dean served as Acting Principal and C. P. Wells served as Nicholas County High School Principal from 1949 to 1973.

Some interesting Nicholas County High School Statistics are from 1950:

- Student Enrollment-Grades 9-12, 670 students, teachers at NCHS-26, Coaches 2

- Cost per student - $500.00 per student, annually,

- Salaries of 1950 were: Superintendent- $4,000 per year. Assistant Supt.- $3,000, Secretary- $1,600, Custodian-$1,000.

- Cost of School Expenditures: Coal per ton- $3.75, Gasoline- $0.23.4 per gallon. Oil- $0.20 per quart, a 60-person school bus- $4,500.

Many Nicholas County High School Graduates have been productive and also professional citizens throughout the history of the school. The quality of teachers from the beginning had been impressive. In 1950, six teachers had Master's Degrees. They were Esther R, Golden, Elizabeth Stephenson, Sybil Champe Miller, Festus P. Drennen, Rotha B. Strickland and Warder Powell.

Cast of the 1950 senior class play at NCHS, Warning Wings: front, seated, Mary Sebert, Joan Wells, Evelyn Morrison, Ann Murphy, Mae Bentley; back, standing, Freda Elkins, Sponsor David Champe, Summers Harrison, Bernard Hendrickson, Charles Doddrill, Harvey Scott, Marsh Deitz, Sponsor Helen Pitzenberger, and Donald Worlledge

41

WALKER BROTHERS OF SUMMERSVILLE — MAKERS OF BRICK AND POTTERY

Early land grants listed land grants in Nicholas County to the following: Elverton P. Walker, 1834, 50 acres on Laurel Creek and 50 acres on Patterson's Fork, 1833. James Walker, 4O acres, Adj. E.P. Walker, 1826, Joel Walker, et al, 50 acres Wts. Elk River, 1833.

Elverton P. Walker had 14 children. His son, Hiram Walker married Fanny Legg, and they had eight sons: William Mack, born 1837 and married Eliza Jane Neal, other sons were Levi, Madison, Marion, Doyle, Taylor, Clark and Irvin all located in Nicholas County.

The first name on Land Books of the County, Elverton P. Walker, came from King George County, Va., about 1806 and located on the Hess Farm on Laurel Creek.

William Mack Walker and Eliza Jane Neal lived in Nicholas County from 1837 to 1870 and then moved to Carr, Missouri and later to Illinois.

In 1873, William Mack and family moved back to Nicholas County by covered wagon. They were the parents of nine children, Viola, Madison Floyd, James, Augustus, Hiram DeVol, Maggie, Maxberry, Minnie and Ernie.

After moving back to Nicholas County, William Mack Walker and his sons started a brickyard called Walker Brothers of Summersville. They harvested the clay to make bricks, churns, crocks, stone jars and jugs. These were important vessels for canning and preservation of foods. The bricks were made of red and yellow clay, fired on the site in the ovens and were used to build brick homes in the area, including the Walker Families, Alfred's Confectionary (near the center of Main Street). The old Catholic Church, which burned, was made of local brick, but it is not certain if Walker Brick or brick from another brickyard in the area was used.

Two of the brick homes were built where the present Summersville Place is located on Main Street.

The Walker Brothers Brick Yard was located on Webster Road where a large pond remains on the site, as the clay was removed, the large hole remained. Pieces of the brick and pottery are still found on or near the location. The bricks were not marked, but the pottery was stamped in blue as Walker Brothers of Summersville.

It was stated in 1931 by a publication that Summersville area had very valuable clay soil, particularly adapted to making brick, crockery and earthenware. It was found in abundant quantities in the "Tinkerville" (McKees Creek Area). The mass production never developed. However, Robert F. Reynolds had a brickyard on the 230-acre farm located on the east end of Summersville.

Hiram DeVol Walker married Ida Hicks in 1898. They were the parents of seven children, Nita (Baber), Altie (Carter), Jewel, Thomas Mack, Ernie, and Opal (Ward), William Madison Walker. The Walker family owned the Walker Store Company on Main Street where they sold groceries and textbooks for the "Free Schools." They also owned tracts of land and the Walker Cemetery adjoining the Groves Cemetery. It is presently known as Walker Memorial Park Cemetery.

There are some members of the Walker Pioneer Family still living in Nicholas County and other locations.

A sixth-generation family member, Ernie D. Walker,
displays a piece of Walker Brothers Pottery.

Stone jars made by Walker Brothers Pottery of Summersville

Walker Brothers of Summersville churn, made of local clay

42

NATIVE STONE BUILDINGS
OF SUMMERSVILLE

The Nicholas County Courthouse was built from native Lower Gilbert Sandstone, which was quarried from quarries in the Summerville area in 1896. John Hamilton donated the land to establish the County Seat.

Architects, Frank and Henry Davis of Baltimore, Md., designed the Nicholas County Courthouse.

The Works Progress Administration (WPA) added a sizeable addition to this building in 1941-42. Through the years of heating the building with a coal furnace and the weathering, the stone took on a dark appearance. The stone was sandblasted to give the clean and early appearance of the native cut stone. The interior of the building has been changed through the years to accommodate the county business and officeholders.

In 1910, a wing was added for the County Jail, which was used until the Regional Jails were established.

According to a January 15, 1914 issue of The Nicholas Chronicle, James A. Plunkett entered into a contract with the County Court of Nicholas County to build a brick courthouse, priced at $22,000 in June 1860.

The brick from Robert F. Reynolds Farm was hauled into Summersville and used by Federal Soldiers for building ovens and etc. and never used by Plunkett because of the War. James A. Plunkett did lay the stone foundation for the Courthouse.

A frame building was built on the foundation that Plunkett laid. That foundation of stones is now the foundation of present courthouse.

The Nicholas County High School was constructed from the native Lower Gilbert Sandstone in 1913 and was designed by noted West Virginia Architect H. Russ Warne and built by P.Q. Shrake and Sons. The building was used from 1914 to 1978 as the High School until a new school complex was built on Route 19, north of Summersville. The stately sandstone building is being restored and used as an art and heritage center. It is also on the National Historic Register. (1989)

Works Progress Administration (WPA) workers built the stone wall along Webster Road in the 1930s from the local quarried Lower Gilbert Sandstone.

**Nicholas County Courthouse built of native
sandstone in 1896 – Photo circa 1920**

Nicholas County Courthouse Photo circa 1950

43

BROCKS FERRY AND
BROCK'S BRIDGE

I n the early settlement of Nicholas County, Virginia, there
were few roads and certainly not any bridges. The pioneers
learned to build ferries to transport people and things from
one side of a river to the other side. Riders on horseback would
cross some streams in the more shallow areas. Wagons could also
cross on the shallow streams, but a ferry was needed for deeper
rivers and streams.

Ferries were small boats, which were rowed with oars or poles
to move people and their possessions across the river. Later they
were moved on the water by engines with less manpower needed.
On larger rivers and lakes, steam and diesel-powered vessels have
taken the place of simple boats.

Daniel Brock, born in 1847, son of Daniel David and
Catherine Brock, continued his father's trade of miller and operated a ferry across the Gauley River, east of Summersville. The
Brock's Ferry continued to operate until 1904 when a bridge was
built at the cost of $9,225, but the correction of a faulty pier on
the west bank of the river raised the cost to over $10,000.

A stonecutter, Tom Leonard, was employed to do stonework
at Brock's Ferry for the construction of a bridge across Gauley
River in 1903. Tom Leonard was a heavy drinker at times and died
after drinking for two days while staying at the Alderson House

Hotel. It was reported that he and two other people drank 22 bottles of lemon and several bottles of palmetto wine on Friday night before his death. He was quite a generous man with money, but was a heavy drinker. At the age of 40, Mr. Leonard was laid to rest in Clarksburg, W.Va.

When the Summersville Dam was built in the mid-1960s, a new Brock's Bridge was constructed over Gauley River on Route 39 East. The bridge required much maintenance for some reason, as the pavement continued to have large potholes.

Recently, in 2006-2007, a new modern approach on both the east and west sides and a four-lane bridge were constructed for the amount of $18,500,000.

The name was changed to Canvas Bridge, but a descendant of Daniel Brock protested to keep the name as Brock's Bridge.

Brock's Bridge

44

LIFE ON DUFFY STREET

For many years, streets in Summersville were not named, except for a few like Main Street, Water Street and Duffy Street, named for the pioneer Duffy Family. Reflections of youth and growing-up years surface, as we call upon those treasured memories. Living on Duffy Street in the 1930s and 40s has many wonderful memories for those families who were fortunate to live, play, neighbor and share whatever they had with others.

Times were very difficult during the Depression. Everyone who could, raised a garden, owned a milk cow and a pigpen, with one or more pigs. Chickens ran freely in backyards, and those who had food shared with their neighbors. Often beggars would knock on a door for something to eat and were fed.

Apple butter making was a neighborhood event, with apple picking, peeling, cooking and stirring the sauce in a large copper kettle over an open wood fire. The women visited while working; the children played when not helping with the apple butter. Most of the husbands either worked at their jobs or at other things, as the women took charge of the gardens, food and the children.

While the adults enjoyed visiting with the neighbors who stopped by on the front porch, the children played on Duffy Street under the street lights, which made a safe play area for children to ride scooters, bikes, roller skate, play ball, kick-the-can, roll-the-hoop and play games. Jumping rope was popular among the girls. Only a few cars were available at that time, which made the streets a safe play area.

Elementary and high schools were just a few blocks away. Walking with friends to school, home for lunch and after school was a great social experience for those who lived on Duffy Street. The Baptist, Methodist and Catholic churches were also close by, as were the stores, post office and banks on Main Street. Small children walked alone to those places, as it was safe to do so. There was a boardwalk on lower Duffy Street onto Broad Street. Most families knew each other, and the children knew not to misbehave, or the parents would hear about it.

There were community cow pastures where families took their cows to pasture during the day and then led them to the barn for milking in the evening. To keep milk production, cows had to be milked at about the same time twice a day.

During the summer, polio threatened many children. Young families stayed confined in their fenced yards to play. Mixing in crowds was threatening, as polio, the crippling disease, often left a patient to live and breathe in an iron lung in special hospitals, or was fatal. It was a frightening time for parents if their children got the virus. The March of Dimes was a major campaign to find prevention of the polio virus. It was about 1954 when Jonas Salk tested a vaccine on thousands of school children. Local children were offered the vaccine in the old Nicholas County High School gym.

August 1991, a successful Duffy Street Reunion was held on the lawn of a longtime resident, the late Frances Sawyers Haynes (1892-1976), known as "Tancy" to all who knew and loved her. Some of the names of former residents who returned to exchange fond memories of living on Duffy Street were the families of Copenhaver, Bailes, Murphy, Coleman, Corbett, Nichols, Hughes, Groves, White, Fahringer, Vaughn, Sawyers, Comer, Vickers, and many guests.

Other who have lived on Duffy Street were Sims, Binns, Bolar, Oliver, Duling, Dickey, Carlyle, Herold, Tinney, Strait,

McClung, Dotson, Bryant, Ford, Hinkle, Boso, Crookshanks, Chandler and Eberly.

In the 1930s and 1940s, gypsies established camps in the Gad area where they helped themselves to the gardens, chickens and the cured hams hung in the meat houses. It was a novelty for the children on Duffy Street to see the gypsies ride their horses across McKees Creek Road onto Duffy Street when they traveled to the town of Summersville. During that period people watched over their possessions while the gypsies were around, as they also set up camp on Webster Road on an empty lot where a water supply from a creek was available for their horses.

Another event of great interest to the children was the annual circus or carnival that set up in the ball field near Oak and Alderson Streets. The older boys got jobs to help with the animals or set up equipment to earn a free pass or a few coins. This summer event brought people from all around to participate in the fair and for the entertainment.

Duffy Street was an exciting, convenient and safe place for families. That early bonding and friendship continues among those who lived on Duffy Street. Although many former residents have passed away or moved, those memories will remain with those who can remember "those good times" on Duffy Street.

Duffy Street Playmates (Circa 1939-40) dressed in long dresses to play "Mrs." or "House" Pictured left to right: Julia Murphy, Ella Jo Coleman, Betty McElwee, Maxine Dickey and Anna Lee Murphy (Located at "Tancy" Sawyer's House on Duffy Street)

"Tancy" Frances Sawyers (1892-1976) —
Duffy Street, Summersville

45

THOMAS J. REYNOLDS

Thomas J. Reynolds was born March 4, 1806, in Cumberland County, Va., to Samuel and Lucy Reynolds. Marriage to Sarah Honaker took place on March 3, 1825, in Monroe County, Va., by Minister J.L. Christy. Thomas J. trained to be a tailor in his youth, but he mostly worked as a minister of the gospel.

Children born to Thomas J. and Sarah (Sally) Reynolds were Robert Ferguson Reynolds, born Jan. 30, 1826, married to Betty Beirne from Ireland; Charles Kenneth Reynolds born March 5, 1827, married Angeline Elizabeth Morris, circa 1853; Mary Francis Reynolds, born Oct. 9, 1830, married Michael Curran; Elizabeth B. Reynolds, born 1831; Frederick S. Reynolds, born 1836 married Roxanna J. Morris; Nancy Jane Reynolds, born 1837-38 married Patrick Maloney; Lucy R. Reynolds, born Feb. 11, 1839, never married and died Jan. 19, 1862; John D. Reynolds, born May 22, 1842, married Asintha E. Frances Jarvis; William M. Reynolds, born 1844, died 1860; Caroline G. Reynolds, born 1847, married Jacob H. Wise.

There were a total of 10 children born to this union. Some were born in Monroe County and then moved to Nicholas County with their parents about 1838-39.

Thomas J. Reynolds is listed as receiving early Land Grants in Nicholas County on 1860. It is recorded that marriages were performed by Thomas J. Reynolds in Nicholas County in 1841-42, continuing through 1861. He was listed as a minister, but it is not known if he was trained as a Methodist Episcopal minister or was permitted to do so as a lay minister. The Methodist Episcopal Church, South Cemetery, in Summersville, Va., was built in 1848 when the trustees were listed were Thomas J. Reynolds and others on the deed.

Thomas J. Reynolds owned a lot of property, much of it located in the Irish Corner area of Summersville, where he resided.

Sarah Honaker Reynolds died Jan. 16, 1862, and is buried in the Methodist Episcopal Church Cemetery in Summersville.

On Aug. 20, 1863, Thomas J. Reynolds married Sarah Humphreys Arritt Dunsmore, age 51, a widow. The marriage is recorded in Monroe County Court House Book 1, Page 44, with Thomas J. Reynolds's occupation listed as Minister of the Gospel. Sarah Humphreys Reynolds and Thomas J. lived in Craig County, Va., near Monroe County, where she died in 1865.

Thomas J. Reynolds returned to Nicholas County, W.Va., where he lived until he died Feb. 8, 1880. He is buried along with his first wife in the Methodist Episcopal Church, South Cemetery, Summersville.

There are descendants still living on some of the Reynolds property, and others are living in Summersville and in many other states.

The Reynolds Log House, Irish Corner

Tom Reynolds (1865-1935), Angeline Morris
Reynolds (1831-1913), Charles K. Reynolds (1827-
1865), "Sein" — Irish Corner, Summersville

46

CHARLES KENNETH REYNOLDS

The second son of Thomas J. and Sarah Honaker Reynolds was Charles Kenneth Reynolds, born May 5, 1827, in Monroe County, Virginia. He moved with his parents to Nicholas County about 1838-39.

Charles K. Reynolds married Angeline Elizabeth Morris, born in Kanawha County, Virginia. She was the daughter of Sarah (Sally) Hughes Morris and Joseph Barnes Morris. Her great-great-grandparents were William Morris Sr. and Elizabeth Stipps Morris of Liverpool, England.

They resided on the Reynolds Property in a log house and were the parents of seven children, three of whom died in infancy. The children were William M. Reynolds (aka Billy M.) born Oct. 6, 1854 and died Nov. 26, 1857. Robert Perbell Reynolds, born May 16, 1856, married Betty Ann McMillion who died, and in 1905 he married Nora Groves. He had no children with his second wife, but he raised a foster son, Grover C. Starbuck. Robert P. Reynolds kept a hotel, was prominent in business and served on the Board of Directors of Farmers and Merchants Bank. He died March 4, 1918 and is buried at Groves Cemetery (Walker Memorial Park) Summersville.

Sarah Frances Reynolds, born Nov. 5, 1858, married John W. Murphy on July 30, 1883, and lived in the Irish Corner where they farmed and had a family of 11 children. Two died as infants. The other children were Annie, Frank, Hattie, Margaret, Robert,

Carl, Rosa, Ernest and J. Ralph Murphy. Sarah Frances died Nov. 3, 1942, and is buried in the Methodist Episcopal Church, South Cemetery, Summersville.

Betty Ann Reynolds, born 1863, married James Alexander McMillion. They were the parents of Bessie, Thomas, Joseph, and Ina Mc- Million. Betty Ann lived about 100 years and died in May 1963. She is buried in the M.E. Church, South Cemetery.

Thomas Oliver Reynolds was born July 1, 1865, in the Log House, located in the Irish Corner. He was known as "Farmer Tom Reynolds" and was well liked and respected by all who knew him. He never married and lived with his parents, Charles K. and Angeline Reynolds, until their death, after which he continued to live alone in the old home he loved. He was self-taught in law and was an avid reader and storyteller. All the young men liked to visit "The Farmer," as he was interested in sharing his wisdom with them. He attended the M.E. Church, South. He was buried in the church cemetery March 4, 1918. The name Thomas lives as a namesake among several relatives and friends in respect to a man with a keen sense of humor who was a philosopher to those who knew him.

Though he has been gone for many years, the name "Farmer Reynolds" is stated in some complimentary ways in many conversations.

**Thomas Oliver Reynolds born July 1, 1865.
"The Farmer" died March 4, 1918**

Sarah Frances Reynolds Murphy Nov. 5, 1858 – Nov. 3, 1942 Betty Ann Reynolds McMillion 1863 1963

47

THE MURPHYS — FROM IRELAND TO THE USA

T he passenger list of May 17, 1850, on board Brig Garland, Galway, Ireland, to Boston, Mass., recorded the following: Jeremiah Murphy, 55, Julia Murphy, 55, Cornelius, 24, Michael, 22 and Julia, 9.

It is believed the father, Jeremiah Murphy, lived in Hartford, Conn., and is listed in the 1870 census. Daughter Julia lived with her parents at 107 Windsor St. Hartford.

Cornelius remained in the northeast as did another brother, John W. Murphy, who resided in Westfield, Mass., and died March 1870.

Michael W. Murphy finally located in Virginia where in 1855 he united in marriage to Barbara A. Baldwin according to Rockbridge County, Va., records. She was the daughter of Peter Baldwin and Eve Ann Keller Baldwin. They moved to Runa, Nicholas County, in 1869. To the Murphy union was born 10 children: six boys and four girls. Two of the daughters died. John W. (1860-1932) married Sarah Frances Reynolds, Mary Jane (1866-1918) married Charles Beirne, Michael (1864-1954), Cornelius "Conn" (1870-) married Ada Jenkins, James A. (1871-1928) married Lucy McClung, Joseph Daniel Murphy (1874-1962) married Florence Burdette, Jeremiah Martin Murphy (1857-1935) married Margaret Jane Curran and Elizabeth Adeline "Eliza" (1880-1935) married Wesley Thomas and Archibald Neylan.

Michael W. Murphy was a farmer in Runa. He was a devoted Catholic and rode his horse or wagon into Summersville to attend church. He raised his family in the Catholic faith. He was a remarkable man in many ways. Endowed by nature with a strong body, he was very industrious. He hewed out of the wilderness his large farm and also accumulated a considerable amount of property. He was frank, at times to the point of almost being abrupt. All knew where to find him after he expressed himself on any subject or defined his views on any position. He was a kind neighbor, a true friend who consistently lived up to his standard of right as he saw it.

He served as a surveyor of roads in Wilderness District for many years and tendered his resignation as surveyor to Nicholas County Court on Dec. 21, 1882.

The following is a letter in part written to Michael W. Murphy from his brother, John W. Murphy, Westfield, Mass., dated May 28,1868:

"When I started for Virginia it was my intention to see you all and if I anticipated the trouble of finding either of you, I would never undertake my last fruitless journey to Virginia. Have a good reason to believe there are but a few Irishmen in your state capable of giving a person correct information on in regard to the proper routes to be taken by travelers in order to reach your residence, and I do not consider yourself any exception to this rule. For instance, you say you live at Snow Hill "Nickless County." Couldn't you write it "Nicholas"? And you write "Luise Berg." Ain't it Lewisburg? Such were Cornelius's directions to me at a time when I was not sure going to you. I started, however ..." "Nobody, far or near, could tell where you lived, except Col. Lewis who told me that a river was to be forged twice. I assure you that if I were back to New York at that time, I would not undertake the journey, but as I was as far as Richmond, did not wish to back down." (Letter to be continued)

Michael W. Murphy, born in Ireland 1826 and died in Nicholas County on May 10, 1907, and Barbara Ann Baldwin Murphy, born about 1838 in Virginia and died Dec. 12, 1917, in Nicholas County. Both are buried in the Catholic Cemetery, Summersville

48

LETTER FROM WESTFIELD, MASSACHUSETTS — MAY 28, 1868

To Michael W. Murphy
"Walking from Spout Spring was way too much for me the morning after reaching Jackson's River (in Allegheny Co. Va.) I could not walk a step — had to stop at Staunton with the double purpose of nursing my foot and seeing if there was any chance of seeing your family. I was compelled to stay there two days before I could go a step and then took the cars (train?) for home very tired if not sick of my journey. When I reached home my purse looked as if an elephant stepped on it and has been looking the same way pretty much ever since. I shall never have such another opportunity. My health is so poor that I suppose the last (trump will turn?) ere long. On my return I went into business with an Irishman in this town but finding him in a bad (pile?) and my health failing I had to sell out last November and have not earned a cent since having spent most of the winter and spring in bed. My esteemed friend of Spout Spring, Col. Lewis wrote me a letter last November, which I have not yet answered.

And you can raise all the pork and potatoes you need in that country without much trouble; it is not like farming on poverty plains. Anyone who gets a living nowadays ought not complain.

My taxes on this house is $50 per year. Potatoes are two dollars per bushel — scarce and poor quality at that. Butter 50 to 60 cents per pound, flour $18 to 20 per bb (barrel), eggs 30 to 50 c, sugar 15 to 20 to 25, beefsteak 25 to 30 and pork somewhere about 20. It has 30 cuts per pound. Anything on a farm is better that trying to live at the above prices.

Now, for your friends with your humble servant who owns a house and three-quarters acre of land, was offered $4,000 last summer but would be glad to sell for that now. Poor as a church mouse, otherwise self sick and both children have not been well lately.

I take much interest in political affairs and hope we will be all right though it often looks blue. We have celebrated the acquittal. Everything looks favorable for the democracy, not withstanding the Republicans have nominated Gen. Grant as their candidate. The thieves want him to save them from the consequences of impeachment, but I think their goose is cooked. Saltpeter won't save that corrupt party. We have a model town here in the heart of this black state: Democrats two to one wish there were many more like it and think will be next fall. Mind your business and don't mind or let wars trouble you.

Yours,
John W. Murphy

Two years after this letter was written to Michael Murphy, John W. Murphy died in Westfield, Mass., in 1870.
Michael Murphy died May 10, 1907, in Nicholas County, and is buried in the Catholic Cemetery, Summersville, near his wife, Barbara A Baldwin, who died on Dec. 12, 1917, at her home in Runa.

49

JOHN W. MURPHY AND FAMILY

The son of Michael W. and Barbara Baldwin Murphy, John W. was born in 1860 in Allegheny County, Virginia, being the third in a family of 10 children. In John W. Murphy's early childhood, he moved with his parents to the Wilderness District of Nicholas County. He helped his father, Michael, to transform the wilderness into farmland.

On July 31, 1883, he married Sarah Frances "Fanny" Reynolds of Summersville. For almost 40 years they resided on a farm in the Irish Corner where the Reynolds family owned property. Raised in the Catholic faith, John W. continued to attend and raise their children in the Catholic faith.

The children born to this union were: Annie Laura (5/1884 – 1/9/62) married Albert Underwood of Cincinnati, Ohio, they had no children; Frank G. Murphy (7/19/1885-1/5/78) married Arta Armstrong, had eight children, farmed and was a business-man; Hattie Marie Murphy, (6/29/1889 – 5/29/80) attended Normal School and Nicholas County High School, never married and was chosen to take care of elderly parents; Margaret Vera Murphy (3/12/1891 – 10/12/78) married Charles W. Gardner, had three sons and lived in Belle, W.Va.; Robert W. Murphy (4/30/1893 – 10/11/57) married Verninnia Cohernour, had one daughter and lived and worked in Nallen; Carl C. Murphy (2/24/1895 – 10/19/68) married Alma Holland, after she died, married Ethel Rader and had two daughters, worked for Nallen

Lumber Company, later was a merchant in Summersville; Rosa "Rose" Murphy (5/28/1896 – 6/10/95) married John L. Evans and had three step daughters; Ernest Murphy (12/24/1889 – 2/24/81) married Ina Keenan, had two children and lived in Irish Corner; James Ralph Murphy (5/26/02 – 6/29/80) married Alice Cavendish on July 3, 1929, worked as a shovel operator, had five children, lived in Summersville and after wife, Alice, died in 1964, he married Inez Harlow on June 17, 1967. J. Ralph died while on his first deepsea fishing trip in North Carolina with his son, John C. Murphy, and others.

Two children died as infants, Cornelius and Ida Frances, born to John W. and "Fanny" Murphy.

Irish families used the same family names, which can be confusing. John W. had an uncle, John W. Murphy, from Westfield, Mass.

John W. and wife, "Fanny" Murphy, moved from the Irish Corner Farm to Summersville circa 1923–24, where he died on Aug. 8, 1932, from a heart attack. He was a quiet and unassuming citizen, a hard worker and friend to those whom he met. He was buried in the St. John's Catholic Cemetery near his parents.

His widow, Frances Reynolds Murphy, and daughter, Hattie Marie, continued to live in their home until she passed away Nov. 3, 1942. Fanny Murphy, as she was known, is buried in the Methodist Episcopal Church, South Cemetery, near the Reynolds Family. Hattie Marie Murphy moved to Belle where she made her home with sister, Margaret Gardner, for many years. Hattie died May 29, 1980, and is buried in the Walker Memorial Park, Summersville.

The Summersville Go-Mart is located on the property that was the Murphy residence.

Back row: Margaret, Annie, Rose, and Hattie Murphy;
seated, Frank, Robert, Carl, Ernest, and Ralph Murphy

The John W. Murphy and Sarah Frances
Reynolds Murphy Family

50

CHILDREN OF MICHAEL W. AND BARBARA BALDWIN MURPHY

Jeremiah Martin Murphy, born 1857, married Margaret Jane Curran, born 1860. "Jerry" was a blacksmith and a shoe cobbler in Summersville. They were the parents of 13 children: Patrick, Leo, Charles, Edward P., William Cornelius, Jesse John, Donald, Annie, Agnes, Mary Frances, Nellie Beirne, Betty Belle, Verna Margaret, Lucille Adeline and Agnes Dell Murphy, all born between 1883 and 1904.

Michael W. Murphy was born in 1864 and married first to Ida Dingess and then wife number two, Mary Alice Scherer, born 1876. To this union was born Vincent Matthew, Edward Philip, Veronica Wanda, Mary Cecillia, Michael Andrew, Rita Jane and Barbara Ann Murphy. They lived in Putnam County, W.Va.

Mary Jane Murphy, born 1866, married Charles J. Beirne and to this union was born Betty, Margaret, Charles, John C., Annie Mary and Patrick L.

Mary Jane married C.P. Sweeney and had children, Gladys, Ruth and Bernard Sweeney.

James Andrew Murphy, born 1871, married Lucy McClung in 1892. Born to this union were: Michael Jennings, Sarah Pearl, James Andrew, Minnie Ethel, John D., Alice Malone, Greeley Sheriden, Kyle and Mary Sybil Murphy.

Joseph Daniel Murphy, born in 1874, married Florence Burdette, born 1879. He died in 1962 and is buried in the St. John's Catholic Church Cemetery. She died in 1965 and is buried in the Sugar Grove Cemetery, Nicholas County.

Cornelius Murphy was born in 1870 and married Ada Jenkins.

Elizabeth Adeline Murphy, born June 24, 1880, married Wesley Thomas, and had a son, Arthus Ray Thomas, 1904-1977. She later married Archibald Neylan and had a son, William A. Neylan, 1912-1994. "Eliza" died March 23, 1935. They are buried in the Methodist Episcopal Church, South Cemetery in Summersville.

There is a separate story on son, John W. Murphy, born 1860, his wife, Sarah Frances Reynolds, and their children.

There are some fourth and fifth generations of the Murphy Family still residing in the Summersville and Irish Corner areas. The name of Irish Street is now used in place of Irish Corner.

Michael W. Murphy, 1864–1954, with niece, Rosa Murphy Evans, 1896-1995

Cornelis C Murphy: born May 31, 1865, Alleghany County, Va. Died Nov. 22, 1952, in Charleston, W.Va. Parents were Michael Murphy and Barbara Ann Baldwin

Ada Jenkins born: March 3, 1873, in Charleston, W.Va. Died Jan. 29, 1946, in Charleston, W.Va. Parents were Lafayette R. Jenkins and Mary J. Jenkins

Dana C. Murphy, born Oct. 8, 1897, in Summersville

51
EARLY IRISH CORNER FAMILIES

The family names of Beirnes, Curran, Murphy, Brock, Reynolds, Hughes and Sweeney were settlers in an area near Summersville, which would later become known as The Irish Corner. There they established family farms and a school. The families were mostly of the Catholic faith, except for the Reynolds, Hughes and a few other families that attended the Methodist Churches.

Elizabeth Reynolds Curran married Logan Sherman Dotson in 1886 and settled in the Irish Corner area. This union produced a large family: Mary Elizabeth, Belle, Caroline, John, Thomas, Margaret, Wanda, Louis, Joseph, Andrew, Vincent and Frederick Dotson. Logan Dotson was a farmer and a lumber-grader-estimator.

Another family that later settled in the Irish Corner was John and Belle Sweeney. The family included nine children: Joseph, Wilma, Paul, Anna Marie, Bernice, Cecilia, Emma, John Jr., and James, who was killed in World War II.

Charles J. Beirne married Mary Jane Murphy (1866-1918). This union produced a large family: Betty, Margaret, Charles, John C., Anna Mary and Patrick. Charles J. died in 1895, and his widow married C.P. Sweeney and had children, Gladys, Ruth and Bernard Sweeney.

John C. and Stella Walker Beirne lived in The Irish Corner and had a family of 10 children: Pete, Margaret, Betty B., Mary

Frances, Elizabeth, William, Ruth, Robert, David and Jimmy Beirne. They also raised a granddaughter, Barbara. John C. was killed in a truck accident in 1942. Stella was a cook at Summersville Grade School for many years.

John W. and Sarah Frances Reynolds Murphy farmed and had a family of 11 children: Annie, Frank, Hattie, Margaret, Robert, Carl, Rose, Ernest, and James Ralph Murphy. Two children died in infancy.

Ernest Murphy was the only one of the late John W. Murphy family to remain in The Irish Corner and was married to Ina Keenan. Their children, Lena Sue, and Leo, still own property that had been owned by the family.

Leslie and Annie Beirne McCutcheon resided in one area of the Irish Corner where Leslie taught in the one room school. Their children were Ida Pearl, Mary Elizabeth, Beirne, Glen, Dana, Otis, James, Lloyd and Boyd McCutcheon. Ida Pearl taught school for many years in Nicholas County.

Oliver and Agnes Murphy Williams resided in the area. Their children were Margaret, Charlie Bob, who was killed in WWII, and Edward Williams who still resides in The Irish Corner. Another family was the French Jarvis Family of Blanch, Luther and Doy Jarvis.

Walter Ray and Amy Legg purchased the John W. Murphy farm and moved there in 1930. The children, Doris, June, Jim, Roy, Bill, Glen and Patty, helped with the farm and walked to attend Nicholas County High School before bus service was established. The farm was sold to the LeRose Family.

Where once croquet was played on the Murphy lawn by the townspeople who visited the John W. Murphy family, it is no longer a working farm. Croquet was a popular game played in The Irish Corner by many families, especially on Sunday afternoon.

Other early residents and owners of a large farm were the Brock family. Later a son, John Brock, took over the large farm. Some of the family were schoolteachers. Annie Brock Pullen was a daughter. Lucy Brock never married and was a well-known schoolteacher. The farm was sold to Elmer Bailes in the 1930s, who moved there to the Irish Corner. The farm now belongs to a son, the late Kermit Bailes and wife, June Legg Bailes. The unusual rock formation known as the "Open Rocks" has been an attraction for visitors for many generations. The Bailes children are Lynn and Tim who continue to enjoy the lovely well-kept farm.

Stuart and Lula Hughes had a farm and were respected neighbors in The Irish Corner. They had a large family: Edith, Ethel, Minnie, Dela, Irene, Betty, Mary and Virgil Hughes. The late Virgil Hughes and his sisters walked to attend Nicholas County High School and the Methodist Church in the town of Summersville. Virgil was employed by the U.S. Postal Department until his retirement.

There have been other families who resided for a period of time in the settlement known as The Irish Corner.

Most of the Irish settlers believed in the importance of hard work, honesty, thrift and neighborliness. The love of music was an important part of life of the Irish. The traditional music from Ireland was enjoyed by those who could play musical instruments and was present at most family or neighborly gatherings.

Through the years, the family farms have given way for the large homes to sit upon the knolls and fields known as the residential developments of Woods at Towns End and Foxfield Farms.

52

THE IRISH CORNER SCHOOL

The first school located in The Irish Corner, Summersville, was a log building built on land dedicated to the Board of Education by Sam and Mary Brock on Nov. 28, 1890. The school was used for 11 years.

The second Irish Corner School was located at the site of the late Louis Dotson. The deed for the property was made on Jan. 1, 1901, between Mary Curren and the Board of Education "for the advancement of society." The school was used until 1913 when it was destroyed by fire during the tenure of Leslie McCutcheon, teacher. The property reverted back to Mary Curren, Logan and Betty Dotson.

The third school building was built on property donated by Logan S. and Betty Curren Dotson in 1915 to the Board of Education. The building was made of oak and poplar lumber cut from the Logan S. Dotson farm. It was sawn into boards at Jerry Murphy's Sawmill and hauled by Vince Dotson to Dan Brock's Planing Mill, all of this within five miles of the school site. The school had lights and outdoor toilets, which were originally located in the woods and were later built near the school. Drinking water came from a deep well in a well house in front of the school.

The teacher and the students walked from home to the school and brought lunches from home. Electricity was added in 1950 as well as a kitchen and a lunch program during the tenure of Lena Dotson, the last Irish Corner School teacher.

Students were taught reading, writing, arithmetic, history, English and grammar. They also participated in exercise and singing. Books, such as the McGuffy Readers, were furnished by the students and passed onto siblings to use. Grades were mostly through the eighth-grade and those who entered High School were tested before attending.

Some of the games played at the Irish Corner School were softball, Red Rover, Drop the Handkerchief, Antne-Over, Ring Around the Rosy, Mother May I? and Simon Says.

Pie Socials were often held to raise money for the school and for the social among the parents.

Some of the teachers who taught at the school from 1914 through 1956 were: Lucy Brock, Edward Dotson, Flora Simms, Harriet Groves, Ada Johnson, Lloyd Johnson, Alice O'Dell, Nancy Murphy, Draper McClung, Joseph Sweeney, Maude Jones Moss, Inez O'Dell, Mary Alice Perkins, Alice Kay Lilly and Lena Dotson, who taught for 10 years at the Irish Corner School.

In 1985, the heirs of Draper McClung donated the building to the Nicholas County Historical Society whose members had the building moved and restored into a one-room school at the Nicholas Memorial Park. The one room school is open to the public, free of charge, from June until the last of September on Wednesdays and Saturdays from 2 - 4 p.m.

Irish Corner School Last Day 1906
Left to right: front row, Ruth Sweeney, Bernard Sweeney,
Rose Murphy Evans, Gladys Sweeney, John Dotson, J.
Ralph Murphy (4-year-old visitor), Ernest Murphy, Carrie
Dotson McClung, John Pauley, Carl Murphy; back row,
Maggie Beirne, Miss Johnson (teacher), Annie Murphy
Underwood, Annie Backus, Hattie Murphy, Willie Hereford,
Margaret Murphy Gardner, John Beirne, Vince Johnson,
Robert Murphy and Mr. Johnson (visitor or teacher)

53

THE REV. ALFRED
FLEMING GREGORY

Alfred F. Gregory was born Dec. 5, 1883, to parents, A. Hinkle Gregory and Roena Cogar Gregory and reared on a farm near Kovan, eight miles northeast of Webster Springs. He attended Fairmont State Normal School, West Virginia University and was a graduate of West Virginia Wesleyan College. From 1914 to 1927 he was principal of Webster Springs High School. He was a brilliant teacher and a tireless worker. The ideals he held before students and the inspiration he gave them had a great impact on the generation he taught, and thus he indirectly influenced the social history of Webster County.

From his youth Alfred was an active member of the Methodist Episcopal Church. In 1927, he resigned the principalship of the school and entered the Methodist Ministry. He served in Webster County before his appointment to serve in Nicholas County.

The Rev. Gregory served as minister of the Methodist Church. on Main Street, Summersville, starting in 1944. The Methodist's Parsonage was located on McKees Creek Road near the Summersville Grade School, where the Rev. Gregory resided with the Irvin family, as he never married.

The young people in the community soon learned that the Rev. Gregory was a good teacher, as he substituted in the Nicholas

County School system when he could do so. He visited the playground when not too busy to visit with the children.

Many men have fond memories of the Rev. Gregory who took them as young boys to the movie theater, to a ball game, to the river swimming hole near Hughes Bridge on Route 19 or to treat a few boys at a time to ice cream or watermelon on a hot day. After 1956-57, he took the boys to swim in a real swimming pool at the Memorial Park.

As a minister, the Rev. Gregory, who was first a teacher and principal, gave much thought to his sermons and advice to young people. The community respected the Rev. Gregory, as he was a trusted friend to all who knew him. He drove a car, but he chose to walk from McKees Creek Road to Main Street so he could speak to people or to invite young friends to an outing or to attend church.

There was a large red maple tree near the road at the McKees Creek Road Parsonage. The Rev. Gregory sat on the ground underneath the shade of the tree and prepared sermons. One of the well-delivered sermons was titled, "The Maple Leaf."

The vision that the Rev. Gregory had after the close of World War II was to plan and build a new Methodist Church. The older church, built in 1906, was small with no facilities or parking. The Rev. Gregory saw a bright future for the Methodist Church. (In 1939, the two churches, Methodist Episcopal Church, South and the Methodist Episcopal Church, north were unified.) Fundraising was started and the building construction started in 1949 on Webster Road, Summersville. The Methodist Church was a modern red brick building with ample parking, a complete kitchen, Parish Hall (social and dining) and many Sunday school rooms. It was dedicated in 1950 and is still very adequate.

The Rev. A.F. Gregory never had a secretary and did his own typing and reports. He had some volunteer help when requested by him. He was efficient, gracious when invited for a meal, well-read and soft-spoken.

He wrote a weekly column for The Nicholas Chronicle titled "Church News" while serving as minister. After the Rev. Gregory retired in 1951-52, he continued to write "News in General." He received a yearly salary of $4,000 until he retired.

His last few winters were spent in Florida and he returned in early spring. The Rev Alfred Fleming Gregory, a great man, teacher and minister departed this life on June 30, 1964, at age 80. The burial took place in Walker Memorial Park Cemetery, Summersville.

The Rev. Alfred Fleming Gregory

Memorial United Methodist Church

54

PIONEER GROCERY STORES

There were small individual grocery stores, which served the populations of Summersville and part of Nicholas County. Some of the early stores were the Bolar- Groves Store, circa 1919 located near Arbuckle Road and the end of Church Street. The Alderson's Grocery Store, located on the first floor of the Masonic Building on Main Street was managed by Joe Alderson and sister, Gertrude Alderson. The Walker IGA Store on Main Street sold groceries, dry goods, books, and school supplies. Vol and Ida Walker owned and managed the business for many years. They sold animal feed and made home deliveries in a pick-up truck. A dry-cleaning business in the downstairs level and an antique store are in the Walker building at this time.

Cecil Groves bought out the Bolar interest in the grocery business, and opened a feed store and a grocery store, Citizens Grocery, in the old Nicholas County Bank Building, which was moved back to make room for the new Nicholas County Bank in 1922. John Sims was co-owner with Cecil Groves for many years. Citizens Grocery also charged groceries and animal feed to their regular customers as well as making home deliveries. The building is now owned and used by attorneys.

The Early Burr Store and Grain Mill, located on the corner of Church Street and Arbuckle Road, sold groceries, animal feed, ground corn and flour at the Mill. The building was built over a creek. The building remains in use today as a residential dwelling.

ANNA L. AND ROBERT B. CAMPBELL SR.

John Binns had a small grocery store near White Funeral Home. Later, Carl Murphy operated the store until his death in 1968.

In the early 1950s, the Aberzino Family of Webster County established the Community Super Market of Broad Street in what was formerly used as the Kaiser-Frazier Garage. The Moose Lodge is now located in the building.

Grocery pioneer Arthur K. Stowers was born Aug. 27, 1895, to John Adams Stowers and wife, Mary Elizabeth Bryant Stowers, near Summersville. A. K. or "Doc" Stowers married Grace Groves on Feb. 4, 1928. They were the parents of one daughter, Helen, born Dec. 24, 1928. The pioneer in the Nicholas County grocery business first brought fresh produce by wagon over Elk Mountain to sell in the store. The first store building was located on Church Street, Summersville, in a small building, which is presently a shoe repair shop. Later, the grocery store was moved to a larger building on Court Street. The same building was used by Arthur Backus as a grocery store and was also used as Dunn's Ben Franklin Variety Store. It is now used as an antique store.

In 1934-35, a two-story red brick building was built on the corner of Church and Main Streets for a larger and more modern grocery store, which had the name on the large glass window, "Summersville Grocery Company," and owned by A.K. "Doc" Stowers. Additional grocery stores were opened in other locations in the late 1930s. A store in Beech Glen, Gauley Bridge, Belle and one on Quarrier Street in Charleston, W.Va., were among the Stowers' Grocery Stores.

The largest modern grocery store in Summersville offered many more things, including refrigeration, a butcher, home delivery, fresh produce, and animal feed in large bags. The feed was in demand as most families had a cow, a pig, and some chickens. Customers could charge groceries, which was a big boost to the grocery business with payments made monthly. Saturday was the busiest day of the week, as customers traveled from all over the county to shop, go to a movie or visit at the Courthouse lawn with family and friends.

The second floor of the Stowers Building was used as a doctor's office by Dr. F.H. Brown Sr. He often sat on the bench on the Courthouse lawn and visited with those nearby while also watching to see if a patient was going up the stairs to his office. Then he walked across the street to attend to his patient. He had no one else working for him. Many of his patients praised Dr. Brown for his medical knowledge and for the safe deliveries of their children. Many still remember Dr. Brown. Other upstairs offices were also rented in the Stowers Building.

In the early days of the grocery store, everything was pickled, salted, or dried, and fresh produce was not available unless locally grown. Dried prunes, apples, apricots, or peaches were packed in large wooden boxes and weighed as requested and sold by the pound.

Fish was shipped salted in a wooden barrel and had to be soaked in water to remove the excess salt. Cheese was in a large round or wheel and cut into wedges and sold by weight. Longhorn cheese was the kind available. Not many items were stocked in shelves until later when canneries were used.

Pork was salt-smoked-cured to preserve the meat and probably was the most consumed meat besides poultry, which most people raised.

In the early days of shopping, people took eggs to the store and traded for other items. The egg basket that transported the fragile eggs, returned with the customer with other necessities from the store. One married couple took a basket of eggs to the store and got items to start their housekeeping and still had a "due bill" for future groceries.

The groceries stocked some items such as ointments and lard in buckets, which were used as "dinner pails" for husbands and children. Also, animal feed sacks were burlap bags and later printed cotton bags were used as fabric for children's clothes, curtains, and other domestic items. Now those much sought after feed sacks are referred to as textile bags. Stick candy, hard candy and orange slices were displayed in large glass jars, sold by the piece, and savored by children who were fortunate enough to get "penny candy." Most items were shipped in wooden grates or boxes and measured and weighed as the customer requested.

During World War II, many grocery items as well as shoes, clothing, cars, gas, and other things were only purchased when available with ration stamps.

"Doc" Stowers and other early merchants experienced many changes in the business through the years. The Stowers Super Market was the beginning of "Super Stores" in Summersville. Now the super stores are everywhere with many items sold under one roof.

The Stowers Grocery Stores were managed by A. K. "Doc" Stowers until his death on Dec. 11, 1963. His daughter, Helen, and husband, B.M. Safreed, took over the ownership and moved to Summersville from South Charleston, W.Va., in 1964. The Stowers Grocery Stores were closed in 1970.

"Shorty" Halstead was another pioneer in the grocery business. He started with fresh produce and a fruit stand, which proved to be very successful. Later, a large building was built on Broad Street, which housed Halstead's Foodland. The store operated for many years in that location until the store was moved to Merchant's Walk Mall. It was very convenient for customers who were served well by Mr. Halstead until his retirement.

Stowers Grocery Store in Summersville on Main Street, A.K. "Doc" Stowers, owner. (Circa 1934; far left - Mearns Building.)

Long time Stowers employee, James "Jim" Hamilton, celebrates circa 1960s retirement with (left to right) A.K. "Doc" Stowers, unknown, and Grace Stowers.

55

SUMMERSVILLE GETS A CLINIC

A medical outpost in the isolation of a rural area, yet at the same time functioning in cooperation with a city-size hospital, was something new, and Summersville had this with the sponsorship of the Laird Foundation. Dr. William Laird was founder of the Laird Memorial Hospital of Montgomery, W.Va., a division of the Laird Foundation, which was established for the relief of suffering, the encouragement of medical education and promotion of medical research.

Prior to the established Clinic, people had to travel long distances for hospital and medical care because physicians and medical institutions shun the isolation of rural and industrial settlements.

To make the clinic a reality, land was purchased from Mrs. F.H. Brown Sr. by Mr. James D. Ireland, who founded Peters Creek Coal Company in 1946. He donated the 5.65 acres for the Summersville Clinic.

The ranch-type building, built of buff colored brick exterior, was complete in every detail in the interior. Minor surgery, traumatic injuries, obstetrics, as well as emergency services, were available. X-ray service and a clinical laboratory were useful services. There were patient rooms for those who needed immediate hospitalization.

The physicians had access to the Laird Hospital, their physicians for consultations and referrals and for other services and training. The cost of the building was in excess of $300,000.

The Advisory Board Chairman Mayor William S. Bryant and committee sponsored a luncheon at the Nicholas County Memorial Park Dining Room at noon, Sept. 7, 1957. Immediately following a brief program, tours of the Summersville Clinic and the dedication was held. The people of Summersville and the surrounding area were present in large numbers to view the first medical facility of its kind.

Those who had young families were grateful for the clinic where children could get medical attention with compassion and efficient service. Many sutures were received, broken bones mended and parents reassured by the caring general practitioners and nurses.

Doctors Donald Groves, Summers Harrison, Studebrink, Rainey, Chang and others served as physicians at the Summersville Clinic.

Later the Summersville Clinic was purchased by William D. McClung, M.D. Those who served with Dr. McClung were Raymond Lim, M.D., Benjamin Belmonte and Myles J. Crowder, R.Ph., who operated a retail drug department.

The clinic served the people until 1971 when a portion of the Summersville Convalescent Hospital (Nursing Home) was converted to a general hospital when Summersville Memorial Hospital became a reality. Many patrons and businesses donated money to make the hospital a possibility.

The former Summersville Clinic building and property operate as an elementary and high school under the ownership of the New Life Assembly Church of Summersville.

Summersville Clinic

56

A.N. BRECKINRIDGE AND FAMILY

Alexander Negus Breckinridge Jr. was born Nov. 15, 1877, in Loudoun County, Va., of Scottish- Irish decent. He worked his way through college and law school.

A.N. Breckinridge, as he was professionally known, came to Summersville in November 1907 by train. He took the K and M train from Charleston, W.Va., to Gauley Bridge, W.Va., where he took the mail hack, operated by Bob Bell. The hack was pulled by horses, and the trip took 11 hours. On the hills, the passengers had to walk and help push the cart.

Breckinridge started his law practice with John D. Alderson in the old offices formerly occupied by John D. Alderson's father, Joseph H. Alderson. After the Farmers and Merchants Bank Building was completed, the Alderson-A.N. Breckinridge Law Office moved to a second-floor suite of rooms in 1919 over the main bank entrance.

Mr. Breckinridge lived at the famous Alderson House, run by Newman and "Cassie" Alderson on Main Street, Summersville. The hotel-boarding room place later was known as the Rader Hotel. The hot meals at the Alderson House cost 25 cents per person. Mr. Breckinridge recalled that the Catholic Church was being built when he arrived in Summersville. The two men in charge, Mr. Swint and Joe Cart, also stayed at the Alderson House.

On Feb. 12, 1912, A.N. Breckinridge married Edith Wright at "Frog Harbor" Williamsport, Md. Edith was born June 7, 1890, in Loudoun County, Virginia. There were no automobiles until sometime later in Summersville, mostly the method of transportation was by horseback or oil field hacks. The roads were dirt. The first automobile garage was built in 1914 in Summersville.

Mr. Breckinridge bought a small farm in Summersville where he had a three-story grey stone house built. The stone was quarried on the property. Mrs. Breckinridge did not like the light-colored sandstone, so a darker grey stone was located, and thus "Greystone" was given as the house name.

The Breckinridges soon introduced Guernsey cattle and Poland China hogs to the area. They established an apple orchard and had a large stable of fine horses on the farm. The horses were very useful, as part of the time the roads were impassable. About 1923, through Mr. A.N. Breckinridge's efforts, Main Street was paved.

An interesting ad appeared in a 1918 Nicholas Chronicle advertising the following: Greystone Berkshires — when you come to Summersville, be sure to see the Berkshires. Visitors always welcome. Pigs have averaged nine to the litter. A few sows to farrow. A.N. Breckinridge, Summersville, W.Va.

Also listed in a 1918 Nicholas Chronicle was the announcement that Delco Light and Service was established by A.N. Breckinridge for the purpose of selling Delco systems for those who wanted a form of light, as there was electricity available for a select few in town from the Campbell Electric Hydro Electric Power Plant, located at Muddlety Creek. A.N. was the factory representative and Grover C. Starbuck was the salesman and supervisor of the installation of the Delco Light System.

As automobiles were available, Mr. and Mrs. Breckinridge owned and drove a car. "Mrs. B," as her friends called her, was one of very few women who could drive, let alone own her own automobile.

As a past-time of Sunday afternoons, a group of people would walk to the Open Rocks or visit farmer Tom Reynolds or go to the Guthrie Fishing Camp in the Irish Corner along the Gauley River.

Alexander Negus Breckinridge Jr.

John D. Alderson Law Office, formerly the law offices of
Joseph H. Alderson, father: man (tallest) in center of photo
Partner A.N. Breckinridge, others unknown. Circa 1908

57

THE BRECKINRIDGE FAMILY

While A.N. Breckinridge Jr. was busy with his law practice, both is Richwood and Summersville, business and farming, wife, Edith, was very busy with their five children and taking care of the large house the "Greystone." The children born to A.N. and Edith Breckinridge were: Alexander Negus Breckinridge III, born Jan. 14, 1913 in Williamsport, Md., married Beverly Watts on Feb. 3, 1951; Robert Wright Breckinridge born July 23, 1914, in Summersville, married Anne Scotzen on Feb. 19, 1940, and Mildred Maynard on July 3, 1964; Mary Van Lear Breckinridge, born Oct. 22, 1916, in Summersville, married Robert J. Mansfield on Dec. 28, 1940, married B.W. Dickinson III and died Nov. 17, 1977; and John Barclay Breckinridge, born Dec. 23, 1919, in Summersville, married Mary Ellen Woodlief on July 20, 1945.

John Barclay Breckinridge attended public schools and graduated from Greenbrier Military School, Lewisburg, W.Va. He received his A.B. LLD and J.D. degrees from the University of Virginia. In World War II he served from 1943 until 1946 in the United States Army Air Corps rising to the rank of captain. He joined his father's law firm and became the senior partner of the Breckinridge Davis and Null Law Firm. John and Mary Ellen had two daughters, Peggy and Polly. John, like his father, A.N. Breckinridge, was active and supportive of civic organizations, a member of the Lion's Club and St. Martins In-the- Fields Episcopal Church in Summersville. John died Nov. 13, 1981.

Casper Shunk Breckinridge was born June 6, 1923, in Summersville. He attended public schools and Greenbrier Military School, Lewisburg, and graduated in 1942. A lieutenant in the 100th Infantry, U.S. Army, he died on the field of battle at Vosges Mountains, France, on Dec. 9, 1944. He was posthumously awarded the Silver Star and the Purple Heart. He was buried in France.

A.N. Breckinridge was active in civic organizations, the Lions Club, Chamber of Commerce, Masonic Lodge, active on politics and supported many local projects. He was prominent in the promotion of the town of Summersville, Nicholas County and West Virginia. A tall man with a friendly smile, he was interested in people from all walks of life. He enjoyed entertaining others in his spacious home, the "Greystone," from farmer Tom Reynolds to the lofty politicians.

Edith Breckinridge, a charming lady, offered a ride to her neighbors who had no transportation to the main part of town, except to walk. Edith often drove her son, Caspar, back and forth to the Greenbrier Military School in Lewisburg. The Campbell Brothers, Robert and William also attended GMS and often rode there with Mrs. Breckinridge and Caspar. They especially liked being entertained by Caspar with his jovial personality.

Mrs. Breckinridge enjoyed playing bridge for years with her many friends. She took time to make a pot of soup for an ill neighbor, or show a young housewife how to prepare a country ham, or just speak a few kind words.

She was instrumental in the development of Breckinridge Heights and donated land and promoted the founding of St. Martins In-the-Fields Episcopal Church on McKees Creek Road, Summersville.

After A.N. Breckinridge Jr. died Sept. 30, 1947, "Mrs. B" sold "Greystone" and moved into a smaller house on McKees Creek Road, where she lived until her death on Nov. 13, 1965. Mr. and Mrs. Breckinridge were truly pioneers in many ways and contributed much to the town of Summersville. They were laid to rest in the Walker Memorial Cemetery, Summersville. All five of the Breckinridge children are deceased.

Caspar Shunk Breckinridge

The Breckinridge Family
A.N. and Edith Breckinridge Family — 1951 Left to right: front, grandchildren Bobby and Peggy Breckinridge, Pat Mansfield and Elizabeth Breckinridge; center, Edith Wright Breckinridge; back, left to right, Anne Scotzen Breckinridge, Mary Ellen Woodlief Breckinridge, Beverly Watts Breckinridge, Mary Van Lear Mansfield, Alexander N. III, John Barclay and Robert Wright Breckinridge.

58

THE ALDERSON FAMILIES

The Nicholas County Alderson family traces its relationship to the Rev. John Alderson, a Baptist minister, who was born in England and came to the United States and settled in Virginia in 1779 in the town of Alderson. He had three sons, George, Joseph and John.

George's son, Col. George Alderson, settled near Lookout, Fayette County. He was married twice and had 28 children. One of those, Joseph A. Alderson, came to Nicholas County in about 1855. A son of Col. George, Joseph A. Alderson Sr. was a lawyer and member of the Virginia Senate. He voted against secession. Two of his sons became prominent in public life. John Duffy Alderson, a lawyer and politician, served in the state in different capacities and was three times elected to Congress. Another son, Joseph A. Alderson Jr., was a teacher, county superintendent of schools and clerk of county court.

John D. Alderson practiced law in his father's old law office with a partner, A.N. Breckinridge, in 1907 and beyond. Later they moved to the upstairs of the Farmers and Merchants Bank Building. After the new Nicholas County Bank was built the law firm moved upstairs. His son, Fleming, a member of the West Virginia State Legislature, introduced the bill creating the Nicholas County High School in the early 1900s.

George Henry Alderson, half-brother to Joseph A. Alderson Sr., later settled at Enon and operated a farm and store. Later,

George Henry established the "Big Hardware Store" on Main Street in Summersville in 1912. In 1915, an ad in The Nicholas Chronicle read as follows: "We do not wish to say this boastingly or even with any degree of regret, but our school tax alone for the year of 1914 was 90 dollars, school purposes only. How much school tax has Sears Roebuck and Company paid? Think a moment and be fair with us." The Big Hardware, Summersville, W.Va.

The Aldersons owned much property in Summersville, including the old Nicholas County High School property and surrounding area. The famous Alderson House (later the Rader Hotel) proprietor was Lewis Newman Alderson. In 1909 an addition to the Alderson House was built with two stories, which added capacity for the popular hostelry. In 1914, some apple trees were removed to enhance the appearance of the Main Street property. P.E. Reynolds leased the Alderson House in 1919 from L.N. Alderson.

Lewis Newman and Catherine "Cassie" Bryant Alderson married on April 17, 1879, had seven children and operated the Alderson House until 1919 when they moved to a new house on Main Street. L.N. died Oct. 7, 1928, at age 73. "Cassie" Alderson kept borders for a few years. She died Oct. 3, 1955.

George Henry Alderson married Sabrina Huffman. He was born Oct. 28, 1844, and died July 9, 1936. They had a son, Roy C. Alderson, born Dec. 21, 1895, and died Aug. 5, 1980, in Summersville. Roy married on May 2, 1917, Hattie Hutchison (1892-1965). They were the parents of five children: Nancy, Betty Jo, Peggy, Dorthea, and John Henry Alderson. Dorthea Alderson Bickerstaff died March 29, 2009.

There is an Alderson Cemetery located on the old Nicholas County High School hill with some family members buried there.

The pioneer Alderson family contributed much to the town of Summersville, were landowners, had many businesses and establishments, were lawyers and politicians and respected citizens. After a century of political and social life in Summersville, there are no Aldersons, only descendants living in Summersville in 2009.

George H. Alderson had the monument for the Morris sisters erected on the Courthouse lawn in Summersville.

George Henry Alderson in 1912 established the "Big Hardware Store" on Main Street in Summersville. The house on the left was built by a doctor and later owned by Lee and Ona Herold.

Lewis Newman and "Cassie" Alderson operated the Alderson House until 1919 on Main and Broad Streets in Summersville. It was later the Rader Hotel and Ramsberger Hotel.

59

DR. FLAVIUS HUGH BROWN SR.

Israel Brown came from Pendleton County in about 1816 to Powell's Creek in Nicholas County. One son's name, John Brown, a pioneer surveyor, adorns many pages of county records. Another son, James F. Brown, a beloved Baptist minister in Nicholas County, had sons, Richard J. Homer and James Flavius, all of whom became physicians.

James Flavius and Sally Brown were the parents of Flavius Hugh Brown, born Sept. 18, 1878, at Birch River. When he was quite young, he moved with his parents to Beaver, W.Va. Flavius Hugh Brown married Elizabeth Huff, who was born Jan. 19, 1889, and the marriage took place on May 5, 1905. Elizabeth, the daughter of Mr. and Mrs. W.D. Huff, was 16 and her husband Flavius was 27 when they married.

For a few years, Flavius H. Brown taught school in Nicholas County and was engaged in the mercantile business at Beaver. He served one term of deputy sheriff of Nicholas County. The first son, Eugene Scott Brown was born March 10, 1906, at Beaver. One year later, Flavius Hugh went to Baltimore, Md., where he was a medical student at the School of Physicians and Surgeons. (later merged with the University of Maryland)

The home at Beaver was sold to Flavius's brother, Pat Brown, and they moved to Baltimore. The traveling was by train. Mrs. Brown and her young sons returned to Nicholas County to spend the summer with her parents and raise a garden and can vegetables

178

to take back to Baltimore for the fall and winter. During this time, two more sons were added to the family, James Dudley, born April 20, 1908, in Baltimore, and John Morrison, born July 1, 1910, in Craigsville. During the summers, Flavius Hugh stayed with his parents and worked on their farm.

Money was scarce while Flavius attended medical school, so Mrs. Brown cooked for "boarders" and cared for the three sons in their little "flat." During the last year of medical school, the Browns borrowed $50 from Mrs. Brown's sister, Molly Brown, a schoolteacher. She was repaid with a year of room and board at their home after Flavius finished medical school.

Dr. Flavius H. Brown graduated from medical school in 1911. He returned to Craigsville where he practiced medicine for 11 years. After receiving his medical degree, Dr. Flavius became ill with typhoid fever and had a long and slow convalescence. Mrs. Brown also contracted typhoid fever but recovered sooner.

Dr. Brown made house calls on horseback, delivered many babies and treated many ailments from his "black bag." His fees were small, and he was paid sometimes with cash and often with chickens, a ham or a sack of potatoes. Sometimes for the delivery of a baby he got an IOU. There is no known count of the number of baby deliveries by Dr. Flavius Hugh Brown, but there are many adults living today who were delivered by Dr. Brown.

The doctor's office was located in Summersville in the main part of the town; at one time the office was upstairs over the Nicholas County Bank and later upstairs from the Stowers Grocery Store. He often sat on a bench on the Nicholas County Courthouse lawn visiting with people until he noticed a patient going into the entry of the Stowers Building. He worked alone and always took time to treat and care for his patients. Dr. Flavius H. Brown was dedicated to pioneering medical care for the people of Nicholas County.

**Dr. Flavius H. Brown, 1911, Graduate of the School
of Physicians and Surgeons, Baltimore, Md.**

60

ELIZABETH HUFF BROWN

Elizabeth Huff was born Jan. 19, 1889, in Persinger. Her parents were farmers with a large farm and had a family of 14 children: George, Guy, Dan, John, Bill, Randall, Fanny, Alice, Bertha, Lula, Anna, Gladys, Beulah and Elizabeth Huff.

Elizabeth learned to cook, wash dishes and care for the younger brothers and sisters. Her family moved to Craigsville and operated a hotel, where young Elizabeth recalled standing on a box at the kitchen sink to wash the dishes.

Her early education amounted to the completion of the set of McGuffey's Readers and a few piano lessons. She was self-educated, an avid reader and probably knew Grey's Anatomy as well as her husband, Dr. Flavius H. Brown, as she read and quizzed him in preparation for medical exams.

Elizabeth, a mature lady for her age, married at 16. She knew how to garden, can, cook and care for her family. The Brown's kept several cows, which Elizabeth milked until some of her sons were old enough to do so. She churned the milk with one hand and held reading material in the other hand while she rocked the baby cradle with her foot. (Now we would refer to all of that as "multitasking.")

After her marriage on May 5, 1905, to Flavius Hugh Brown, she gave birth to nine children. While Dr. Brown attended medical school in Baltimore, Md., they had Eugene Scott (March 10, 1906) born in Craigsville; James Dudley (April 20, 1908) in

Baltimore; John Morrison (July 1, 1910) in Craigsville, and after returning to Craigsville the following sons were born: Flavius Hugh Jr. (Oct. 2, 1912), Paul Huff Brown (Sept. 21, 1916), William Herbert (Oct. 1, 1919) and Robert Ray Brown (Nov. 8, 1922) in Summersville, two daughters, Elizabeth Ann (Born Oct. 18, 1925) and Alice Marie (born Nov. 18, 1928). An interesting note: all seven sons were born on weekdays, and the two daughters were born on Sundays.

The children were each given chores to do in the house, and outside chores were mostly for the boys. However, the boys had to help in the house with many chores. The kitchen was a hub of activity for the Brown family.

Dr. Flavius Brown Sr. was busy as he covered a large area of the county to see patients, either by horseback or later in his Chevy automobile.

He provided material things for his family, but the strength came from wife and mother, Elizabeth Brown. She calmed the fears and cured the ills of her children. Her life's philosophy was shared often from the kitchen, as that room took care of many needs.

Elizabeth nursed her family of nine children through such dreaded diseases as diphtheria, pneumonia, cholera, infantum, scarlet fever, smallpox, whooping cough and many colds, flu and other illnesses. The deep faith sustained Elizabeth as she kept vigil and nursed each child back to health.

Mrs. Brown had a love of horses and rode sidesaddle. Before the days of the automobile and in weather when cars could not be driven, she went to the barn, saddled and prepared the horse while her husband, Dr. Brown, dressed and got ready to make house calls. He made many house calls to the sick in the middle of the night.

Elizabeth Brown always wore an apron, as she found many uses for the apron in her busy life as a wife and mother of nine.

Dr. Flavius Brown Sr. Family Left to right: Robert, William, Paul, Flavius Jr., Morrison, Dudley, and Eugene; front, left to right, Alice, Marie, Elizabeth Ann, and Elizabeth Huff Brown (mother)

61

THE F.H. BROWN FAMILY HOME

S pring 1922 the Brown family moved to Summersville from Craigsville. It was an exciting time for the family of seven boys along with the parents Dr. Flavius H. and Elizabeth Huff Brown. In 1923, a new two-story house was built on the original 25 acres of land.

The stone for the west and north steps was quarried on the edge of Arbuckle Creek near the north boundary of the grounds. The oak tree covered knoll is the perfect setting for the Neoclassical Revival style modest 2,400 square foot home. The hipped roof with asphalt shingles and the unusual scupper system instead of gutters are part of the house, which also has a full basement. A garage was completed in 1934 at the end of the great Depression with sleeping rooms over the garage for the older sons. The foundation is made of Walker brick made by Walker Brothers of Summersville and was laid by Jim Walker. Dr. Brown and his sons built the remainder of the garage "Jenny Lind" style. When built, the house faced the main road, which was replaced with Old Route 19 in 1937-38.

After the family moved to Summersville, a son, Robert Ray, was born Nov. 8, 1922. Two daughters, Elizabeth Ann, born Oct. 18, 1925, and Alice Marie Brown, born Nov. 18, 1928, were both born in the new house.

The sons also learned to press their own trousers, polish shoes and assist with many household chores. Mrs. Brown starched, sprinkled and ironed many shirts over the years and even did so while the sons were in college. They mailed home dirty laundry, and when Mrs. Brown completed the laundry, it was mailed back to the sons.

Four of the Brown sons became medical doctors, and three were dentists. It was a close family, with competition in the family croquet games, known as the "Oak Bush League." The games started in the spring and ended in the fall. Scores were kept, and plaques were given over the years.

Christmas was observed in the Brown home, always with a freshly cut pine tree from the woods and wreaths hung in the clean windows with lots of goodies baked in the kitchen. Mother Brown ordered gifts for the children from Sears and Roebuck and the Montgomery Wards catalogs. That is where Santa got most of the children's presents in those days.

On June 8, 1945, the whole community was saddened to learn that their beloved physician, Dr. Flavius Hugh Brown Sr., had died from a stroke at home at the age of 66. The funeral service was held at the Summersville Baptist Church, where Dr. Brown had been a devoted member. Interment was made in Groves Cemetery. (Now Walker Memorial Park, Summerville)

Elizabeth Brown later moved to Morgantown to keep house for the two daughters, Elizabeth Ann and Alice Marie, until they graduated from West Virginia University. In 1949, Elizabeth Huff Brown was selected Mother of the Year for West Virginia, an honor rightfully deserved for a mother who raised nine children, all college graduates and all seven sons with medical degrees.

In 1954, the Brown house was purchased from Mrs. Brown by son, Dr. Flavius H. Brown Jr., and his wife, Josephine Hill Brown, who lived and raised their three children, Mary Jo, Betty and Hugh, there among the strong oaks on the knoll. Mrs. Elizabeth Brown also sold five acres in 1956 to the Laird Foundation for the Summersville Clinic.

After Mrs. Brown moved back to Summersville from Morgantown, she lived in a smaller house and was active in the Summersville Baptist Church and civic affairs. She was known to always wear an apron, and due to her many domestic chores, she found the apron not only kept her dress clean, but she found many uses for the apron.

Daughter Elizabeth Ann wrote of her mother, "She possessed a limitless capacity to recognize and cultivate the best of each of us, had the objectivity and patience to accept and to love each of us, together and individually."

Daughter, Alice Marie Brown wrote her memories of her mother and quoted from Mrs. Brown's diary, "Enough, Is As Good As a Feast," as she often shared food with those in need. Alice Marie wrote a story, "My Mother's Apron," which was published by West Virginia Golden Seal Magazine in Spring 2004.

Dr. Eugene S. Brown followed his father, Dr. Flavius Brown, in that he established his medical practice in Summersville for many years. He had more conveniences that his Dad had as well as a reputation for being an outstanding physician, as did Dr. F.H. Brown Sr. The people of Summersville and the surrounding area were most thankful to have had two dedicated doctors to serve the people for many years.

Dr. Eugene Brown, after his retirement, moved to California with his family where he died Feb. 22, 1966.

Dr. Flavius Brown Jr., a dentist, practiced in Summersville for many years. His dental office was located upstairs of the Walker Store Building on Main Street. He died on Feb. 2, 1980. The interment was in Walker Memorial Park Cemetery.

Dr. Flavius H. Brown Sr. and Elizabeth Huff Brown and eight of their children are deceased. Alice Marie Brown Juergens in the only survivor.

The lovely Brown home was sold, rented, and was partly damaged by a fire. The City of Summersville purchased the property in 1999. It was about to be torn down, when some interested citizens, who knew the Brown family and the wonderful history, voiced, "The Brown House is worthy of restoration." A dedication of Brown Oaks was held on the front lawn June 22, 2002, with Mayor Stanley Adkins leading the ceremony. A large crowd and any extended Brown family members attended and toured the lovely restored house. It is used as a meeting place, for wedding and receptions and other events, with a Board of Directors and Summersville Mayor and Council in charge of the maintenance and use.

This concludes the story of the wonderful Brown Family and how they helped to shape and enhance the lives of so many people in Summersville.

The Dr. F.H. Brown home, built 1923 and restored in 2002, is listed on the National Register of Historical Places.

Alice Marie Brown Juergens with her father's "Dr. F.H. Brown" office sign

62

WILLIAM HENDERSON (HUNTER) CAVENDISH

William Henderson (Hunter) Cavendish was born in Ireland about 1740 and came to America between 1756 and 1760 with his mother and two sisters. The story is that he was eligible for the House of Lords in parliament and that his mother had been sent to Ireland from England before his birth so that in case the child was a boy, he could become a Member of Parliament directly from Ireland. However, growing up, his sympathies were so pro-Irish that is was thought advisable to get him out of the country.

The Cavendish Family members, who became Dukes of Devonshire, not only have been at the center of English political and cultural life for centuries, but were also remarkable in their own right. Some were magnificent as the stag, and others were as cautious as the serpent, the beasts that appear on the crest of the Devonshire Arms (Coat of Arms) that represent the Cavendish name.

The Cavendish Family left England and came to America and settled in Virginia on the James River, not far from Lexington and settled on a farm, known as the Cavendish Farm. William H. Cavendish's sisters married and from one of them descended George H. McClintic, Judge of the U.S. District Court of Southern West Virginia and the Arbuckles of Lewisburg and Glenville.

William H. Cavendish was a quartermaster general during the Revolutionary War 1778-82. He was appointed on the first board of visitors at Washington College, Lexington, Va., in 1796. The proof of this is contained in the Laws of Virginia, Page 44, Chapter 41, "An act for erecting Liberty Hall Academy into a college." This act was passed Dec. 21, 1796, and names of board of visitors were to appoint the president and professors, remove and suspend the same for a good cause, fix their salaries, make inspections and have control of all property belonging to the college.

Lord William H. Cavendish, as he was known, served in Assembly of Virginia 1802-1805 with the exception of two years when he was Sheriff of Greenbrier County at which time he lived in Lewisburg. He lived in Lewisburg for some time. He was busy dictating deeds and wills of his countrymen to a Clerk Court. He witnessed the "X" marks made by pioneer men and women on courthouse documents and decided to start a school to combat illiteracy of early Greenbrier residents. His compassion for others and his skills as a lawyer made him a most respected and successful gentlemen.

The question of Lord William H. Cavendish's wives is still debated by his descendants. Only Church of England marriages were recognized until after the Revolution. His marriage to Jane McCoy Murphy on June 13, 1780, is documented. To this union were born five children, of whom we have record of two sons and three daughters. After the death of Jane McCoy Murphy in 1804, William H. Cavendish married Alice Mann in Bath, Va., in 1804. This union had no children.

Descendants of Lord William Henderson (Hunter) Cavendish will be continued.

THE CAMPBELL COAT OF ARMS, FEATURING THEIR FAMOUS SERPENT AND STAG. The motto "SAFE BY BEING CAUTIOUS"

63

FAMILY OF WILLIAM HENDERSON (HUNTER) CAVENDISH — SECOND GENERATION

T he children of William Henderson (Hunter) Cavendish were Mary Cavendish born in Greenbrier, Va., married Isaac Callison Aug. 25, 1792, and died 1840; William Cavendish Jr. born 1776 in Greenbrier, married Jane McCoy Feb. 6, 1794, first Clerk of Kanawha County and a lawyer; Jane Cavendish, born 1779 in Greenbrier, married Joseph McClung on May 1, 1804, and died in Nicholas County, Va., Dec. 4, 1828; Rebecca Cavendish, born March 28, 1790, in Greenbrier County, married Alexander McClung Jan. 25, 1816; Andrew Cavendish, born March 24, 1787, in Greenbrier and attended Washington College at Lexington, Va., where he finished in about 1809.

On April 27, 1809, Andrew and Jane (Janet) McClung were married and settled on Big Clear Creek in Greenbrier County near Lewisburg. Andrew was the father of 13 children, five sons and eight daughters, and practically all were born in Greenbrier County, Va. In 1935, Andrew Cavendish moved his entire family to Fayette County and settled near Wood's Ferry on Gauley River where he purchased 1,000 acres of land at 50 cents per acre.

Andrew cleared the land and built a home one mile from the Gauley River. He farmed and taught a subscription school for a few years, teaching only a few months per year. He died in

1870 and was buried at Christ Cemetery in Fayette County. His land was divided among some of his children and has since been divided into several farms.

The children of Andrew and Jane (Janet) McClung Cavendish were Alex (Alexandria) born Feb. 25, 1812-1899, at Bucks Lick, Nicholas County, W.Va.; Abigail Cavendish, born 1812 or 13 and died Oct. 1, 1866, in Greenbrier County; Rebecca Cavendish, born Nov. 7, 1814, and died Sept. 15, 1891, in Greenbrier County; Nancy Cavendish born Oct. 2, 1816, and died Dec. 10, 1896, in Greenbrier County; Sarah Cavendish born Sept. 2, 1818, and married John Kincade; Margaret Cavendish, born March 1821 and died in 1904 in Fayette County, W.Va., married Charles Walkup in 1846; Joseph Cavendish, born 1822 and died 1892 in Fayette County; John Cavendish, born March 2, 1824, and died 1897 in Fayette County; Isaac C. Cavendish, born Sept. 22, 1834, married Talitha Ann Dorsey in 1859, served as a minister in Fayette County, where he died at Mills Creek in 1909; Minerva Cavendish born April 15, 1826, and died 1876 in Greenbrier County, married Robert Dorsey; William Cavendish, born Feb. 4, 1810, married Rachael Hull, died July 14, 1876, in Fayette County; Mary Cavendish born Feb. 22, 1830, and died Feb. 1, 1906.

The Cavendish families that remained in Fayette County are recorded in the Cavendish Family Genealogy by Hugh Cavendish. A copy is filed with the Fayette and Raleigh County Genealogy Society, Oak Hill, West Virginia.

64

CAVENDISH FAMILY — THIRD AND FOURTH GENERATIONS

William Cavendish, eldest son of Andrew and Jane (Janet) McClung Cavendish, was born Feb. 4, 1810, and died July 14, 1876. William married Rachael Hull and they had nine children. During most of his married life, he lived near Edmond, Fayette County, where he was killed while working in timber. Their children were: Frank, born 1845, married Virginia Tully, had children, and lived at Lookout where he operated a store, later moving to Huntington, where he died; James Cavendish, born about 1845, died at Fort Delaware and was a Confederate POW; George Cavendish, served in the Confederate Army and died in 1929 in Florida; Andrew, born about 1847, died about 1861, murdered near Raven's Eye along with another youth named William Crane; Nancy Cavendish, born 1853 and married ? Withrow; Edgar Cavendish, born in 1859 and died in infancy; Edna, a twin to Edgar married and lived at Edmond with their family; Jane Cavendish born circa 1863, married J.S. Johnson and had a family; Francis (Fanny) Cavendish born about 1867 and married? Harshbarger and after husband's death married? Wheatly.

The second son of Andrew and Jane (Janet) Cavendish was Alexander (Alex), born Feb. 25, 1812, in Greenbrier County, Va., married Sarah A. (Sallie) Dorsey on May 20, 1841, in Bucks Lick,

Nicholas County. Sarah was born in 1821 in Nicholas County and died Nov. 20, 1897, in Bucks Lick. Alex and Sarah Cavendish are buried at the Dorsey Cemetery, Drennen. The children of Alex and Sarah Dorsey Cavendish were: Samuel H. Cavendish, born on May 5, 1843, married Elizabeth Lewis and had children, Joseph, Homer D., Esther, Florence and Thomas H. Cavendish; Benjamin B. Cavendish, born Aug. 5, 1845, in Nicholas County, married Martha Legg and later Mary E. Koontz, died in Nicholas County in 1894; Andrew (Andy) Cavendish born on July 31, 1847, married Sarah Tully; John M. Cavendish, born Dec. 1, 1849, in Nicholas County and married Agnes Dunbar and later died in Montgomery; Robert L. Cavendish born Nov. 1, 1852, in Nicholas County, married Sarah Legg and died on Feb. 5, 1933, in Fayette County; Socrates Clark Cavendish, born March 14, 1856, married Ida Koontz and died Feb. 10, 1901, at Bend of Gauley, W.Va.; Nancy Jane Cavendish, born June 10, 1863, in Nicholas County and married Finley Koontz and died in 1947; Joseph Finely Cavendish, born Feb. 1859, in Nicholas County and married Ermina Jane Legg (Sis) and he died in 1928.

Alexander and Sarah Dorsey Cavendish settled in land near the Dorseys on Panther Mountain, Nicholas County, and raised seven sons and one daughter (all listed above). There were some Civil War incidents in the community. There are several unmarked graves in the Grose Cemetery on Panther Mountain. Some of the Cavendish family members buried there are: Henry Cavendish, Joseph Finley Cavendish and Benjamin B. Cavendish.

John M. Cavendish and wife, Agnes Dunbar Cavendish, operated a store in Montgomery. John was killed while delivering supplies with a horse and wagon when hit by a train at the lower crossing. John and Agnes had six children: Kennie, Albert, Grafton, Grace, Nora and Vida and are buried at Pratt Cemetery.

Benjamin B. Cavendish (Bud) married twice. To the first wife, Martha A. Legg, two children were born, Charles W. and Ermina L. Cavendish. Martha died May 29, 1881. Mary Elizabeth Koontz was the second wife who had six children with Benjamin. The children were Newton, Essa May, Everette, Elsa, Edward H.

and Burley Sylvanus Cavendish. Benjamin in buried at Grose Cemetery, Panther Mountain, Nicholas County.

The youngest son of Alex and Sarah (Sallie) Dorsey Cavendish was Joseph Finley Cavendish, married Ermina Jane Legg on March 18, 1882. Their son Harry B. drown in 1908 and son Theodore A. Cavendish, born Dec. 30, 1884, was a teacher and active Republican business owner in Cabell County and died Sept. 4, 1968, in Culloden, W.Va. The other children of Joseph F. and Ermina were Otis, Orbin, Esa, Lavina, Lola Ann, Oliver, Leora B. and Leona L. Cavendish.

Robert L. and Sarah Legg Cavendish had five children: Dessie, Mintie, Ona, Dana and Trennie Cavendish.

S. Clark and Ida Koontz Cavendish had six children: Mona, Ivy, Erma, Mae, Chauncey and Hallie Cavendish.

Nancy Jane Cavendish and Finley Koontz married on Oct. 31, 1883, and had five children: Ora, Festus, Elbert, Bertha and Tony Koontz.

Some of the first settlers in Edmond, Fayette County, were the Cavendish Family. The chief industries of that area were farming, coal mining and timber. The churches were Baptist and Methodist and there was a one room school for the early settlers. The Cavendish Family partly remained in Fayette County, Greenbrier County and some settled in rural Nicholas County.

65

SAMUEL H CAVENDISH AND FAMILY — FOURTH AND FIFTH GENERATION

S amuel H. Cavendish, son of Alex and Sarah Dorsey Cavendish, was born May 5, 1843, in Nicholas County, Va. He married Elizabeth Lewis, born Jan. 9, 1844, in Greenbrier County, Va. The marriage took place in Greenbrier County on Oct. 12, 1865. To this union five children were born: Sally Esther Cavendish, born Aug. 29, 1866, in Nicholas County; Joseph A. Cavendish, born April 1, 1871; Homer Dickinson Cavendish, born Nov. 10, 1874, in Vinton, Nicholas County; Thomas Hampton Cavendish, born Feb. 25, 1879; and Florence Cavendish, born July 5, 1882.

According to the obituary of Samuel H. Cavendish on Nov. 2, 1897, he died of "consumption" at his home after a long illness, with his aged parents, Alex and Sarah Dorsey Cavendish, staying to care for him for several days before his death. Samuel was buried at the Donnally VanBibber Cemetery, Camp Fork, Nicholas County. He was 54 years old.

On Nov. 21, 1897, Sarah Ann Dorsey Cavendish died at Tipton after a brief illness. The mother who helped care for her son, Samuel, during his illness, only lived 19 days until her death. Sarah "Sallie" was survived by husband, Alex, and four children. She was buried in the Dorsey Cemetery, Drennen.

The widow of Samuel H. Cavendish, Elizabeth Lewis Cavendish, married George S. McCutcheon in 1900. After her second husband's death, Elizabeth resided with her son, Homer, and wife, Julia Harlow Cavendish, until her death on Jan. 5, 1923, in Zela. She was buried at Keenan Cemetery, Zela.

Sally Esther, daughter of Samuel and Elizabeth Lewis Cavendish, was born Aug. 29, 1866, married John Bailes and died June 15, 1889.

A son, Joseph Alexander, born April 1, 1871, married Mary Elizabeth Hughes. They had one adopted daughter, Agnes, born Nov. 11, 1913. Joseph died Sept. 2, 1963. Mary Elizabeth died 10 years earlier on May 28, 1953. Both are buried in Dotson-Simpson Cemetery, Keslers Cross Lanes, Nicholas County.

Homer Dickenson Cavendish, son of Samuel and Elizabeth L. Cavendish, was born Nov. 10, 1874, in Vinton. He married Julia Alice Harlow, April 25, 1900, in Summersville. They lived on a farm at Keenan's Branch near Zela, where they had 12 children: Clara Esther, born March 4, 1901; Verna Elizabeth, born March 27, 1902; George Burl, born Aug. 1, 1903; Lon Henderson, born May 3, 1905; Levi Bonnie, born Dec. 27, 1906; Ada Alice, born June 11, 1908; Queenie Adelaide, born April 6, 1910, Phala Loraine, born Feb. 28, 1912; Jennings Woodroe, born Nov. 5, 1913; Homer Kyle, born Feb. 5, 1916; Charles Franklin, born May 9, 1918; and Theodore Landon, born Dec. 27, 1920.

Thomas Hampton Cavendish, son of Alex and Elizabeth Cavendish, was born Feb. 25, 1879, married Bessie Holt, resided in Greenbrier County and had five children: Aubrey, John, Obed, Mrs. David Welch, Mary C. Simpson. Thomas H. was a blacksmith and died Aug. 10, 1956, and was buried at the End of the Trail Cemetery, Greenbrier County.

Florence V. Cavendish, born July 5, 1881, at Zela, married Mr. Bailes and later married Wellington Grose. They resided in Victor, Fayette County. She died Oct. 10, 1949, and is buried at Keenan Cemetery, Zela.

Joseph A. Cavendish (1871-1963) Elizabeth
Hughes Cavendish (1871-1953)

Homer D., Julia, and Clara Cavendish in 1902

66

HOMER DICKENSON CAVENDISH AND FAMILY — FIFTH AND SIXTH GENERATIONS

Homer Dickenson Cavendish was born Nov. 10, 1874, at Vinton, Nicholas County, West Virginia, to parents Samuel and Elizabeth Lewis Cavendish. He married Julia Alice Harlow on April 25, 1900. She was the daughter of George Washington and Clara Ellen Hickman Harlow of Summersville.

Homer and Julia lived on a farm on Keenan's Branch Road, Zela, where they farmed and had a large family of 12 children. The first born was Clara Esther, born March 4, 1901; Verna Elizabeth, born March 27, 1902; George Burl, born Aug. 1, 1903; Lon Henderson, born March 3, 1905; Levi Bonnie, born Dec. 27, 1906; Ada Alice, born June 11, 1908; Queenie Adelaide, born April 6, 1910; Phala Loraine, born Feb. 28, 1912; Jennings Woodroe, born, Nov. 5, 1913; Homer Kyle, born Feb. 5, 1916; Charles Franklin, born May 9, 1918; and Theodore Landon, born Dec. 27, 1920.

The large family required much work, as the older children helped to care for the younger children and work on the farm. The farm contained cattle, sheep, horses or mules and small coal mine, which was the fuel source for the fireplace and cooking stove.

There were no modern conveniences such as running water (a well) or bathroom or electricity. Oil lamps were used for light in the two-story house.

Julia Alice and daughters raised a vegetable garden and canned pickles and dried fruits and vegetables. There was a cellar to store root crops, such as potatoes and sweet potatoes. The cool area also kept the fresh milk and churned butter from spoiling. The family also attended to the chickens and gathered eggs from a nearby chicken house. The meat house kept the cured pork from several hogs for the winter use. A grainery housed the grains for the family's use and also for the animals.

The clothes for the family were made by Julia Alice by hand. A Sunday outfit for each and a weekday outfit was about all they had with some "hand-me-downs" from the older children. The family outing other than school was usually once a week to church and in a wagon.

Later, Homer D. Cavendish had an automobile, which he briefly drove, and when he drove into a ditch, he never attempted to drive again. He depended upon one of the seven sons to drive the car, until they left home for the service or to work, then a neighbor would drive Homer and Julia to Summersville to get groceries, such as sugar and flour and other things that the farm did not provide.

Homer and his sons used the blacksmith's shop on the farm for shoeing horses and making and repairing farm implements.

The surplus vegetables, apples, eggs and dressed chickens were carried by horse by Homer D. to sell down Route 39 West to customers. He also sold some coal from his coal mine, which was mined by "pick and shovel" by him and his sons. Some cattle were sold and always the sheep were sheared for the wool and sold. This is how the family was cared for, no extras, but the children all grew into adulthood, were educated in a one-room school and most attended high school.

To have raised 12 children on a farm with no domestic conveniences or assistance, Julia Harlow Cavendish, was a remarkable and innovative woman, was well respected as a friend, mother, grandmother, and neighbor. Julia Alice Harlow Cavendish died of a heart attack on Sept. 25, 1947, at her home on Keenan's Branch Road, Zela. She was buried at the Keenan Cemetery, Zela. She was survived by her husband of 47 years, Homer D. Cavendish and all 12 children.

Homer D. Cavendish continued to live at the farm with son, Homer Kyle, for several years. In declining health, Homer D. stayed with a daughter, Alice Cavendish Murphy in Summersville for some time until he was cared for at the Christian Home, Fayetteville, where he died on Sept. 2, 1960.

Homer D. Cavendish was survived by his 12 children and buried beside his late wife, Julia Alice Cavendish in the Keenan Cemetery, Zela. Homer and Alice Cavendish had 38 grandchildren.

Front row, Queenie, Jennings (on lap) Julia Cavendish, Homer D. with Phala, Bonnie; middle, Alice; back, Clara, Verna, Burl and Lon (Circa 1915-16)

Homer D. and Julia Harlow Cavendish Family: back
row, Clara, Verna, Alice, Queenie, Phala and Jennings;
front row, Burl, Bonnie, Theodore, and parents Julia
and Homer D. Cavendish, Charles, Kyle, and Lon
Cavendish. Circa 1940s, Cavendish Farm, Zela, W.Va.

67

FIVE CAVENDISH BROTHERS
SERVE IN WORLD WAR II

T he five sons of Homer D. and Julia Harlow Cavendish served in the Military Service during World War II. It was a difficult time for the parents to see their sons off to war in 1942, and the loss was also felt on the Cavendish Farm.

Five of the seven sons, George Burl, Jennings, Home Kyle, Charles F., and Theodore L. Cavendish were in the service. A flag with five stars hung in the farmhouse window during World War II. All five sons returned home following their discharges in 1945. Only Homer Kyle was seriously wounded and required a lengthy hospital stay for recovery. He received a Disability Discharge from the U.S. Army.

**PFC Jennings W. Cavendish
648th Medical Clearing Co.**

Induction: June 12, 1942 — discharge Oct. 29, 1945
Campaigns and battles: Northern France, Ardennes,
Rhineland, and Central Europe
Decorations: Good Conduct Medal, Am. Theater Service
Ribbon, WWII Victory Ribbon, European, African and
Middle Eastern Service Ribbon

**PFC Theodore L. Cavendish
Battery "B" 322 Field Artillery Battalion**

Induction: Nov. 21, 1942 — discharge Dec. 6, 1945
Campaigns or battles: Normandy, Northern France, Ardennes,
Rhineland, and Central Europe Decorations: Good Conduct
Medal, Am. Theater Service, European, African, Middle
Eastern Service Ribbon. World War II Victory Ribbon

PFC Homer Kyle Cavendish
Co. I 327th Glider Division Infantry

Induction: March 24, 1942 — discharge Oct. 12, 1945
Campaigns of battles: Normandy, Bastone, Germany, and
Belgium
Decorations: Four Bronze Stars, Oak Leaf Cluster, Purple
Heart, Unit Citation, Glider Badge, and Combat Infantry
Badge. Awarded certificate of disability discharge

George Burl Cavendish
U.S. Navy
Medical Discharge

CPL. Charles Franklin Cavendish
Corporal Detachment "B", 52nd Fighter Control Squadron

Induction: April 28, 1942 — discharge Oct. 1, 1945
Campaigns or battles: Air Offensics, Europe, Normandy,
France, Rhineland, Ardennes, and Central Europe.
Decorations: European, African, Middle Eastern, Service
Ribbon, Good Conduct Medal, Oak Leaf Cluster, and
Distinguished Unit Badge

68
HOMER D. AND JULIA ALICE HARLOW CAVENDISH FAMILY

H omer D. and Julia Alice Harlow Cavendish grew up on the Cavendish Farm on Keenan's Branch Road near Zela. The first-born was Clara Esther, born March 4, 1901. She taught school before her marriage on April 29, 1923, to Albert Jennings Bailes. They lived their early life together at Gad, W.Va., in the McKees Creek area. They were parents of six children: Howard Calvin born Feb. 25, 1925, never married and died on July 23, 1997; Albert Jennings Jr. born Oct. 26, 1926, married Patricia Venth and after her death, married Loreda Cochran on Sept. 9, 1999; Hilda Ruth born Dec. 10, 1930 married Gayle Van Hoy and had four children, Nancy, Betty Jean, Teresa, and John R. VanHoy; Esther Elaine, born March 19, 1938, at Gad, married Daniel L. Clark on June 3, 1961, parents of two children, Lewis and Lisa Clark; Helen Naomi, born July 28, 1939, married Bernard Staats on April 11, 1959, and are parents of two daughters, Jill and Monica Staats; Charles Landon born Nov. 17, 1936, married Frances Ramsey and he died in an accident on Jan 13, 1987. They had four children, Charles L. Jr, Charlotte, Cheryl, and Charlene Bailes.

The second child, Verna Elizabeth Cavendish, born March 27, 1902, taught school and married James Allen Hamilton on Aug. 6, 1927, parents of Laura Elizabeth born Aug. 2, 1930, and

James Eugene, born March 9, 1932. They lived on Armstrong Road near Summersville. James A. Hamilton died Jan. 15, 1983, and Verna E. died Dec. 10, 1996. Both were buried in Grose Cemetery on Armstrong Road.

The third child, George Burl Cavendish, was born Aug. 1, 1903, and married Irene Brillhart on July 23, 1942. They had two daughters, Julia Ann, born July 15, 1945, and Norma Ruth born Feb. 12, 1947. They lived at South Charleston, W.Va., and later in Summersville. George Burl died May 15, 1984. Irene died Nov. 18, 1984. Both are buried at West Virginia Memorial Gardens, Calvin.

The fourth child, Lon Henderson, was born May 3, 1905, and married Elsie Gray on Jan. 20, 1935. They had three children: Ezzelle May, born March 16, 1936, Orvin Leon, born Oct. 12, 1939, and Thelma Ann, born March 26, 1946. Lon Henderson died May 17, 1980, and Elsie died Sept. 27, 2003. Both are buried at West Virginia Memorial Gardens.

The fifth child, Levi Bonnie, was born Dec. 27, 1906, and married Lura Tyree on Nov. 15, 1936. They had two daughters, Charlotte, born June 19, 1940, and Patricia, born June 13, 1945. Bonnie died Nov. 30, 1990, and Lura died Oct. 5, 2007. Both are buried at West Virginia Memorial Gardens.

The sixth child, Ada Alice, was born June 11, 1908, and married James Ralph Murphy on July 3, 1929. They were the parents of five children: James Leo, born Dec. 31, 1930, Anna Lee, born Aug. 23, 1932, Julia Frances, born Aug. 8, 1933, and twins John Calvin and Jeannean Carolyn, born Jan. 21, 1943. J. Ralph and Alice Murphy lived in Summersville. Ada Alice died Oct. 13, 1964, and J. Ralph died June 29, 1980. Both are buried in Walker Memorial Park Cemetery in Summersville.

The seventh child, Queenie Adelaide, was born April 6, 1910, married Thomas C. Dorsey on Dec. 26, 1935. They were the parents of 10 children: Shelba Jean, born Sept. 10, 1937, Jo Ann Dorsey, born Aug. 7, 1938, Thomas Dickerson, born Feb. 16, 1941, James Robert, born June 5, 1943, Shirlene Doris, born Nov. 8, 1945, twins Pauline Sue and Claudine Lou, born July

9, 1948, John David born July 26, 1950, Brenda Joyce, born April 8, 1952, and Julia Louise, born Jan 16, 1954. They lived in Gilboa on the Dorsey Farm. Thomas and Queenie are buried in the Keenan Cemetery, Zela.

The eighth child, Phala Loraine, was born Feb. 28, 1912, and married Patrick L. Grose on May 5, 1933. They were the parents of five sons: Gerald Leon born Sept. 9, 1936, Charles Russell born April 21, 1938, twins John Hamilton Grose and James Hamilton Grose, born Jan. 21, 1941, and Homer Samuel, born June 11, 1943. Phala and Patrick Grose are buried in the Grose Cemetery on Armstrong Road near Summersville.

The ninth child, Jennings Woodroe Cavendish, was born Nov. 5, 1913, married Virginia Grey in June 1944. They were the parents of two children, Freda Mae, and Jennings Woodrow Jr. born Sept. 1947. Jennings and Virginia are buried in the Dotson-Simpson Cemetery, Keslers Cross Lanes.

The 10th child, Homer Kyle Cavendish, was born Feb. 5, 1916, never married and served in World War II where he was wounded and received a disability discharge in 1945. Kyle died Jan. 31, 1993, and is buried in Keenan Cemetery, Zela.

The 11th child, Charles Franklin Cavendish, was born Feb. 9, 1918, and married Loretta O'Dell on Dec. 31, 1949. They had two children, Mary Ann, born June 23, 1958, and died in infancy; and Mark Charles, born December 1959. Charles Franklin died Jan 14, 1962, and is buried at Keenan Cemetery along with daughter, Mary Ann. Loretta moved to Tucson, Arizona, where she died Aug. 18, 1994. Son, Mark Charles Cavendish, resides in Arizona.

The 12th child, Theodore Landon, was born Dec. 27, 1920, and married Hazel Ford. They had no children. Theodore L. Cavendish died Sept. 25, 1981, and Hazel died Feb. 26, 2006. They are both buried in the Dotson-Simpson Cemetery, Keslers Cross Lanes.

An interesting note that all 12 Cavendish children were single births, but there were three sets of twins born to three daughters of Homer D. and Julia Harlow Cavendish. All 12 children are deceased. Clara Bailes died May 14, 1984, Lon H. died May 17, 1980, Levi Bonnie, died Nov. 30, 1990, Queenie Dorsey died Feb. 9, 1998, Ada Alice Murphy died Oct. 13, 1964, Phala Grose died Sept. 11, 1978, Jennings W. died Jan 5, 1980, Homer Kyle died Jan. 31, 1993, Charles F. died Jan. 14, 1962, and Theodore Cavendish died Sept. 25, 1981.

Homer Dickerson (Dickinson) Cavendish seldom used his middle name. It is recorded on the marriage license and it is difficult to read the handwritten spelling of the name. The Cavendish Farm has completely returned back to nature, as there are no buildings or monuments to the land that once sustained the large Cavendish family. The property is now owned by a Cavendish heir.

Julia Harlow Cavendish and daughters, Clara
Bailes, Verna Hamilton, Queenie Dorsey, Alice
Murphy and Phala Grose — 1940

Theodore, Charles, Kyle, Jennings, Bonnie, Lon, and Burl
Cavendish with their father, Homer D. Cavendish — circa 1940s

69

THE HARLOW FAMILY FROM
BOTETOURT COUNTY, VIRGINIA

"**B**otetourt County and Its Men," 1780-1786 By Charles T. Burton, lists John Harlow as a member of the Militia Company No. 40 and the same name appears in the 1820 census. In the 1850 census is listed William Harlow, born circa 1820, and James Harlow, born 1819.

The Harlow Family that we shall follow is the James Edward Harlow (1819) and wife, Minerva Painter, who were bonded July 28, 1845, to the Governor of the Commonwealth of Virginia for the sum of $150.

The eight children of James Edward and Minerva Painter Harlow were born in Botetourt County, Va.: George Washington Harlow, born June 15, 1845 d. 1926; Mary Harlow, born 1848; Ruby Keenan Harlow, born July 16, 1857, died 1925; Samuel A. Harlow, born 1860, died 1931; Susan Harlow, born 1865, died 1959; John Harlow; Lewis Harlow; and General B. Harlow, born 1865, died 1924.

Samuel Harlow married Sallie Clinebell in 1887. They purchased the Cartsmill's Farm in Purgatory, his birthplace, and spent his entire life there. They had children: Lewis (1888-1963), Lon (1889-1972), Edd (1896-1979), Charlie (1896-), Sidney (1895-1950), Daisy (1902-) married Morris Campber and Leonard (1906-) who lived on the home place in Purgatory, Va.

George Washington Harlow married Clara Ellen Hickman March 7, 1878, in Rockbridge County, Va. Their first child, Julia Alice Harlow, was born Dec. 11, 1879, in Rockbridge County, Va.

The Harlow Family first appeared on the Federal Census of 1880 in Nicholas County, W.Va. George Washington and Clara Ellen moved with their young daughter, Julia Alice, along with three younger brothers: Lewis, Rubin and John Harlow; and sister, Susan, to Nicholas County where he bought a farm on Peter's Creek.

General B. Harlow came later to Nicholas County and married Minnie Bowyer (1876-1955) and they had seven children: Gussie (1898-1995), Irene (1900-1940), Clyde (1903-1981), Lee (1905-1976), John Paul (1908-1964), Mary Pearl (1911-1989), Ruby (1915-1987). Most of his family is buried in the Backus-Fitzwater Cemetery, Salmon Run Road, near Summersville. John Paul and wife, Inez McCutcheon Harlow, are buried in the Walker Park Cemetery, Summersville.

Rubin (1857-1925) married Cora Ann Lively (1872-1937). They were the parents of five children: Joseph Carroll Harlow (1899-1987), Ada, Alice, Ida May, and Keith (1887-1906). Rubin and Cora Harlow are buried in the Southern Methodist Cemetery, Summersville.

Susan Harlow (1865-1959) married Mr. Blake and had two children, Jack and Rebecca. Susan lived in Summersville and is buried in the Backus-Fitzwater Cemetery.

Lewis Edgar Harlow married Henrietta Bryant. They were the parents of Elmer Lewis Harlow (1905-1983); Harry Harlow, who lived in Maryland; Velma lived in Illinois; Opal lived in Little Rock, Ark.; and Ruth lived in Pennsylvania.

When the long trip by horse and wagon was possible, the Harlow Families would return to Purgatory, Va., for a Harlow Reunion with the family who remained in Botetourt County. Carving out a life in the mountains of Nicholas County in the early years was a challenge for those who chose to cross the mountains from Virginia to West Virginia.

Harlow Family Reunions were held almost each year either in Botetourt County, Va., or near Summersville. This would be the only opportunity to see and visit with relatives.

According to a written account of a Harlow Reunion on the Harlow Farm in Summersville, they were entertained with beautiful songs, played on the violin by J. W. McHenry, husband of Rose Harlow McHenry.

The Harlow Reunion is currently held at noon on the third Saturday of July at the Summersville Dam Shelter Picnic area.

Next will be the family of George Washington Harlow.

George Washington Harlow b. June 15, 1845 — d. Nov. 20, 1926
Clara Ellen Hickman Harlow b. Sept. 2, 1859 — d. Nov. 7, 1924

Descendants of James E. Harlow and wife, Minerva Painter Harlow, General Harlow and Family and George Washington Harlow Family 1925 Front row: Louise Gray, Buster Gray, Charles Cavendish, Julia Harlow Cavendish, Theodore Cavendish, George W. Harlow, Bennett O'Dell, Dennis O'Dell, Paul O'Dell, Dimple Bragg, Bernard Bragg and Barbara Bragg; Row two: Owen E. Gray, Queenie Cavendish Dorsey, Sally Ann Harlow Gray, Homer D. Cavendish, Juanita O'Dell, Jennings Cavendish, Kyle Cavendish, Phala Cavendish Grose, Clara Cavendish Bailes, Katherine Bragg, Omar Bragg, Verna Cavendish Hamilton, Kitty Harlow, Jake Harlow, Minnie Holcomb Harlow; last row: William Harlow, Joe Harlow, James Gray, Rose Harlow McHenry, Alice Cavendish Murphy, Gussie Harlow Bailes, Elmer Bailes, Paul Bailes, Lewis Harlow, Velma Harlow and Opal Harlow

70

GEORGE WASHINGTON HARLOW AND FAMILY

Clara Ellen and George Washington Harlow and young daughter, Julia Alice (Dec. 11, 1879) arrived in Nicholas County after a long trip by wagon across the mountains from Virginia to start a new life. A farm near Peters Creek, west of Summersville, was purchased. The family increased with James Edward Buck Harlow (1882-1958), Rose Josephine (1883-1961), Annie Mae (1885-1971), Molly (1884-1976), Catherine (1888-1960), Sally Ann (1889-1955), twins Jake (1890-1968) and Frank (1890-1911), George William (1892-1970). The family lived in a two-story house about one-half mile below Summersville where George Washington Harlow farmed to care for his large family.

Julia Alice Harlow married Homer D. Cavendish on April 25, 1900. They were the parents of 12 children: Clara (Bailes), Verna (Hamilton), George Burl, Lon H., Bonnie, Alice (Murphy), Queenie (Dorsey), Phala (Grose), Jennings, Homer Kyle, Charles F., and Theodore Cavendish. Julia Alice died Sept. 25, 1947 and had 38 grandchildren.

James Edward Buck Harlow married Bertha Morriston on April 3, 1910. They had 10 children: Jake Eugene, Lewis Mason, Edith A., Lambert, Ellen Mae, Heber, Ruth Anne, Alice L., Dana E., and Phyllis. They lived near the Bend of Gauley. Bertha died in 1933, and Buck married Halcie Hyer from Clay County,

W.Va. Buck died in 1958 and is buried in the Dotson- Simpson Cemetery, Keslers Cross Lanes. Annie Mae Harlow married Everette O'Dell on Nov. 15, 1905. They raised a family of six children: Kelly O'Dell, Juanita Hughes, Lanty, Paul and twins Herbert Dennis and Bennett O'Dell. Everett O'Dell died Jan 16, 1948, and Annie Mae died Sept. 18, 1971. They are buried in Dotson-Simpson Cemetery.

Molly Harlow married Marshall Gray on Dec. 27, 1910. They were the parents of five children: George Marshall Gray, Gladys, Sylvia, Beulah, and Crynthia Bell Gray. The family lived near Drennen and Molly and Marshall Gray are buried in Montgomery Memorial Park, London, W.Va. Catherine "Kate" Harlow married J. Oscar Bragg on Sept. 30, 1908. They were the parents of eight children: Beatrice, Bernice, Fred, Barbara, Dimple, Omer, Bernard, and Betty Lou (died in infancy). They lived near Summersville. The parents are buried in the Backus Fitzwater Cemetery on Salmon Run, Summersville.

Rose Josephine Harlow married James William McHenry on Aug. 8, 1910. They resided in Lockwood, W.Va., where they raised a family of 11 children: Cecil W., twins Lilly M. and William J., Glen W., Earl, Mary Rose, Mildred, Harlow, Daisy, Shearl and Virginia. The parents are buried at Sims United Methodist Church Cemetery, Swiss.

Sally Ann Harlow married Owen E. Gray on Sept. 20, 1909. They were the parents of seven children: James Edward, Lottie Mae, Dainty Virginia, Audrey Rae, Reba Ann, Louise and Owen M. Gray.

Twin Frank Harlow died at 21. His twin Jake Harlow married Minnie Holcomb on Jan. 25, 1926. They had five children: Olia, Nola, Delano, Flavia and Randall. They lived on the George Washington Harlow Family Farm. They and some of the children are buried on the farm on the Harlow Cemetery.

In 1925, the two-story house and granary on the George Washington Harlow Farm were destroyed by fire, which originated in the kitchen. The water supply was exhausted and the fire could not be extinguished, but some furniture was saved. A large sum of money in the house was lost. There was no insurance carried.

According to the death certificates, Clara Ellen Harlow died from stomach cancer on Nov. 7, 1924, at 76. George W. Harlow died on Nov. 20, 1926, from pneumonia fever at 80. Both are buried in the Harlow Cemetery on the Harlow Farm, Summersville.

George Washington and Clara Ellen Harlow had 64 grandchildren.

Daughters of George W. and Clara Ellen Harlow, circa 1940: L. Sally Gray, Kate Bragg, Mary O'Dell, Julia Cavendish, Molly Gray and Rose McHenry

George William Harlow (1892-1970) and Jake Harlow (1890-1968)

James Edward Harlow (1887-1958) and wife

Frank Harlow 1890-1911

71

THE MCCLUNG FAMILY

The early record of the McClung Family located them in Galloway, Scotland. Tradition says that three brothers, James, John and Robert, left Scotland on the account of religious persecution and settled in the Province of Ulster, Ireland, in about 1690. Some of the family members located in other parts of Ireland, and some immigrated to America.

The first to settle near Christiana, Pa., in 1729, was Tom McClung from Moate, Ireland. Others followed in about 1731. John McClung settled in Brookfield, Mass., and later went to Lancaster County, Pa. His father and the rest of the family joined him in about 1740. The father, James, and wife, and their eight children: James, William, Hugh, Charles, Matthew, Mary, Isabel, and John. Later in 1742, James, William and Hugh settled in Augusta County, Va., (now Rockbridge County). Other members settled in other areas of Pennsylvania, and from there the descendants went north, east and west. Other emigrants of the McClungs from Ireland followed within a decade or so to America.

The McClung families started their families and married wives from other families in the many areas they settled. Many family names are repeated in following generations, which becomes confusing. So to distinguish the many Williams, James, Josephs and etc., another descriptive name was attached, such as Samuel "Nicholas Sam," Joseph "Fear Not," William "Grandfather Billy," John "Lame John," and also the county location was used. They referred to Nicholas, Greenbrier, Pennsylvania, Tennessee, Canada, Dublin, Belfast and other McClungs.

The McClung Genealogy, by the Rev. William McClung, written on 1904, refers to several encounters with the Indians. Some were killed; others were wounded and escaped. William McClung "Grandfather Billy" born about 1738, died Jan. 18, 1833. He emigrated from Rockbridge County, Va., to Greenbrier County. He took a tomahawk entry for 1000,000 acres and was the first to settle on the Meadow River. The Indians were so troublesome that he plowed his fields with his rifle tied to his shoulder, while his wife with her musket and three children took refuge in the dense swamp during the day and returned to the cabin at night when her husband was there to defend them.

In partnership with General Andrew Moore and Alexander Welch, William McClung patented a tract of land of 43,000 acres between Meadow and Gauley River in Nicholas County. Many of "Grandfather Billy" McClung's descendants settled in Greenbrier and Nicholas Counties. He married Abigail Dickinson who had 11 children. She died Nov. 7, 1820. A daughter, Janet "Jane" McClung was born Oct. 4, 1788, and married Andrew Cavendish on April 27, 1809.

There were many members of the McClung families who married prominent names and settled in Nicholas County. Samuel McClung married Georgiana Alderson. Sarah Martha McClung married Edward Tyree. Catherine McClung was born in 1803 and died in 1883. She married Daniel Brock. Margaret Jane McClung married John Richard Tyree on March 15, 1873. Mary Eliza McClung was born Feb. 16, 1856, and married Henry Herold of Summersville on April 19, 1877. John Tyree moved from Fayette County to Nicholas County where he married Elizabeth McClung on May 19, 1842. She was the daughter of "Lame John" and Deborah Rader McClung.

Talitha McClung, born April 14, 1827, married Anderson C. Herold on July 4, 1850. They had a child, H.W. Herold. Many McClung families settled in the Mount Lookout, Nicholas County area. The Rev. Charles Allen McClung, born Jan 10, 1862, married Mary Lewis Champe on April 19, 1883. They were the parents of nine children: Ona, May 14, 1884; Judson L., April 24, 1887; Clinton, Oct. 7, 1888; Cynthia L., April 14, 1890; Burton, March 24, 1893; Jay R., Jan. 8, 1895; Draper, Dec. 3, 1896; Fuller, Jan. 14, 1899; and Milton, Nov. 21, 1900.

Another McClung line from John McClung, who died about 1788, was James McClung (1700-1824) who married Sarah Evans. They had Dickenson Carpenter McClung, and his son was Matthew Thomas Mc- Clung (1841-1890). His son was Caleb Watts McClung (1867-1943) who married Marinda Abigail Mc- Clung in 1890 and lived in Mount Lookout. They had four children, William Elton, Hallie Francis, Verda Louella and Clarence Springston McClung, who was born April 9, 1897, and died Dec. 9, 1955. Clarence Springston McClung married Pearl Ramsey on July 26, 1923, in Summersville. They lived in Winona, W.Va., part of the time and were the parents of four children: Gory, 1926; Glendell, 1928; Sharon, 1931; and Lowell Gale McClung, 1924. Gale married Mary Louise Amacker of Poplarville, Miss., in 1946, after serving in World War II. They spent most of their married life in Summersville and were the parents of a daughter, Susan Gail, b. 1946. Gale McClung died in Jacksonville, Fla., on July 17, 2008. Louise and daughter, Susan, live in Jacksonville.

There are many McClung families in Nicholas County at this time with numerous family connections. The McClungs followed many professions as farmers, merchants, educators, doctors, ministers, and lawyers and were very successful and respected.

William Scott McClung, born July 26, 1880, married Florence Tyree Dec. 11, 1910. William Scott McClung was the son of Andrew Davis McClung (1832-1903) and Sarah Ann Tomlinson McClung (1840-1919). They were also the parents of Lucinda, Ruth, Edward, and Jennie McClung. W. Scott and Florence McClung were parents of Lena (Baker), Lelia (Bostic), Grace (Mills), Ruth (Bailey) and William Edward 'Bill" McClung. The family resided in Canvas on a farm.

After the death of the first wife, Scott McClung, married Nora Groves (Reynolds) (Nutter) and lived in Summersville until his death on May 8, 1965. Son William E. 'Bill" lived in the house on Church Street.

More information of the McClung Family will be included with the Tyree Family stories.

Scott (1880-1965) and Florence McClung (1890-1942), married on Dec. 11, 1910

The McClung -Tyree Home Left, Florence Rader McClung,
daughter Carrie, wife of Henry McClung; in chair, Martha
Woods McClung, wife of Anthony McClung; Sarah Martha
McClung Tyree, married to Edward Tyree; baby Ida; Samuel
McClung (sitting in chair); and Georgia Alderson McClung,
wife of Samuel McClung. On the porch are Ellie Cottle and
Annie White. (Location Phillips Run, Summersville)

72

THE TYREE FAMILY

L ike many families that immigrated to America, the Tyree name appeared in Scotland. Tyree Family records are shown in New Kent, County, Va., by 1759. The early spelling believed to have been spelled Tyrie and Tirie.

William Tyree made his settlement in Charles City County, Va. He had four sons: Richard F., married Sally (Sarah) Johnston on April 3, 1804, settled in Lewisburg and kept the first hotel "Long Ordinary," which describes the size, 10 x 75 yards long. The other three sons, Frances, John and another stayed in Virginia.

Richard F. Tyree bought a farm near Mountain Cove, Fayette County. They had nine children all born in Lewisburg: Mary Jane (Feamster), John George, Samuel, Martha (Wells), Sallie (Sarah) (McClung), Francis, Rebecca and William. The father died in 1834 and Sarah (Sallie) died in 1839, and both are buried in the Tyree Cemetery at the foot of Sewell Mountain near the Stone House residence.

Col. William Tyree, born in 1807, had an impressive life beginning with an early education at the Lewisburg Academy. He married Rebecca McClung and four children were born to this union. Rebecca died in 1841. Col. Tyree was first Sheriff of Fayette County from 1831 until 1846 and served in the Virginia Legislature in 1855-56. He was Colonel of the 142 Regiment of the Virginia Militia. He married Sarah McClung, who was the daughter of Andrew McClung of Greenbrier County. They had one son, Charles W. Tyree. Col. William Tyree, a member of the Methodist Church, was granted 656.75 acres of land. He died of cancer in 1883.

John Tyree, born in 1811, was the son of Richard F. Tyree. He moved with his parents to Fayette County as a young boy and lived in Mountain Cove. He moved to Nicholas County at the age of 29. There he met Elizabeth McClung and was married May 19, 1842. She was the daughter of "Lame John" McClung and Deborah Rader McClung. John and Elizabeth Tyree lived on Muddlety Creek, four miles northwest of Summersville. John purchased 560 acres of land that he farmed. They were the parents of six children: Sarah Rebecca (b.1844), John Richard (1846-1920), George J. (1850-1877), Fiedling Mc Tyree (1852-1935), James W. (1854-) and Mary E. Tyree (Betty) (1856-1923).

Sarah Rebecca Tyree married Charles A. McClung. Their children were Mary, Anne, George, James R., Charles and Nellie McClung. Some of this family moved to Kansas about 1871.

John Richard Tyree married Margaret Jane McClung on March 15, 1866. Their children were Charles Allen Newman, George Emerson, Rebecca Ann, Hudson Dickson, Richard Flem, Marshall L., Eugene N., Mary Ella and Aminta Tyree. The mother, Margaret Jane died June 28, 1927. John Richard Tyree died Feb. 24, 1920, and they are buried on the George Allen Groves Farm in Enon. George Emerson Tyree married Alice Groves on April 20, 1889. Their children are Chessie (Groves), Clara (Harvey), Lela (Groves) and Nellie McMillion.

Rebecca Anne Tyree married Joel Hill Groves on April 27, 1899. The children born to this union were: George Arnett (1900-1967), David Flem (1903-1982), Virgie Irene (1901-1999), Martha Jane (Mason) (1906-), Leonard (1908-1969), Kyle (1910-), Mary Glenna (Fitzwater) (1913-), and Gladys (Chapman) (1915-2007).

Hudson D. Tyree married Emily Brown on Nov. 5, 1909 and had a son, John Herman Tyree (1912-1925). Hudson D. also married Lysia Cox Woods on July 20, 1921, and they had Kathleen Ruth (Smith).

John Richard Tyree married Margaret Jane McClung
in 1866. She died June 28, 1927. John R. died
Feb. 24, 1920. They had 10 children.

73

THE TYREE FAMILY – PART TWO

The Tyree Family emigrated from Scotland and settled in Virginia. They moved to Fayette County and into Nicholas County where many married into the McClung and Groves families.

Marshall Leonard Tyree married Mertie Welmer Bell on June 9, 1912. Their children were born on the old Tyree Farm Place. They were Ezelle (Hypes) (1913-), Mary (Nugen) (1917-2007), John B. (1918-), and Marshall Paul (1922-1968) who married Eloise Rapp and had two sons.

Mary Ella Tyree married Richard Groves Sept. 28, 1905. They were the parents of Verta (1907-), Nita (Bell) (1909-), Verner (1911-), Virgil (1916-), Vada M. (Baker) (1913-), Heber V. (1918-), Virginia (Dodrill) (1924-), and Velda Groves (1927-).

Arminta Tyree married Goff Groves Aug. 25, 1915. Their children were Zelda Groves (1917-), Thelma (McClung) (1918-), Hugh (1921-), Clyde (1924-1983), and Myrtle Groves (1920-2006).

George J. Tyree never married and died in 1877.

Fielding Mc Tyree married Susan Davis on Oct. 10, 1872, from Fincastle, Va. They lived on the Tyree Farm near Summersville, which was willed to him by his father, John Tyree. Their children were Walter Lee (1873-1933), his twin William W. (1873-1955), Edward (1876-1966), John Davis (1878-1951), Mary E. Tyree

(1882-1943), Sallie A. (1884-1904), Otis McGee Tyree (1887-1972), and Florence Tyree (1890-1942).

Several members went west and settled in South Dakota, Arizona, Iowa, Minnesota, California and Oklahoma.

Edward Tyree married Sarah Martha McClung, born Sept. 14, 1876, to Georgiana Alderson and Samuel McClung. They were farmers in Nicholas County and are buried in the Tyree Cemetery near Summersville. Their children were: Owen F. (1898-1971), Ida Mae (1899-1977), George H. (1902-1976), Mamie Anna (1904-1993), Ollie (1905-1983), Sam (1906-1907), Otis Paul (1908-1985), Georgia F. (1909-2003), Charles Edward (1911-1958), Vesta D. (1913-2002), and Coleman Newman (1915-2002).

Owen Fielding Tyree married Ocie Williams Jan. 28, 1921. Their children were: Hubert (1922-), Leon (1925-), and Lloyd (1927-). Owen married the second time to Clara Belle Hamrick on Feb. 13, 1936, and their daughter, Agnes, was born Aug. 31, 1939. Agnes Tyree married Clyde Dale McClung on Sept. 12, 1958. Their children are: Merry Lynn (1960-). Melinda (1962-), and Matthew Dale McClung (1974-), who is an ordained United Methodist Minister.

Otis Paul Tyree married Ruth Bryant on Aug. 12, 1933. They had three children, Shirley, David and Linda Tyree.

Ollie Susan Tyree married Everette W. Perrine on June 25, 1827 and lived in Ohio. Their children were Edward, Vera, Berwyn and Delmas Perrine.

Georgia Frances Tyree married Wade Woods on June 4, 1932, and had a son, Newman Hill Woods (1942).

Charles Edward Tyree married Ida Faye Smith on June 18, 1938. He had some health problems, which required surgery at Johns Hopkins Hospital, where he died in surgery. The children born to this union were Martha Jean (1940-) who married Edward Suss on Nov. 15, 1963; Charlene Ann, born (1942-) and married Lester Perry on April 16, 1965. They lived near Cleveland, Ohio, until retirement when they moved back to Summersville. Ida Faye married Elton Rapp.

Vesta Della Tyree married Floyd F. Rock on June 26, 1939, and lived at Glade Creek, Nicholas County.

Cleleman Newman Tyree married Retta Faye Murphy on Feb. 28, 1945. He was in World War I and retired from Peerless Eagle Coal Company and resided at Phillips Run Road near Summersville. Their children were: Sharon (1946), Suzanne (1948), Edward Allen (1951) and Frances Waynew Tyree (1957-).

John Davis Tyree married and lived in Oklahoma.

Mary E. Tyree married Adolphus Bostic on Dec. 25, 1907. The children born to this union were: Earl Bostic (1910-), Edith (1915-), Everette, Irene (1922-), Madeline (1921-) and Alice Bostic (1925-1945).

Sallie A. Tyree (1884-1904) was unmarried and is buried in McClung Cemetery on Phillips Run Road near Summersville.

The Tyree Brothers

The Tyree Family

74

THE NICHOLAS COUNTY
TYREE FAMILY

Otis McGee Tyree married Hester V. Groves on July 4, 1914. They lived in the Fielding Mc Tyree home, which was built in 1861. They had eight children: Lawrence Mc Tyree (1915-1963), Lula Tyree (1916-), Lee Tyree (1917-), Lura Tyree (1918-2007), John Lundy (1919-1998), Leslie (1921-1985), Laura Belle (1924-1924), and Leonard Otis Tyree (1931-) Hester Groves Tyree was born in 1893 and died in 1957. This family lived in Phillips Run, near Summersville.

Lawrence Tyree married Hester Brewer on Nov. 29, 1936, and had: Betty (1933-2007), Shirley (1937), William Jr. (1940) and Charles Barr (1955).

Lee Tyree married Jean Hartley on April 24, 1948, and he served in World War II and had one son, Robert Wayne Tyree (1950).

Lura Tyree married Levi Bonnie Cavendish on Nov. 15, 1936 and lived on Phillips Run near the Tyree home. Bonnie worked for Ely-Thomas Lumber Company. The children born to this union are Charlotte Cavendish, who was born June 19, 1940, married Dale Allman on Aug. 19, 1962, and had one daughter, Cynthia Kay Allman. Patricia Cavendish born June 13, 1945, married Dencil Backus on Aug. 13, 1966, and had children, Shane Backus born Nov. 14, 1970, and Shanita Backus born Oct. 15,

1975. Patricia married Richard Kalt on April 5, 1980. Richard Kalt died April 22, 2008.

John Lundy Tyree married Marjorie Monroe in 1942. She was born on June 3, 1920 and died Feb. 1, 2001. Their children are: Helen Ruth (1943), Glenn Allen (1947) and Lundy Tyree (1950). Helen Ruth married Fred Roberts in 1962. Glen Tyree married Pam Walker in 1967, and Lundy married Barbara Conrad in 1972.

Leslie Howard Tyree married Lenora Carte on March 14, 1944 and served in World War II. They are the parents of Bonita (1947) and Sandra Tyree (1953).

Leonard Otis Tyree and Geraldine Groves were married June 23, 1962. Geraldine taught school, and Leonard served as school principal. They live at the Fielding Mc Tyree Farm on Phillips Run. Children born to them are: James (1963-1963), Leonard Otis Tyree Jr. (1965), Charles Tyree (1971).

After retirement, Leonard has established a painting business in the area.

Florence Tyree married William Scott McClung on Dec. 11, 1910. He was born July 26, 1880 and died May 8, 1965. They lived on a farm at Canvas, where they are buried in the family cemetery. Their children were Lena Baker (1911-1994), Lelia (Bostic) (1914-), William E. (1918-2006), Grace (Mills) (1920-), and Ruth V. McClung (Bailey) (1923-).

William E. "Bill" McClung was born Sept. 18, 1918, at Canvas. He married Mary Hennessy, and they were the parents of William E. McClung Jr., Elizabeth McClung Reynolds, and James Michael McClung. Following the death of the first wife, Mary, William E. McClung married Shirley Hughes on July 3, 1959. They are the parents of a son, Mark Allen McClung. "Bill" Mc- Clung passed away May 28, 2006, in Summersville. "Bill" and Shirley resided in the Scott McClung House, which was a rooming house for many years. After Florence Tyree McClung passed away, Scott married Nora Groves Reynolds (Nutter), a widow of Robert P. Reynolds of Summerville.

There are several generations of the Tyree Families who married and remained in Nicholas County. Others went westward, where some generations remained. It is interesting to note how many of the Tyrees married McClungs, Groves and other Nicholas County families. Those who traveled to other states changed the pattern to other names native to a particular area.

There is a Nicholas County saying, "you don't say anything negative about a person, as they are probably related."

Note: A special "thank you" to Charlene Tyree Perry for sharing information of her ancestors.

Seated, "Mac" Fielding McTyree, Susan Davis Tyree, standing, Edward Tyree, Mary Tyree Bostic, Florence Tyree McClung, and Otis Tyree

Tyree Home place Fielding Mc Tyree and wife, Susan Davis Tyree, in front of their home on Phillips Run Road. Built circa 1861.

75

JAMES D. IRELAND AND PETERS CREEK COAL COMPANY

After World War II the demand for coal production increased to be used in steel mills and manufacturing of things needed to build cars, bridges, buildings and etc. Nicholas County had coal reserves that were needed and would bring prosperity to the rural area.

James D. Ireland was born Dec. 1, 1913, in Duluth, Minn., and grew up in Cleveland, Ohio. He attended Hawken School, St. Paul School, Kent School and Cornell School of Engineering. His professional career began in 1937 in the coalmines of M.A. Hanna and progressed to Division Superintendent.

In 1946, he came to Nicholas County, W.Va., to start a coalmine named Peters Creek Coal Company. Location of the operation must have suggested the company name. James D. Ireland and wife, Cornelia, stayed at the Rader Hotel on Main Street in Summersville, until they established a small home near Enon.

Cornelia Ireland and young son joined her husband and established their home near Enon near the operation. The office of Peters Creek Coal Company was located upstairs over the Farmers and Merchants Bank Building on Summersville for many years.

Young men who served in the military services and defense work were eager for a job. Experienced miners also heard about the new company and traveled from Kentucky, Ohio, Pennsylvania, and other counties in West Virginia to find work in Nicholas County.

Other coal companies were being established, which was an encouragement to the people of Nicholas County. There was much "buzz" about the young couple, the Irelands from Cleveland, Ohio, who had come to a rural area, which had been known mostly for timbering and farming.

After much planning, preparation and contacts, Mr. Ireland's Coal Company was ready to mine the seams of coal known as "Peerless and Eagle." Coal production was ready to begin in Nicholas County.

Transportation was needed to get the mined coal to the mills, power plants and wherever it was ordered to be shipped. The coal was trucked to loading docks in the beginning where the transfer to railroad cars took place.

In 1948-49, the New York Central and C & O Railroads jointly constructed a railroad in Nicholas County. The new rail line ran from an initial turnout on the existing C & O Railroad Line near the confluence of the Gauley and New Rivers. The track was located along State Route 39 toward Summersville. There were bridges and culverts along the line as it weaved in and out of the hollows. The track was constructed by Royce Kershaw Company of Montgomery, Ala. The bridges and concrete work were contracted by Vicellio Company, who hired many local people and college students to do the work. It was a labor-intensive project to build the railroad but opened the door for much employment on coalmines and related jobs in Nicholas County.

James D. Ireland was particularly interested in the development and operation of highly mechanized coalmines with an emphasis on safety. He had a strong commitment to civic and cultural activities, which boosted things in Summersville. In 1950, James D. and Cornelia Ireland and family moved back to Cleveland. Jim, as he was known, commuted during the workweek by piloting his airplane to an airstrip near the operation, until he had a landing in a river near Whitesville, W.Va., in 1954. From that time forward, he was "grounded" by his wife, Cornelia, and he drove a car from Cleveland to Nicholas County. A local merchant made a statement that Peters Creek Coal Company had very little impact on the economy of Nicholas County. The remark got to Mr. Ireland, who found an innovative way to prove that his company, which employed about 200 men at the time, certainly contributed greatly to the local economy. The miners took vacation time near the July 4th holiday and were paid their regular wages plus vacation pay. This particular year, they each received the entire amount of pay in uncirculated $2 bills and were required to pay their bills and spend the $2 bill everywhere. The circulation of the $2 bills revealed the Peters Creek Coal Company's impact and importance to the economy of Nicholas County. Merchants grew weary of counting their money with so many $2 bills.

Peters Creek Coal Company shut down the operation for a period in 1958, and was the predecessor of Peerless Eagle Coal Company in 1961. The mine produced metallurgical coal, which was sold on the domestic market and abroad.

Peters Creek Coal Company Christmas Party for children held at NCHS in Dec. 1951 President James D. Ireland (owner)

76

PEERLESS EAGLE COAL COMPANY

T he Peerless Eagle Coal Company, formed from Peters Creek Coal Company in 1961, continued to employ many people and boost the economy of Nicholas County and support many local activities, organizations, and when the Summersville Municipal Building was completed in 1964, James D. Ireland and wife, Cornelia Ireland, agreed to furnish and equip the new library, which was located upstairs in the second floor of the building. This was a substantial contribution to the community. They attended the Municipal Building dedication in Summersville on Oct. 24, 1964.

In the mid-1970s, Peerless Eagle Coal Company, through the leadership of managers, substantial labor and equipment were supplied to build a football stadium for Nicholas County High School at Memorial Park, near Summersville. This joint effort, with the Nicholas County Board of Education, businesses and volunteers made the first class stadium a reality.

The Summersville Clinic was established in 1957 on land purchased and donated by James D. Ireland. Ten years later, Sept. 27, 1967, the Summersville Area Convalescent Hospital was dedicated. Mr. Ireland matched dollar for dollar the money raised to build the facility. In 1988, again, James D. and Cornelia Ireland presented a check of $25,000 to the Summersville Memorial Hospital Building Fund.

A philanthropist that has contributed in many ways and over time to Summersville, was James D. Ireland and wife, Cornelia. They have been among the biggest boosters of Nicholas County.

The employees and their families were honored each Christmas in the early years with a party with a special wrapped present for each child and served with Christmas goodies. They were supportive of the employees and their families. Later a summer picnic was organized for the families with entertainment and lots of good food.

As time moved on, Mr. Ireland who had other business interests in Cleveland and other locations, sold the Peerless Eagle Company to A. T. Massey Company of Richmond, Va., in 1975.

James D. Ireland, of Peters Creek and Peerless Eagle Coal Company died at his home in Cleveland Heights, Ohio, of an apparent heart failure in January 1991. They were the parents of four children: James D. Ireland III, Lucy E. Ireland, Cornelia I and George R. Ireland.

On Aug.7, 1997, Cornelia Ireland passed away in Cleveland, Ohio, after a brief illness of lung cancer.

Some managers and employees of Peters Creek and Peerless Eagle Coal Company had their entire career with the company for more than 35 years. They too made great contributions to the welfare of the community and to Nicholas County.

The office building, former Nicholas County Bank Building, which housed the Peerless Eagle office from 1976 was used until A.T. Massey shut down the company prior to 1998. The once modern coal tipple, which processed many tons of coal from both the Peerless and Eagle seams of coal is now rusty and idle on Camp Fork Road near Enon. Once it was a very busy hub of activity cleaning, loading and hauling by rail and large trucks to customers. The coal tipple shut down operation in November 1998.

Once a year, former employees get together for a reunion and to revisit those memories of comradery and their devotion to a company that offered them a good life. Peerless Eagle Coal Company was a loyal employer and certainly had many loyal employees for their long careers.

You know that the beginning of Peters Creek Coal Company took place more than 60 years ago, when the telephone numbers were four digits: 3871 (General Office), 4441 (Mine Office), and 4442 (Warehouse).

Summersville Municipal Building Library — Oct. 25, 1964
Left to Right: Mitch Haddad, Chamber of Commerce,
businessman; Congressman John Slack; Cornelia Ireland;
James D. Ireland; son, Jamie Ireland; "Buffy" Ireland,
daughter; Summersville Mayor W.S. Bryant; and Sen. Robert
Byrd. The Irelands donated the library furnishings.

77

SUMMERSVILLE
MUNICIPAL BUILDING

With the population increase in Summersville, W.Va., to 2,408 in 1960, the Mayor and Council Members decided to apply for a grant from the Federal Government under the Accelerated Public Works Program, which would supply 66 percent to the cost per project. A building to house offices for the City's business was much needed.

The American Legion donated their corner lot on Water and Broad Streets for the construction of the building in exchange for a meeting room for the members of the American Legion.

The Summersville Volunteer Fire Department raised money to buy a second fire truck in 1958. When it arrived, it was too long to fit in the garage. So, a hole was knocked into the partition to accommodate the truck. A garage for the fire trucks was planned for the proposed new building.

Young people complained that they had "Nothing to do and no place to meet friends." So, the proposed building would also provide a large recreation room, a kitchen and adequate facilities and furnishings.

A central room with a stage was included on the second floor for meetings and organizations to use.

Adequate offices and Council Chambers were proposed, and the City Policemen would also have space for their business.

This was an exciting idea with 66 percent of the cost by the Federal Government, and 34 percent would also need to be raised to build the Municipal Building at a cost of $205,000. The Town Council called for an election to pass a bond for the purpose of increasing the property tax of 6 percent on Dec. 18, 1962. The citizens were agreeable.

The money raised by issuance of the bond was directed to be used as follows: 34 percent cost of building, $70,000; furniture and fixtures, $10,000; and cost of issuing bonds, $5,000, which totaled $85,000.

The building, built of masonry and concrete, was under the direction of General Contracting, E.P. Fogleman and the architect was Donald Moses.

The Mayor W.S. Bryant, Councilman Robert B. Campbell, Harry Trent, Joe B. Boso, Joseph Sweeney, W. Clinton Halstead, Larry Tucker and Thomas L. Dotson all had and carried through their vision for progress of the town of Summersville. The dedication of the Municipal Building was held on Oct. 25, 1964. The Elizabeth Stevenson Memorial Library furnishings were provided by James D. and Cornelia Ireland of Cleveland, Ohio, and they also attended the dedication along with Representatives John M. Slack Jr. and U.S. Sen. Robert C. Byrd.

The Municipal Building has served the citizens of Summersville for 45 years and was recently remodeled and changed to meet current needs.

The Library, which also serves the New River Community and Technical College, was moved to a larger building north of Summersville on Route 41. The auditorium was closed to make more rooms, an exercise area, a local television and visual center and an elevator to access all floors.

The fire trucks also have a separate building on Route 39 East where the volunteer firemen have more storage space for the updated equipment.

Main Street is mostly for conducting business in Summersville, as the retail stores have moved out in different directions. Banks, attorney offices, the Courthouse, and annexes and the

Summersville Municipal Building are much needed and used by the citizens of Nicholas County.

Summersville has continued to grow, the needs have changed, and the Mayor and Councilpersons will supply a vision to meet the future needs of the community of Summersville.

Dedication of the Summersville Municipal Building and the Elizabeth Stevenson Memorial Library, Oct. 25, 1964 Left to right: The Rev. Riker Bennett (Methodist Minister), Ben Brown (lawyer), Councilman Robert B. Campbell (back row), Congressman John Slack, Councilman Harry Trent (back row), Recorder Boyd McMillion (back row), James D. Ireland (Cleveland, Ohio; donated furnishings for library), Mayor W.S. Bryant, Contractor/ builder E.P. Fogleman (back row), Sen. Robert C. Byrd (speaker), Mary Louise Kincaid and Cornelia Ireland (donated library furnishings).

78

A PIONEER LOG HOUSE

After 1795, settlers from Greenbrier, Monroe Counties and from other parts of Virginia and Pennsylvania began to rapidly occupy the lands that in 1818 were formed into the new county of Nicholas.

The selection of land and the building of his cabin was the first objective of a home seeker or settler to the area. A spring of water, a good source of building material, as well as fertile land for crops was important.

The cabin, constructed of logs, usually was 20 feet by 24 feet in building a log cabin. The roof was laid of clapboard made from suitable timber. The cracks between the logs in the wall were daubed with clean clay mixed with water.

In 1817, the poplar log house was constructed on Panther Mountain. The cabin was home to several people at that location for many years. One family had 11 children to live in the cabin.

The split log house was purchased and moved about 12 miles to a location on Route 129. Each log was numbered and photographed before the relocation took place in 1968.

When the building was taken down, it was discovered that chestnut logs had been used for sills under the first floor. These were carefully squared off into sections at a sawmill and used for upper and lower mantle boards. Some one-inch thick boards were used to make a door.

All of the original glass with "waves and bubbles" was used except for a few replacement panes. The weathered wood shutters were added to protect the original glass. The stone in the chimney and fireplaces is native, hand-quarried from the Dotson, Gilbert and Mahoning sandstone.

The first or main floor is one large room with a fireplace, stairs to the second floor and one closet with a door made from one sideboard. This room was the parents' bedroom and also the living room for the family. A screened porch is accessed from the main room.

The second floor was the girls' bedroom with a fireplace. The boys' bedroom was located on the third floor.

There was no running water or indoor plumbing when the house was located on Panther Mountain. The kitchen was located off the back porch, usually away from the main house, as there was a fear of fire from the wood-burning stove.

Pioneer living was a challenge, but there were innovative ways that kept the families from the elements and homemade cures for illness. There were few comforts or conveniences for those who survived the cold winters.

The clothing was handmade with only an outfit or two per person, so closets were not included in pioneer log houses.

Pioneer families sacrificed a lot to raise a family. Many family cemeteries attest to the loss of young children.

A log house is a monument to those pioneers. It would be interesting to know how many "lived in" pioneer log cabins still remain in Nicholas County.

Pioneer Log House, Route 129, Summersville, WV

79

A LOG CHURCH — A CATHOLIC CHURCH

I n 1818, some few Catholic families were already in what is now Nicholas County, near the town of Summersville. The County of Nicholas was formed in 1818 from parts of Kanawha, Greenbrier, and Randolph counties of Western Virginia. The State of West Virginia was formed June 20, 1863.

The first established mission was in 1846 when a young Irish priest, Father Thomas Farrell, was appointed by the Bishop of Richmond, Va., to care for the Catholics living in Nicholas, Braxton, Fayette and Kanawha Counties.

Father Farrell died in Summersville in 1847 after serving one year in the mission field. The Catholics of the area continued with services under Bishop Whelan.

The first Catholic Church was a small log building. Mainly through the efforts of John H.H. Duffy, a brick structure was built on a hill in Summersville in 1848.

After a few years, the mission was in disorder because of the Civil War. Nicholas County was on the dividing line between north and south. Some citizens joined in with the Union, and others fought under the Confederate flag. The armies of both sides dug trenches on the hill behind the Catholic Church, which was used as a fort and base hospital. The Union forces later destroyed the church by fire so it could be useless to the enemy.

It was a trying time with a shortage of priests, but the Catholics gathered for prayer and held instruction classes in Catechism for the children.

The Marist Fathers arrived about 1902 and established their residence in Richwood and served the Catholic families in Summersville.

In 1908, through the efforts of Sen. Frank Duffy and Andy Horan, the U.S. Government awarded the parish an indemnity for the destruction of the original church during the War Between the States. John Duffy donated an adjoining lot to enlarge the plot on which the new Catholic Church was built and served the community until fire destroyed the building on Jan. 1, 1953.

The beautiful stained-glass windows were gone, as nothing could be saved from the fire.

The congregation met in the Groves Theater on Court Street in Summersville, while holding services and planning for a new St. John's Catholic Church. A pledge drive, voluntary contributions and the sale of some of the property at the foot of the cemetery helped raise building funds.

On Oct. 5, 1954, the construction contract was awarded to E.P. Fogleman to build a brick church on Webster Road. The total cost exceeded $62,000 with future plans for a social hall and a kitchen.

The first mass was held by Father Kellerman under temporary conditions on Oct. 16, 1955. The Dedication Service was conducted at Mission Church of St. John the Evangelist on Sunday, Aug. 4, 1957.

The Catholic Church has continued to grow and to expand in Summersville.

The Former St. John's Church: In 1908 with money
obtained from the Federal Government, as indemnity for
the church destroyed during the Civil War, the above brick
church was built. It was this edifice that was completely
razed to the ground in a matter of minutes on the fateful
and unforgettable day, Jan. 1, 1953, the Feast of the
Circumcision of Our Lord. In the foreground is St. John's
Cemetery, in which many former members are buried.

The small frame church was built a few years after the
destruction of the original brick church by the armies during
the Civil War. This church stood until 1908 when it was
replaced by the church ravaged by fire on Jan. 1, 1953.

80

JOHN F. BAYS AND FAMILY

John Fielding Bays was born in 1794 in Maryland to parents, John Franklin Bays (b.-1774) and Mary Ann Knight Bays (b.-1775). He married Margaret "Peggy" Hall on Oct. 29, 1816, in Giles County, Virginia. They settled on Meadow River near Nallen and raised seven sons and seven daughters. John F. Bays died in 1866 in Nicholas County.

Their children were: William Bays (b. Sept.11, 1817), married Louise Stewart; Thomas Bays (b. Sept. 8, 1833), married Eliza Dotson (b. Feb. 22, 1843) — children, Augustus, Rebecca, Susan, Ella, Austin, Jacob Russell, Nora, Edgar, Tildon, Mary, Lemon and Arthur Bays; John F. Bays Jr. (b.1822), married Catherine Amick and were the parents of 14 children: Samuel died while in the Confederate Army in Ohio, Moses moved to Missouri, Lewis married seven times and lived in Kanawha County, George Washington Bays (b. Feb. 23, 1839), married Virginia Whiteman (more information to come), Isabell Bays married Joe Haynes, Betsy married George Dotson, Mary married Henry Haynes, Margaret married Newton Haynes, Jemina (b. 1845) married Isaac Dotson in 1865, Lucy married Miletus Woods and Rebecca Bays married William Dotson. All seven sons served in the Confederate Army.

George Washington Bays was born Feb. 23, 1839, to John F. and Margaret "Peggy" Hall Bays in Fayette County and married Virginia Louise Whitman on Feb. 1, 1866. He owned land on

Hominy Creek and cleared out a large farm where he and his wife raised a family of 12. The children were: Lizzie M. Bays (Jan. 1, 1867-1924), married Thomas B. McCutcheon; Charlotte Lottie Bays (b. Aug. 5, 1870-1936), married Arthur McCutcheon; Nannie Isabell Bays (b. Nov. 14, 1868-1936), married John W. Groves; Rebecca Ann Bays (May 22, 1872-1958), married M. R. Groves; Samuel J. Bays (b. Oct. 30, 1875-1954) married Ida Copeland; Henry Thomas Bays (b. Nov. 3, 1873), married Julia Frances Sevy on March 15, 1896; William Newton Bays (b. Oct. 5, 1877-1948) married twice to Ms. Deal and Ms. Hobbs; Mary Susan Bays (Nov. 3, 1879-1953), married J. W. Campbell; Martha Virginia Bays (b. Sept. 16, 1882-1888); Grover Cleveland Bays (b. Sept. 9, 1884-1957), married Clara Haynes; Fannie Lemon Bays (b. Sept 18, 1886-1938), married Bill Burdette; Ada Evelyn Bays (b. Jan. 4, 1889-1969), married Samuel Arnold and later Ben Tackett. She was a schoolteacher.

George Washington Bays enlisted in the Army for the Civil War and served from 1861 until March 17, 1865, as a mechanic. It was noted that he was known to be "shifty and thrifty." After living on Hominy Creek for some time, he sold the property and purchased property at Big Glade at Lookout and moved there in 1890. He and his wife, Virginia, built almost entirely themselves a Methodist Church at Lookout named Mount Olive Methodist Church, South. His funeral was held at this church in October 1908. Virginia Whitman Bays (b. Nov. 26, 1845) was the daughter of Robert and Elizabeth Whitman. She raised the family of 12 children. One daughter died, and a young son, Henry, was killed in the mines at Keeny Creek. Virginia Bays had 65 grandchildren and 10 living children when she died on March 9, 1924.

Grover Bays and friend, possibly Clara Haynes (1884-1957)

George Washington Bays (b. Feb. 23, 1839 —
d. Oct. 23, 1908) and Virginia Whitman Bays
(b. Nov. 26, 1845 — d. March 9, 1924)

81

EXTINCT PLACES OF NICHOLAS COUNTY

At one time in Nicholas County, each small settlement of people had its own Post Office, school and a church or two. Most of these villages or settlements no longer have a Post Office but are included within a larger area Post Office.

Earl was located near Deer Creek, east of Summersville. The Post Office disappeared in about 1917. The name was changed to Canvas. The United Methodist Church recognized a District as the Earl Charge, which consists of several United Methodist Churches.

Kirkwood had a Post Office and now is known as Phillips Run and is a part of Summersville.

Vinton and Panther Mountain areas had a large settlement west of Summersville. There were land patents listed as early as 1800 to Captain George Fitzwater who later sold the land to Charles W. King. Some of the early pioneers of the area were the families of Brown, Dunbar, Backus, Mason, Legg, Hess, Grose, Dorsey, Cavendish, Renicks and others. There was both a Methodist Church and a Baptist Church in the area of Panther Mountain. The Arnette Methodist Church was built on 1903 and no longer serves the people.

Albion was near the above settlements. The Grose Cemetery is the resting place for many of the pioneer families. Some of the family names are Grose, Copeland, Nutter, Renick, Pierson, Legg, Backus, Harrah, Mason, Cavendish and several unmarked graves. Many members of the families received higher education and moved to other areas as teachers, preachers, and other professions.

The Summersville Dam displaced Gad and Sparks. The places that were there are now mostly under water. Both places were thriving communities with large farms, stores, Post Offices, schools, and homes.

Other communities that are without Post Offices, schools, and stores are: Cambria, Greendale, Harriet, Burl, Dade, Opal, Delphi, Nile, Donald, Coal Siding, Dain or LaFrank, Grassy Falls, Tolbert, Hominy Mill, Coe and Ophelia. Bamboo was located in the lower part of Nicholas County. Curtin was a booming area with timber operations.

Perhaps some of the readers of this story might know of other extinct areas not mentioned.

These post cards were sent from the Ophelia, Hominy Falls and Deepwell Post Offices.

82

EARLY DRUG STORES AND CONFECTIONERIES

I n Summersville, there was a restaurant owned and managed by Alfred Groves on Main Street, near the corner of Broad Street, in 1905. He advertised that his place of business would be opened during the session of the Nicholas County Court. He also advertised that he would have for sale at the District Conference, which convened at Mount Vernon Methodist Church on Glade Creek, the following items: ice cream, soda water, cakes, lemonade, cigars, bananas and oranges. This was the beginning of "Alfred's Place" Soda Fountain. He sold meals for 20 cents at the restaurant.

To make ice cream the year round, lots of ice blocks were needed. In the winter, blocks of ice were cut and stored in an "ice house" under sawdust and wood chips. Young boys were hired for an ice cream serving to turn the crank on the ice cream maker. This was a real treat in those days to have a taste of ice cream, so there was no shortage of "crank turners."

In 1913, Richwood Pharmacy, owned by L.N. McCutcheon, M.D., claimed to be the only drug store in Nicholas County.

May 1919, Moore and P.A. Herold advertised best Drugs and Patent Medicines, confectioneries, toilet articles, magazines, newspapers, Kodak cameras and supplies, with the business located in the Old Farmers and Merchants Bank Building. (Located about mid-Main Street in Summersville)

Some patent medicines were sold at the Walker Store Company as early as 1916-17.

About 1920, Fitzwater and Mollohan Store advertised and sold Edison Phonographs and records, Kodak cameras, toilet waters and face powders. "Alfred's Place" (Groves) was a popular hangout location for young people who liked to dance to the jukebox music in a small area near the soda fountain area in the 1930s and 40s.

About 1946-47, Glen Webb from Beckley, W.Va., came to Summersville and started "Webb's Cut Rate" in the former Alfred Groves Building on Main Street. Harry Daniels and Wallace Davis were business partners in "Webb's Cut Rate." Later, Harry Daniels sold his interest in the business to Wallace Davis who continued to operate the store for a short time until he went out of business in Summersville. Another place, which was popular during the 1930s and 40s was Crislips Drug Store. Later this business was purchased by "Shorty" and Lucy Carroll. They named the drug store Carrolls Confectionery. Sometime in the late 1940s, " Fuzzy" and Virginia Walkup purchased the business from the Carrolls and operated a drugstore as Summersville Drugstore with a pharmacy. Dr. Russell Winkler operated the pharmacy for several years. The new building opened in December 1948.

The soda fountain with chrome padded stools was a popular place for students and business people to sit for refreshments of Cokes, fountain sodas, ice cream, milk shakes or coffee. Ham and cheese salad sandwiches were made and sold at the drug store. Ice cream in several flavors was kept in large drums in freezers and sold by the scoop for 5 cents. Flavored Cokes were popular, such as vanilla, cherry and chocolate.

Summersville Drugstore was located about where the present radio station is located on Main Street. There were tables and chairs beyond the soda fountain with shelves and showcases stocked with beauty products, patent machines, magazines, newspapers, and other things on either side of the wall. At the end of the long room was the pharmacy.

The jukebox (a coin-operated phonograph with push-buttons) was most always playing a popular tune of the time, while people were visiting and meeting others at the drugstore. The pinball machine was busy after school with young boys using their skill to beat the game.

In the mid-1950s, Paul Taylor and associates established the City Cut Rate Drugstore in the Alfred Groves Building and later remodeled the Ward Theater Building and moved to that location near the St. Nicholas Hotel, where the business remained until the 1960s. They sold the business to Lee Drennen who continued to operate the business for some time.

Main Street, Summersville, was the hub of activity for many decades until change started more rapidly and eventually most of the businesses moved to the outer areas of town.

The independent stores and restaurants were important to the citizens and visitors and served several generations in Summersville. The Main Street drugstores and confectioneries promoted a place to socialize and were missed by those who had known the pleasure of meeting at those places.

Summersville Drugstore 1951 — Policeman Sam Boley checks the locked door. On the left is a Hot Dog Place and, on the right, Johnson's Department Store.

Summersville Drugstore — Circa 1949-50

Fuzzy and Jenny Walkup 1949

83

THE DUFFY FAMILY OF NICHOLAS COUNTY

About 1821, a group of the Duffy Family, Michael, Peter and John Duffy came from Monaghan, Ireland, to Nicholas County as immigrants. A few years later, some cousins arrived from Ireland. They were Catherine, Owen, Francis and Phillip.

The Duffy family members were of the Catholic faith and were instrumental in the establishment of the Catholic Church. There was no established mission until 1846 in Nicholas County. A small log church served the Summersville Catholics until 1848 when a brick church, through the efforts of John H. Duffy, a pioneer member, had become a reality on donated land. That church building was later ravaged by fire and a new building inspired by Sen. Frank Duffy, was awarded money from the government to finance a new church in 1908. John Duffy donated additional land for the church and Catholic cemetery.

The 1850 Census listed the following Duffy family: Owen Duffy (age 49), Ann Duffy (42), Margaret Duffy (21), Robert (16), Hugh (14), Mary Duffy (10), Sam Duffy (8), Alice Duffy (6), Charles Duffy (3), John Duffy (age 52), Mary Duffy (47), Mary Susan (19), Rowena Duffy (14), Andrew Duffy (12), John Duffy (11), Sarah F. Duffy (8), Teresa Duffy (6), Peter Duffy (age 36) and Ann Duffy (age 52).

John and Phillip Duffy in partnership with Patrick Beirne, operated the largest store in Nicholas County for many years.

John Duffy's son, John H.H. Duffy (1839-1936), a lawyer, and wife, Sally J. Patteson Duffy (1841-1910) had children Cora E. Duffy (B-1872), John Kane (B- 1876-1944) and Annie L. Duffy (B-1878) married Alfred Groves. John Kane Duffy and Grace Champe were married Dec. 20, 1905.

John Duffy's will is recorded at the Nicholas County Courthouse, Book No. 1, Page 143, which names a son, John H.H. Duffy and three daughters, Mary, wife of Joseph H. Alderson; Sarah, wife of Felix J. Baxter; and Teresa, wife of John F. Campbell.

Owen Duffy's son, John Duffy Jr., had sons, Robert and John Duffy, and seven daughters.

The children of John Kane Duffy and Grace Champ Duffy (1882-1953) were Blanch N. Duffy (1909), Catherine Lucile (1912) and John Hamond Duffy (Dec. 18, 1914–Feb. 20, 1990).

A marriage bond is listed in Nicholas County Records for Catherine Duffy and John Groves Jr. on June 3, 1833.

John Duffy married Ann Thorton on Oct. 21, 1866, and had the following children: Lola (John Binns), Oct. 8, 1886 and died Sept. 12, 1959; Patrick Duffy, born April 14, 1888, and died July 15, 1919; Madora A., born Dec. 10, 1880; and Rebecca Duffy, born Oct. 25, 1883. Lola Duffy Binns served as a nurse during the WWI. She is buried in the Catholic Cemetery as is her husband, John Binns, and his brothers who all came from England.

Some other Duffy marriages recorded are: Alice Frances Duffy (8-12-1931) to Basil O'Dell; Georgia Duffy (7-3-1904) to Henry Kidd; John Gladstone Duffy (12-20-1906) to Mary Frances Hereford; Patrick Owen Duffy (6-17-1923) to Ada Marie Atwood; Thomas Osker Duffy (7-12-1909) to Milda Gay Hamon; William Duffy (8-02-1911) to Agnes Cronin; Owen Harvey Duffy (7-15-1867) to Medora McComley; Peter Duffy (7-17-1877) to Martha J. Wright; Charles D. Duffy (1-14-1898) to Erma Catherine Harris; Owen H. Duffy (6-9-1934) to Eva Bragg; Patrick Lee Duffy (12-31-1868) to Margaret Susan Duffy; Peter Duffy (4-5-1842) to Ann C. Warren; Maurice Duffy (2-11-1935) to Susan Williams; Eugene Duffy (8-8-1937) to B. Evelyn Lewis; and Robert Duffy (12-17-1961) to Connie C. Satler.

The children of Robert E. Duffy and Althea Thorton Duffy were Celia Duffy (B. 7-4-1904); Anna Duffy (B. 3-27-1903); James P. Duffy (B. 8-12-1908); Ethle Gertrude Duffy (B. 12-11-1908); James Porter Duffy (B. 10-3-1911); Joseph P. Duffy (B. 11-10-1912) and Robert Owen Duffy (B. 12-17-1915).

Thomas Osker and Milda G. Duffy had children Lawrence A. Duffy (B. 10-6-1913) and Donald N. Duffy (B. 12-23-1915).

The Duffy Family owned land on Peters Creek in Summersville and nearby areas. There is an older established Duffy Street in Summersville and also land referred to as Duffy Hollow, which had coal reserves north of town.

The Duffy family, a pioneer family with origins in Ireland, is connected by marriage to many other pioneer families of Nicholas County.

Annie L. Duffy (B 1878-1955) and husband, Alfred Groves (1878-1950) were well known for many years with the "Alfred's Place" Restaurant, which was operated on the corner of Main and Broad Street in Summersville. The Groveses are buried in the Walker Memorial Cemetery, along with their two daughters, Mary Eugenia Groves (B 1903) and Monica May Groves (1905-1969).

84

MAIN STREET SUMMERSVILLE
OF THE PAST

For many years Main Street, Summersville, remained the same, as business did not change, only ownership.

The Confection, known as "Alfred's (Groves) Place was a most popular hang-out and later became Webb's Cut Rate, started by Glenn Webb and later sold to Harry Daniels and Wallace Davis about 1946-47. Later, Harry Daniels sold his interest to Davis.

A Pure Oil Service Station opened on Main Street, located near Robinson's News Stand and later a restaurant The Dinner Bell. The station was a place where the customer received full service for the automobile. A gas fill-up, tires and oil checked, and windows washed was expected in the 1940s and 50s. Later, the station became Dooley's Esso Service Station and was operated by Pearl Dooley for many years. He also offered full service to customers. Often a drinking glass or a gadget was offered as promotion when the service was offered to loyal customers.

Main Street in the early 1900s had hotels, which were used during the sessions of Court and by those who traveled to Summersville. The Summersville Hotel, the Fitzwater Hotel, the Alderson House, Skaggs Hotel, Rader Hotel, and the St. Nicholas Hotel were well known.

The St. Nicholas Hotel was started by Sarah Dixson and later purchased by Mr. Junutalo. Clara Chapman Buckland worked and managed the hotel. Later, she purchased and managed the hotel for many years. The building housed the Summersville Post Office on the front right side. Later, Thelma Roop had a dress shop in the former Post Office. In the basement of the hotel, in the 1930s, housed a Government sponsored kindergarten taught by Gearldine Herold. Part of the basement of the St. Nicholas Hotel housed a dress shop owned by Peg Bennett, and later she ran a floral shop from the location.

Main Street, Summersville — Pure Oil Station, S.M.E. Church (Broad Street) and the R. Sweeney Residence

Webb's Cut Rate Drugstore, Main Street, Summersville: Fountain Room: left, Wallace Davis and Harry Daniels, owners, circa 1947-48

Webb's Cut Rate Drugstore, Main Street, Summersville: left,
Harry Daniels and Wallace Davis, owners, circa 1947-48

St. Nicholas Hotel, Main Street, Summersville — Started by
Sarah Dixson, circa 1930s and purchased by Mr. Junutalo
and managed by Clara Chapman Buckland. Clara Chapman
Buckland bought the hotel and managed it for many years until
it was sold. Summersville Post office was in the right front.

85

THE PIONEER GROVES FAMILY

According to H. D. Groves History of the Groveses, John Groves the emigrant born in England in about 1710, came to America and settled in Virginia and had a land patent of 400 acres in 1741. Nothing is known about his wife, but a son John Groves II (born 1750-1783), married Mary Craig (1758-1830) in 1776.

John Groves II and Mary Craig Groves had children. 1.Elizabeth Groves (1777-1802), married Joseph McClung about 1796 or 1799, had one daughter, Margaret (1820-) who married John Rader. 2. Martha Groves (1779-) married a Mr. Jarrett. 3. John Groves III (1781-1861) married Jane McClung in 1804. Their children were William (1805-1878) married Margaret McClung. Nathan (1807-1871) married Nancy McCoy and had six children. Elizabeth Groves (1809-1830) married William D. Cottle and had three children.

John Groves IV (1811-1881) married Catherine Duffy; Alexander (1813-1877) married Lydia McMillion; Jane Groves (1816-1846) married William Bryant; Jackson (1818-) married Carolyn Hanna; Harrison (1821-1892) married Rebecca Jones and Sarah E. Davis; Mary Groves (1823-1887) married Frederick Kessler; Alfred Groves (1826-1872) married Elizabeth Hill and Evelyn Hill; Mansfield (1828-1896) married Miram McCue, Martha Hill; Austin (1830-1889) married Liza Hill.

William Groves and Margaret McClung Groves had 10 children: Ruth (1832-1862) and never married; Washington Groves (1834-1914) married Elizabeth Campbell; Franklin Groves (1836-1924) married Sarah Jane Chapman; Elizabeth (1838-) married John Dorsey; Jackson Groves (1839-1903) married Sarah M. Rader; Jefferson Groves (1841-1863) never married; Samuel Groves (1843-1886) married Elizabeth Chapman; Harvey Groves (1846-1911) married Ruth Cottle; John Groves (1850-1927) Married Frances Moore; Virginia (1853-1932) Married John K. Bryant.

John Groves III was the pioneer who settled in Summersville in about 1804 with his mother who had married Robert Martin, who brought Mary, her two daughters and son, John Groves III, to Nicholas County. John Groves III had a slave, Joe Crow. Before the death of John Groves III, he freed Joe Crow and gave him a farm. According to W.G. Brown's Nicholas County History, the son, John Groves III, first located on McMillion's Creek, sold to John McClung, and located in Summersville.

Many of the Groves descendants were from the John Groves II and Jane McClung Groves family. Their sons, John IV, Nathan, William, Alfred, Mansfield, Alexander, Harrison, and Austin all located in Nicholas County. One son, Jackson, went to Illinois.

Many descendants of John Groves were farmers, merchants, and educators in Nicholas County. There are many ties with other pioneer families of Nicholas County with the Groves families.

John Groves came from England and was a
pioneer settler in Nicholas County.

The John Groves Family
It is unknown which John Groves is in this picture.

86

FRANKLIN GROVES AND FAMILY

A son of William and Margaret McClung Groves, Franklin Groves was born Nov. 11, 1836, and married Sarah Jane Chapman in 1860. Sarah Jane was the daughter of Andrew F. and Jane Fockler Chapman.

Franklin Groves purchased several acres of land from Austin Groves in 1867 in the Promise Land section of Kentucky District, Ophelia Post Office. On that property, he farmed and raised a family of seven children.

1. John W. Groves, "John Billy," 1861-1945, married Elizabeth O'Dell and they settled near Beckley Church, Ophelia, W.Va., and had six sons and two daughters, Franklin, Washington, George, Alvin, Ray, Prudence and Lola J. Groves.

2. Andrew Groves, born 1863, married Georgia O'Dell and settled near the Beckley Church, Ophelia. They were the parents of five children: Addie, Alderson, Beirn, James M., and Effie Groves (White).

3. M.R. Groves, born Sept. 25, 1865, died Jan. 17, 1954, a.k.a. "Dock" Groves, married Rebecca Ann Bays (1872-1958) on Oct. 7, 1871. They lived on part of the Franklin Groves Farm. They had six children: Lottie

Groves (Eakin), Luther Groves, Guy Groves, Edna H. Groves (Campbell), Porter Groves and Hobert Groves.

4. Nora E. Groves (1870-1953) married first to Robert Reynolds, second to Noah Nutter and third to Scott McClung. She had no children.

5. Franklin Beckley Groves, March 8, 1875-May 8, 1924, married Sarah Rebecca O'Dell. They had six children: Stanley, Otis, Esther, Roy, Beirne and Ralph Groves.

6. Stewart Groves, died 1920, married Nancy Dooley; they were the parents of Delta, Arlin and Velda Groves.

7. Martha Jane Groves Dec. 7, 1883-Feb. 8, 1965, married George Spencer and lived in Richwood. They had three daughters: Glenna, Audra and Mary Evelyn Spencer and sons, Frank and George Spencer.

After Sarah Jane Chapman Groves died in 1912 of typhoid fever, husband Franklin Groves lived with son and daughter-in-law, M.R. "Dock" and Rebecca Bays Groves, near Deepwell, W.Va., until his death on April 8, 1924. They are both buried in the Groves Cemetery on the Groves Farm.

Nora Groves, Stewart Groves, and Martha Groves Spencer

Franklin Groves

The Groves Family: George, Alvin, Prudence, John Billy, Harrison, Ray, Liz, Washington and Frank (Lola deceased)

87

MORMION RUSH GROVES
"M.R." OR "DOCK"

On Sept. 25, 1865, a son, Mormion Rush Groves, a.k.a. M.R., was born to Franklin and Sarah Jane Chapman Groves in the Promise Land of Kentucky District, Nicholas County, W.Va.

M.R. "Dock" Groves helped his father, Franklin, clear the fields and farm the land. Until the surfaced highways were made, the Groves Farm was on a road, which was one of the main thoroughfares of the county. It led to the Deepwell and Hominy Falls sections, a thickly settled part of Nicholas County. After the completion of the "good roads," the original road was seldom traveled.

Oct. 7, 1891, M.R. Groves married Rebecca Ann Bays (born May 22, 1872). They built their home on the Franklin Groves Farm near Deepwell, W.Va. Rebecca Ann Bays had a limited education of the third grade but was an avid reader, self-educated and with a knowledge of many domestic skills. She established a home for their family of six children.

1. Lottie Groves, born Nov. 20, 1892 — died Jan. 23, 1953. She was a teacher for many years and married June Eakin. She had one daughter Helen Eakin, who

was born Oct. 9, 1919, and married Lee Otis Bobbitt Jr. She died June 21, 1979.

2. Luther Groves, born Aug. 14, 1894, died Dec. 12, 1961. He married Cora Arthur. They were the parents of 11 children: Raymond (B-1918), Thomas A. (B. 1920 — D. 2002), Carl Hall (B. 1921 — D. 1946), David Hugh (B. 1922), Marguerite (B. 1924 — D. 2008), Genevieve (B. 1928 — D. 1987), Herbert (B. 1930), Luther Jr. (B. 1932 — D. 2009), Sylvia (B. 1934), Imogene (B. 1935) and Kenneth (B. 1941).

3. Guy Groves, born Dec. 31, 1899 and died May 7, 1973. Married Gussie Perkins and had three children: Irene (B. 1924) married James Callahan, Howard Buster Groves (B. 1926 — D. 1989), married Mary Frances Wood, Eugene (B. 1936 — D. 1997) married Carolyn Blake.

4. Edna Hall Groves (B. 1902 — D. 1961), married Eugene L. Campbell and had three children: William Eugene (B. 1924 — D. 1998), married Alice Anne Meckes, had three children; Robert Burns Campbell Sr. (B. 1926), married Anna Lee Murphy, parents of two children; and Carolyn Campbell (B. 1930), married T. S. Hoffman, parents of two children.

5. Porter Groves (B. 1904 — D. 1986), married Ruby Ward and had one stepdaughter.

6. Holbert Groves (B. 1918 — D. 1936)

M.R. "Dock" Groves was a Republican and served as the Deputy Sheriff of Nicholas County. He farmed the land that had been in the Groves name for many years, as did his father, Franklin Groves.

The children walked a few miles to attend the one-room school. Mother Rebecca Groves taught them many things, and reading from the Bible was done daily. Mr. Groves offered long prayers while each member remained on their knees. They were Methodist Church members and were a well respected and a religious family.

The passage of time has rendered the land back to nature. There is no evidence of the land that offered abundant life to so many of the Groves family members since the 1800s.

M.R. Groves died Jan. 17, 1954, and Rebecca Bays Groves died May 18, 1958. A daughter, Edna Groves Campbell cared for her parents in her home in Summersville from 1950. They are at rest in the Memorial Park Cemetery, Summersville, W.Va.

M.R. and Rebecca Groves and Family in 1903-04: l-r, Luther, Guy, M.R., Rebecca, Lottie, and baby Edna Groves.

Oct. 6, 1941 — 50th Anniversary for M.R. and
Rebecca Bays Groves (seated); standing, left to right,
are children, Porter Groves, Edna Groves Campbell,
Guy Groves, Luther and Lottie Groves Eakin.

88

JOHN WILLIAM GROVES
AND FAMILY

John William Groves was born in 1866 to parents, Washington and Elizabeth Jane Campbell Groves, who settled in Hominy Creek, Wilderness District, Nicholas County, W.Va.

Nancy "Nannie" Isabell Bays was born Nov. 14, 1868, to George Washington Bays and Virginia Louise Whitman Bays. She was one of 12 children born to that union. The other children were: Lizzie M. Bays, Charlotte (Lottie) Bays, Rebecca Ann Bays (Groves), Henry Thomas Bays, Samuel J. Bays, William Newton Bays, Mary Susan Bays, Martha Bays, Grover C. Bays, Fannie Lemon Bays and Ada Evelyn Bays (Tackett).

John William Groves and Nancy Nannie Bays married and settled on Hominy Creek, Wilderness District in Nicholas County, W.Va. They were parents of seven children. Irvin Groves married and lived in Alaska and South Africa, where he died. Orange Groves married and lived in Alaska and Washington. Ira Claypool Groves, married Annie Mary Neff and was the parent of eight children: Zela, Willy, Oliver, Vada, Viola, Anna, John and Mary (Bailes). The parents are buried in the Hickory Groves Cemetery.

Lester Groves married and lived in Saint Albans where he worked as a policeman. Effie Groves married Camden McClung and had children, Olive McClung (O'Dell) and James McClung.

Mary Groves married Jeff Moore. The seventh child was Maggie Groves.

John William Groves died in 1935 and Nancy "Nanny" Groves died January 13, 1936.

In researching the Groves Family Genealogy there are many John Groves in several generations. John Groves III who settled in Nicholas County was a true pioneer. He settled on many acres of land and passed it on to his many descendants to carry on the Groves name.

A special thank you to Glenna Bailes Burr of Summersville and to Anna Bailes of Cottageville, W.Va., for their assistance in the identification of the John William Groves and Nancy "Nannie" Bays Groves family photo in the Oct. 29, 2009, issue of The Nicholas Chronicle.

Glenna Bailes Burr is the granddaughter of Ira Claypool Groves and a daughter of Mary Groves Bailes and Waldo Bailes.

Son of Washington Groves, John William Groves; wife,
Nancy Bays Groves; baby on lap, Lester Groves (was
Policeman in St. Albans, W.Va.); girl on left, by father, Mary
Groves (married Jeff Moore); girl between parents, Maggie
Folks; back row, Ira Claypool Groves and Effie Groves,
who married Camden McClung. Information furnished
by Glenna Bailes Burr, granddaughter of Ira C. Groves.

89

HARRISON GROVES AND FAMILY

Harrison Groves was born in 1821 to William (1805-1878) and Margaret McClung Groves. Harrison Groves (1821-1892) married Rebecca Jones in 1844 and had several children, Henry (1845-1905), Nancy Groves (Milam), Margaret Groves (Milam), Cleora Groves (Summers), Elizabeth Groves (Summers), Henrietta Groves (Hamilton) and Kyle Groves.

The second marriage of Harrison Groves (1821-1892) was to widow Sawyers Dyer. They had no children.

Harrison Groves (1821-1892) married the third time to Sarah Elizabeth Davis. They were the parents of Alex Groves, Harrison Groves Jr., (born Nov. 19, 1875) and Alfred Groves, who married Annie Duffy. Harrison Groves Jr. (1875-1969) married Annie May Mc-Queen on April 1, 1901. They were the parents of nine children. Thelma Groves (1902-1979) Pugh, Henry Groves (1904-1904), Margaret Rose (1905-1980) Savilla, Sarah Alice (1909-1909), Henry Harrison (1910-1910), Owen Groves (1911-1965), Alfreda Groves (1915-1994) Wild, Louise Groves (1920-) Still, and John Harrison Groves (1924-1994).

Harrison Groves Jr. was a schoolteacher and Nicholas County Superintendent of Schools for many years. He was director of Nicholas County High School in 1916-17. He attended Summersville Normal School in 1893 and engaged in mercantile business for many years, owning and managing the Groves Department Store on Main Street in Summersville. The store was first owned by Oscar Stanard and Harrison Groves Jr. as the Stanard Department Store. After the Groves Department Store was sold to new owners the name remained the same until the store closed for business. The building remains, but is not occupied on the first level.

Annie May McQueen Groves and husband Harrison Groves Jr. lived on Main Street between the Groves Department Store and the first Masonic Building. The front porch was most inviting to friends who passed by when either Mr. or Mrs. Groves was sitting on the porch. The house is no longer there on the present empty lot.

John Harrison Groves operated the Groves Movie Theater on Court Street in Summersville from the 1940s until it closed.

Many of the Groves Family members are buried in the Groves Cemetery, which is now known as Walker Memorial.

Harrison Groves, Jr. (1875-1969) Summersville, W.Va.

Stanard Groves Store
Some offices in the Groves Store Building, second floor:
attorneys, Judge Dana Herold, Brooks Callahan, Gordon Duff,
and John McCutcheon; Dr. J.O. McQueen; Justice of the Peace
Mike Maloney; Mary Corbett's Sewing Shop; Jewelry Repair
Shop; Groves Insurance, and others throughout the years

90

THE CHERRINGTON
GROVES FAMILY

Cherrington Groves, born March 28, 1861, was a son of Alfred Groves (1826–1872) and Evaline Hill Groves (1823-1900). Cherrington Groves married Lola McCue and settled near Canvas, Nicholas County, where he farmed and raised a family. He was killed while squirrel hunting when a tree limb fell on him Dec. 24, 1901, and is buried in the Groves Family Cemetery on Groves Ford Road near Summersville.

The children born to this union were:

Richard Groves, born May 31, 1884, married Mary Ella Tyree and settled on the home place near Canvas. They had seven children, Neita, Vernor, Vada, Herbert, John Verl and Virginia Groves.

Emma J. Groves, born Nov. 12, 1885, died 1973 and married Stewart McClung and settled in Canvas. Alfred Groves, born 1887 and died 1960, married Ophelia Chapman and settled in Canvas, had children, Helen, Lena, Hardy, William, Alfred Jr., and Carl Groves.

Goff Nathan Groves, born Oct. 5, 1889, died Sept. 25, 1987, married Mintie Tyree, settled in Canvas and raised family, Zela, Thelma, Myrtle, Hugh and Clyde Groves.

Cecil Groves, born June 6, 1885, married Mary Pearl Stewart, daughter of David Thomas Stewart and Elizabeth Hyer Stewart, in 1915. Mary was born on Nov. 20, 1894, and died June 6,

1987. Cecil died March 26, 1858. Cecil was in the mercantile business for many years. In 1919, Cecil Groves and C. S. Bolair started a grocery store business together. They also sold animal feed along with produce, meat and other groceries. In 1921, Cecil Groves operated the grocery store in the Harrison Groves Building and started to build behind the Nicholas County Bank in Summersville. Later the bank building was moved in 1923 back to the lot behind the Main Street location and became known as Citizens Grocery, operated by Cecil Groves and John Sims for many years. Cecil and Mary Stewart Groves were active members of the Methodist Church in Summersville and raised a family of seven children.

1. Paul Groves (1916-2003) married Iva Tingler and was involved in the Grocery Business for many years in Summersville and Canvas. Iva Groves died in 1994 in Summersville. They had no children. A niece, Norma Copenhaver Damron and husband, Charles Damron, moved into the Groves house and cared for Paul until he died Oct. 26, 2003. Cecil Paul Groves served as a volunteer for many years after retirement at the Summersville Memorial Hospital.

2. David Cherrington Groves (1918-1994) married Thelma Perkins, had five daughters, operated a gas service station in Summersville before moving to Belle, W.Va. Thelma Perkins Groves was born in 1922 and died in 1985 in Belle. David married Beatrice Allman Webb who passed away in 2009.

3. Margaret Ellen Groves, born Sept. 8, 1920, married Harvey Copenhaver and settled near Canvas. Five children were born to this union, Betty, Joseph, Eugene, Norma, and John Copenhaver. Margaret and Harvey divorced, and she married a Mr. Burke. She died Oct. 14, 1967.

4. Donald Groves, born April 11, 1923, married Wanda McClung. Don Groves became a well-known physician in Summersville where he practiced medicine at the Summersville Clinic and in private practice until his death from a boating accident on Summersville Lake June 26, 1977. They were the parents of three children, Gary, Dwight, and Patricia Groves. Gary became a dentist and Dwight Groves, a medical doctor.

5. Joan Groves, born in 1928, married Al Parsons and have a family of two children, Mary and David Parsons. They reside in Ohio.

6. Dana Watt Groves, born Dec. 3, 1925, and died Feb. 19, 1992, married Gale Lilly Ellison. They were the parents of Larry, Dana Mike, Robert, Joe and Sherry Groves. Dana Watt worked for Peerless Eagle Coal Company.

7. Claude Otis Groves was born in 1929 and married Ruth Piercy and had a military career. They were the parents of five sons, Steven, Timothy, Denny, Dean, and Gregory Groves (1963-2002). Otis and Ruth Groves and their family lived in many places during his military service including France. After retirement from the service, they resided in Florida. Otis died Jan. 3, 1990, in Orlando, Fla., and interment is in Chapel Hill Cemetery, Orlando.

Several members of the Groves Family are buried in the Groves Cemetery, Groves Ford Road, near Summersville and also several are buried in the former Groves Cemetery, now Walker Memorial Park Cemetery in Summersville.

The pioneer, John Groves III, who settled in Summersville in 1804 and wife, Jane McClung Groves, are buried in the Groves section of Walker Memorial Park Cemetery, Summersville.

Note: The Cherrington Groves Family History, which appeared in the Dec. 10, 2009, issue of The Nicholas Chronicle, omitted

Linda and Roger Copenhaver, children of Margaret Ellen Groves and Harvey Copenhaver. Also omitted were Linda and Larry Ellison, stepchildren of Dana W. Groves. Alfred Groves (1887-1960) married Mary Ophelia Chapman who was known as Mary O. Groves. Cecil Groves was born June 22, 1895, and died March 26, 1958.

The Groves Family

Mary Pearl and Cecil Groves

91

A PIONEER STORY

This is a true story that occurred in O'Delltown in Nicholas County during the War Between the States in 1863. Andy J. Groves was born July 21, 1863, to Franklin and Sarah Jane Chapman Groves who lived down on Hominy Creek and later moved to Ophelia, which is now O'Delltown.

The peculiar situation of his birth is alarming. The soldiers came through the area and earlier had taken Franklin Groves' horses. He slipped around the camp, got the horses and put them under a rock cliff on Hominy and left them during the winter. He carried feed and water for them.

Earlier on July 20, 1863, Sarah Jane Groves spied the soldiers and raised a plank in the floor, tossed a ham of meat under the floor. It was well that she hid the ham, as that was all the meat from the meat house. Next thing that Sarah Jane did was to go for her riding horse and brought the horse to the porch.

The soldiers came to the porch of the house and demanded her horse. She refused to give up the horse and the soldiers could tell that she was heavy with a child and did not take the horse by force. She informed them that she would remain on the porch to keep the horse. They planned to wait until she went into the house to give birth to her child. Late in the evening the soldiers left the house. That evening Sarah Jane Groves delivered her son, Andy J. Groves, a healthy baby boy.

The next morning, Sarah Jane got up from her bed and built a fire and made breakfast for her husband, Franklin, who had been hiding in the woods to keep from being taken prisoner.

The story was shared from a daughter of the late Andy J. and Georgia Groves, Effie Groves White (born 4-24-1903 — died 9-12-1999).

ANDREW J. GROVES

Andrew J. Groves married Georgia Ann O'Dell and lived near Beckley Church on O'Delltown Road near Nettie. They had a family. Addie Groves died at age 3. Alderson Groves died at 1. James M. Groves was born Jan. 18, 1906, and died Oct. 23, 1992. He remained single and was a farmer. He is buried in the Groves Family Cemetery on O'Delltown Road in Nettie.

Their daughter Effie Groves was born April 24, 1903. She married Edward L. White and they had one son, Eddie Lee White. Effie was schoolteacher for many years. After her retirement, she made many lovely quilts, which she enjoyed giving to family members and special friends. Effie Groves White died Sept. 12, 1999. Mr. White passed away Sept. 29, 1976. Interment was in Wallace Memorial Cemetery Clintonville, W.Va.

Andrew J. Groves, born July 21, 1863, son of
Franklin and Sarah Jane Chapman Groves

Effie Groves White, born April 24, 1903, died Sept. 12,
1999, daughter of Andrew J. and Georgia Groves

92

THE W.G. BROWN LAW
OFFICE BUILDING

On the corner of Main Street and Webster Road is located a two-story building with a loft or attic that was used on the lower level as the office of Attorney W.G. Brown. His secretary and second wife was Evie Cutlip Brown. It was there that the History of Nicholas County by William Griffie Brown was written and published in 1954. The typewriter, on which the manuscript was typed by Evie Cutlip Brown, now is in the Nicholas County Historical and Genealogical Museum in Summersville.

W.G. and Evie Cutlip Brown lived in the upstairs apartment for several years. Mr. Brown died in 1957, and Mrs. Brown continued to live in the apartment.

Later, the street-level part of the W.G. Brown Building was used by the Monongahela Power Company, under the management of Ralph Jones until the company moved to another location.

Mabel Brown Rowe lived in the upstairs apartment after she moved back to Summersville from Arizona and worked for the Nicholas County Mental Health Department during the early organization. Dama Brown Langley and sister, Mabel Brown Rowe, were daughters of W.G. Brown and first wife, Margaret Groves Brown. Their other children were Margaret, Heber, and Reginald Brown. All are now deceased.

Through the years, other businesses and offices were located in the lower level of the Brown Law Building, while the apartment was rented to many different people over the years.

While living in Arizona, Dama Brown Langley wrote books about the West and was interested in the Hopi Indian tribe. Her books published were Hopi Girl, I Married a Stranger, and Indians of the Southwest.

In Summersville, Dama and her husband, Harry Langley, lived in the brick home, which had belonged to her father, W.G.Brown. The house, made from Walker Brick, is now owned by Dr. and Mrs. Bob Stanley.

W.G. Brown's Law Office —has been used by Reedy, Surveyor; bottom floor was Power Company Office

Professor William G. Brown Founder and Principal 1864-1957 Author of Nicholas County History Book Published 1954

93

HARVEY GROVES AND FAMILY

Harvey Groves (1846-1911), son of William (1805-1878) and Margaret McClung (18 0 - 1862) married Ruth Cottle (1851-1942) in 1868. Harvey and Ruth Cottle Groves settled on a farm in Kentucky District of Nicholas County where he farmed and raised livestock. Harvey owned 1,100 acres of land. In later years, he sold the land and timber and moved near the Methodist Church in Canvas.

They were the parents of children: Alice (1869-1926) who married George Tyree; Emerson (1870-1902) married Henrietta Bryant; Scott (1874-1929) married Mary Etta Groves (1888-), daughter of Allie and Lola Rader Groves; Melvina Jane (1875-1945) married Austin Bryant in 1899; Homer David Groves (1877-1961) married in 1910 to Inez Myrtle Ward (1887-1924) and married a second time to Elizabeth Black, a teacher, of Rupert, W.Va.

Emerson and Henrietta B. Groves had children May, Okey and Reva; and two sets of twins, Dana and Dennis and Ruth and Rose Groves. Scott and Mary Etta Groves had daughters, Blanch and Rachael Groves. After Scott died, Mary Etta married Leonard Groves.

Melvina and Austin Bryant had children: John, Bertha, Lawrence, William, Homer, James, Effie, Ruth and Mary Bryant.

Homer David "H.D." Groves and Inez Ward Groves had children Lucille Ward Groves who married A.E. Burnside of

Milton, W.Va. Virginia Ward Groves married Charles Zabel of Youngstown, Ohio; Eloise Ward Groves (1923-1994) married Harold B. "Buster" Hughes and lived in Huntington, W.Va., and had three children, Mary, Agnes, David Joseph and Hames Herold Hughes.

After the death of first wife, Inez M. Ward Groves, Homer David "H.D." Groves married Elizabeth Black who taught at Nicholas County High School. H.D. Groves taught at public schools, Summersville Normal School and Glenville Normal School and served as principal of Nicholas County High School from 1929-1935.

Many of the early Groves History from Augusta County, Va., to the Nicholas County West Virginia History was written by Homer David "H.D." Groves.

Special thank you to Russell Jarrett of Buckhannon, W.Va., who wrote of his appreciation of the Groves Family Genealogy in the Passage of Time. He shared unknown information about Martha Groves (1779-1855) who was born in Augusta County, Va., to John Groves II and Mary Craig Groves. Martha Groves married Squire Jarrett (1776-1860) on Feb. 4, 1804.

James Jarrett (1741-1822) and David Jacob Jarrett Jr. (1740-1811) were brothers. Squire Jarrett was a son of David Jacob Jarrett Jr.

Virginia Groves (1853-1932) married John K. Bryant. She was a daughter of William Groves and Margaret McClung Groves. They had nine other children: Ruth, Washington, Franklin, Elizabeth, Jackson, Jefferson, Samuel, Harvey, and John Groves.

94

GROVES GENEALOGY

The many stories about John Groves I, II, and III, which were printed in "The Passage of Time," covered only part of the Groves Families. Since John Groves III had nine sons and three daughters, they also had large families and married into Nicholas County families. There are numerous connections of the Groves name remaining in the area. The early generations married into the Tyree, McClung, Chapman, Rader, McCue, Cottle, Bryant, Duffy, McCoy, McMillion and other pioneer families.

Alexander Groves (1813-1877) fourth son of John Groves III, married Lydia McMillion of Greenbrier County and settled on Glade Creek, Nicholas County, and raised several children. Some descendants are living in the area.

A descendant of Alexander Groves (1813-1877) was John Milton Groves (1866-1936) who married Virginia Cutlip (1867-1951) on Dec. 8, 1887. Their children were: Troy Groves (1898-1959), Jarrett (1862-1927), Gus (1902-1965), Grace (1902-1979), Ada (1894-1960), Hunter (1890-), Joe Groves (1896-1944).

Mansfield (1828-1896), eighth son of John Groves III, married Miriam McCue. He was married a second time to wife, Martha Jane Hill of Hillsborough, W.Va. They were the parents of three sons: George Allen (1859-1922), Joel Hill Groves (1861-1941) and Homer Holt Groves (1869-1938). Joel Hill Groves married

Rebecca Anna Tyree (1874-1958) and were the parents of eight children: George Arnett, Virgie Irene, David Flem, Martha Jane (Mason), Leonard, Kyle, Mary Glenna (Fitzwater) and Gladys Groves (Chapman).

The Groves name remains prominent in Nicholas County. Many Groves Family members have been teachers, farmers, merchants, and other professions.

It would be difficult to research and write of all the Groves. It is a known fact that the Groves' name has not only populated Nicholas County but has contributed to the education and welfare of the Nicholas County citizens for many generations.

95

THE HAMILTON BAKERY

John Hamilton of Scottish descent was born in Pennsylvania and later moved to Virginia with his parents. In 1805 he came with his family of seven children to Cross Lanes. He was a man of wealth at that time.

In 1818, Nicholas County was organized at his home where meetings were held in the log structure. The five-member commission recommended that public buildings should be erected on a tract of land known as the Arbuckle tract. John Hamilton donated 30 acres of the tract for the county seat of Nicholas County. The pioneer settler, John Hamilton, died in September 1818. His heirs carried out his plan.

John A. Hamilton's sons were Robert, Edwin and Samuel Hamilton. Edwin and Elizabeth McClung Hamilton established a bakery in the basement of the Farmers and Merchants Bank Building (Now BB&T). The freshly baked aroma of bread permeated that part of Main Street, Summersville in the 1920s and 1930s. Walter Baker made bread deliveries for the bakery. Customers could walk into the Bakery and purchase fresh bread. It is unknown when the Bakery is closed.

Edwin and Elizabeth (Lizzie) McClung Hamilton had one daughter, Sarah Ann Hamilton, who was the first women elected to public office in Nicholas County as a Circuit Clerk. She was serving her third term in 1975 when she was killed in a traffic accident on the way to a Clerks Convention in Martinsburg,

W.Va. She was a great-great-granddaughter of the pioneer John Hamilton.

Robert Hamilton settled in Washington. Samuel Hamilton settled and raised a family in Summersville. Part of the old Route 19 on Broad Street was located on some of the Hamilton property until it was sold into lots where homes and businesses are located. When the Hamilton farm was farmed it was a popular sledding place for the children in winter.

Sarah Ann Hamilton — born 1918, died June 11, 1975

Young boys (unknown) stand in front of the Edwin Hamilton Bakery located in the basement of Farmers and Merchants Bank, fronting Main Street in Summersville. Note the basement windows. Photo circa 1920s and 1930s.

Edwin Hamilton and Elizabeth "Lizzie" Hamilton — picture taken at Bakery in basement of Farmers and Merchants Bank

96

PIONEER BRYANT FAMILY

I t is believed that William Bryant, of Irish decent, who settled in Rockbridge County, Va., and with his wife and children were the first ancestors of the Bryants to come to Nicholas County. The two sons, William H. and James Bryant, came to the west, now known as West Virginia. William H. Bryant worked with his uncle, Fielding Bryant, as a tanner, which is the process of making hides into leather.

William H. Bryant married Jane Groves, daughter of John Groves and settled in Summersville. In 1868, he was conveyed a tract of land on what is now known as Camp Fork, by the John Groves heirs. The sons to the first wife were Harrison and John Bryant. The second wife was Ruth McClung. Their children were: Lizzie (Copenhaver), Letitia (Graves), Cassie (Alderson) and Richard E.M. Bryant.

James Bryant settled in Kentucky District of Nicholas County. His sons were Joseph M., John K., Austin, George and Fielding Bryant. All acquired farms in Kentucky District of Nicholas County.

Edward M. is the son of Joseph M. Bryant. Aaron Bryant is the son of Austin Bryant. The sons of George Bryant are Hayes, Dexter, Harrison and Irving Bryant. Fielding Bryant's sons are Burt and Dayton Bryant.

John K. Bryant, who married Virginia Groves, had sons, Walter and C. W. Bryant. Their daughter, Mary Elizabeth Bryant, married John A. Stowers of Summersville.

C.W. Bryant's son, C.Z. Bryant, was a teacher in Nicholas County High School and had a business in Summersville.

Edward Ferguson Bryant married Mary Estaline Hutchinson of the Muddlety area of Nicholas County. She was the daughter of Leroy and Martha Herold Hutchinson. Edward F. and Mary Estaline Bryant bought a place on Peter's Creek near Enon on a branch of water called Bryant's Branch. There they established a tanning business and made leather into shoes. A man, by the name of Turner who was passing through the county, stopped by the Bryant's home. He was also a tanner and made shoes. He remained there with the Bryants for many years. They also made harnesses and saddles.

Mary Estaline was a seamstress and made men and women's clothes. She continued to sew until her later years.

After shoe companies were established the handmade shoes were no longer in demand. The Bryants moved into Summersville, where they lived until the first World War. During the War the tannery in Richwood needed tanners for the big production of leather. The Bryants moved to Richwood, where Edward F. Bryant worked rolling leather during the war.

Mr. Bryant died in 1935 and Estaline moved in and lived with her daughter, Martha Bryant White (Handley) for many years until her death at the age of 102. Estaline remained active in her later years and walked often to visit friends on Duffy Street and to Oak Street where she visited her sister-in-law, Sarah "Sally" Hutchinson, widow of Cameron F. Hutchinson.

97

NICHOLAS COUNTY SHELTERED WORKSHOP

The Articles of Incorporation of the Nicholas County Workshop was issued on July 1, 1977, in Summersville. The incorporators, Ms. Debbie Burkett, Ms. Anne Leamon, Michael Leamon, Samuel Sapp, and Dwight McMillion, all of Summersville, were listed on the document.

The purpose of the non-stick, nonprofit corporation was: a. to provide a facility that is worked-oriented rehabilitation sheltered workshop with a controlled environment and the necessary related services in order that the individually handicapped person can obtain the required skills so that he can be placed into remunerative employment, thus becoming a fully participating member of our society, b. to serve our trainees and customers as efficiently as possible, c. to provide intelligent, aggressive and capable management, d. to provide a maximum degree of satisfaction on the part of our staff in their assigned tasks, e. to cooperate with all public, private and religious agencies and professional groups in the furtherance of these ends, f. to solicit and receive funds for the accomplishment of the above purposes.

Meetings were held and a Board of Directors appointed to plan for a location. The Board of Directors met monthly at the Episcopal Church and the Nicholas County Mental Health Building on McKees Creek Road. The Board of Directors who served during 1977-78 were John and Kathy Stevens, Bishop W.C. Campbell, Sam Sapp, Betty Sapp, Beverly Cutlip, Carol Dunkley, Dwight McMillion, Debbie Burkett, Ralph Dado, Hal Slaughter, Michael and Anne Leamon, Edgar Kitchen, Etta Morrison, Coleman Murphy and Charles Hughes.

In 1978-79, the following names were added to the Nicholas County Sheltered Workshop Board of Directors: Peggy Tucker, Tim Salvati, Robert Dunlap, Moody J. Goff, Bill Hypes, Dave Withrow and Mrs. Robert B. Campbell (Ann). The President of the Board was John Stevens and the Secretary elected was Ann Campbell. She served as secretary for five years.

The business consisted of building options, acquirement of land by lease or by donation and securing funding by grants and donations. Accounts were set up by the Nicholas County Bank, Summersville. The Board of Education was consulted on any vacant buildings that may be available.

The names of members added to the Board 1980-81 were Carol Salvati, Robert Kamm Jr., David Groves, Kyle Groves, Malcolm Vaughn, Fred Kraft, the Rev. Russ Ward, Curt Mullens, Luther Baker, Larry Bradford, Jinks Hinkle and Jay Comstock.

As members either resigned or moved from the area, more names were added to the Board in 1981-82. They were Daniel Phillips, Camilla Whitlock, Neil Gambo, Bill Bright, Huling Spencer, Robert Bailey, Kathy Cardullo, Dr. Robert Fleer, Ben O'Dell and Mary Groves.

Members of the Board of Directors of the Sheltered Workshop visited Sheltered Workshops in several counties in West Virginia to learn about the successes or failures and how best to proceed in Nicholas County.

Board Members Moody J. and wife, Mona Goff, moved before
the Nicholas County Sheltered Workshop Dedication

98

NICHOLAS COUNTY SHELTERED WORKSHOP, INC. – PART TWO

Many options for a location were considered including the Tannery School in Richwood. Board Member Larry Bradford toured the school and reported that a committee be appointed to look into the possibility of using the school building. It was reported to the Board of Directors that the repairs to make it accessible and functional would be too costly. It was not considered for the Sheltered Workshop. Other options were to be considered.

A coordinator of the Sheltered Workshop under a Title Funding was recommended by the committee of Moody J. Goff, Dwight McMillion and Ann Campbell. This position was under the CETA Grant. The position would be for 18 months with a temporary office space in the mobile unit near the Nicholas County Mental Health Center on McKees Creek Road, Summersville. Linda Little assumed the position of co-coordinator and served until August 1979.

At the meeting, May 21, 1979, Bill Futten, director of the Sheltered Workshop of Fairmont, W.Va., was guest speaker to the Board of Directors about starting, funding and operating a Sheltered Workshop.

In August 1979, at the monthly board meeting, Beverly Cutlip of Craigsville offered to donate some front property to the

Nicholas County Sheltered Workshop if acceptable. The motion was made and accepted to accept the land offer from Dr. and Mrs. R.L. Cutlip on Route 41, Craigsville.

Larry Bradford, director of the Region IV Planning and Development Council offered information and plans for grant applications for funds for building and operation of such buildings. His service and knowledge were very valuable to the Workshop. His leadership moved the plans for a Sheltered Workshop forward.

Robert Dunlap and associates surveyed the land in Craigsville for the future site of almost three acres for the Sheltered Workshop. Committees were appointed and functioned for funding, building plans, excavation and sire preparation. Moody J. Goff reported on a Grant Application for $50,000 for a 40x60 metal building. A deed was prepared for the land in September 1979.

Board members, Coleman Murphy Sr., Dave Groves and Robert Dunlap worked on the site preparation plans. Tim Salvati, President of Island Creek Coal Company, Northern Division, donated the use of equipment to prepare the donated land and 20 of their employees donated their time to assist with the site preparation for the future Sheltered Workshop of Nicholas County.

Gov. Rockefeller advised by letter of Sept. 5, 1980, that an additional $13,500 in Community Partnership grant funds were given to the Nicholas County Commission for overrun costs of construction of Sheltered Workshop in Craigsville. Also, in 1980, a grant for $15,000 was received from the Claude Worthington Benedum Foundation for payment of the first year of operation.

The mobile unit from the Nicholas County Mental Health was available for the Sheltered Workshop to be moved to the site for the cost of $100 by Mr. O'Dell in 1980. Connection of water, sewer and other utilities was an added expense. The mobile unit was accepted from the Seneca Mental Health. Seedling of the land was done by Edward Williams and Company.

Contracts with companies were discussed and proposed by Moody J. Goff. Many letters were written, requests made, donations sought, plans made, job descriptions written, co-coordinator hired and procurement persons hired, organizations contacted — just to name a few jobs for the Board of Directors in 1980-81. Under the able leadership of Moody J. Goff, many things were achieved for the progress of the Sheltered Workshop.

**Sheltered Workshop Nicholas County Site, Craigsville
Land donated by Dr. and Mrs. Robert Cutlip**

**Bob Dunlap, surveyor, at the future location
of the Sheltered Workshop, Craigsville**

Site of Sheltered Workshop of Nicholas County,
Craigsville — pictured, left to right, Jim Spurlock, Tim
Salvati, L.A. Moses, Bob Dunlap and Tim Oxley

99

NICHOLAS COUNTY SHELTERED WORKSHOP – PART THREE

S en. Larry Tucker communicated with Gov. John D. Rockefeller IV on behalf of the Sheltered Workshop in support of the facility. It was a community and county effort that made the Sheltered Workshop in Nicholas County a reality.

Four years after the organization of the Sheltered Workshop a Dedication Ceremony was held on July 19, 1981, at 1:30 p.m. at the location in Craigsville on the land donated by Dr. and Mrs. R.L. Cutlip and prepared by donated equipment and labor.

There was music, history, speeches and a ribbon cutting led by Gov. Rockefeller. Refreshments were served by Nicholas County Garden Clubs. Benediction was given by Board Member the Rev. Russ Ward. The Sheltered Workshop Director was Fred Curry.

The Dedication Committee, Beverly Cutlip, Larry Bradford, Marsha Fraley, Director Fred Curry and Secretary Mrs. Robert B. Campbell (Ann) were very pleased that the Sheltered Workshop was so well supported by the citizens of Nicholas County.

Jim Gamble served as Director of the Sheltered Workshop for many years and built in into a useful facility that fully serves the purpose so well and offers beneficial services to the clients and to the County. After the retirement of Mr. Gamble, Robert Johnson was appointed Director of the Sheltered Workshop of Nicholas County.

It is rewarding to know that all the efforts and careful planning from July 1, 1977, when the Articles of Incorporation were established, to the present time, 2010, that the Sheltered Workshop has been very successful and continues to serve both clients and the communities with services and jobs. The Sheltered Workshop continues to offer new services with new equipment and more funding available.

Left: Ann Campbell, Kathy Cardulo, Camilla Whitlock, Neil Gambow, Gov. Rockefeller, Larry Tucker, Beverly Cutlip and Larry Bradford; back, Bishop W.C. Campbell; front, a Sheltered Workshop client

Sheltered Workshop Board of Directors Member
Larry Bradford, speaker; seated, Bishop W.C.
Campbell, Beverly Cutlip and Sen. Larry Tucker

Left to right: Beverly Cutlip (donated land), Gov.
Jay Rockefeller and Sen. Larry Tucker

100

THE JAMES AND BETSY BAKER FAMILY

The picture featured in "The Passage of Time" in The Nicholas Chronicle of Jan. 21, 2010, has been identified by Ella V. Cox of Ft. Lauderdale, Fla., Amy Baker Pellegrin of Fairmont, W.Va., and Mary Baker Frazier of Summersville.

The following information was written by Ella V. Cox, whose grandmother, Ann Selina (Baker) Hickman, was a daughter of James and Betsy Robinson Baker.

James Baker (1845-1900) and wife Betsy Robinson Baker (1845-1928) were married on Jan. 15, 1866, in the St. James Church in the Parish of Walleston in Worcester, England.

In December 1879, James Baker and Henry Robinson left England on the Germanic. Their wives, Betsy R. Baker and Mary Robinson, joined their husbands in the United States in 1880 on the ship Baltic.

Mrs. Cox's grandmother, Ann Selina (Baker) Hickman, told her grandchildren about the trip on the Baltic. At age 6, she recalled that it was not a happy journey. On one occasion the ship had stopped, and it was a long fearful night. The crew worked tirelessly throughout the night in the fog and darkness, but the passengers were left to guess what was amiss.

However, at the first crack of dawn, there stood several large icebergs. Her mother, Betsy Baker, explained to her how frightful it would have been if the crew had not been alert. At her adult age, Grandma Ann Selina would also recall the Titanic and the story of a much bigger and more powerful ship as the smaller English ship, Baltic, as they braved the great Atlantic. That trip was frightening for Grandma, even though her mother, Betsy, tried to convince her that God was on the water as well as on the land. At last, they sighted land, and what a joy they felt. They certainly were ready for an introduction to their new homeland, the United States of America.

At the time of arrival in the U.S., James and Betsy Baker had five children. They were Jemina, Bessie "Betsy" and Ann Selina (Grandmother of Ella V. Cox), Joseph Henry and Clara Alice Baker.

James, Betsy Baker and family settled near Pittsburgh, Pa. James was a good blacksmith, and a good blacksmith was in demand in those days, so he had a job. (A blacksmith makes and repairs iron objects by hammering them on an anvil, after the iron has been heated to a red glow in a forge. The most important article made were horseshoes.)

James (1845-1900) and Betsy Baker (1845-1928) are seated
in the front center. Little boy on the left is their son, Harry
Baker. The little boy on Betsy's right is Fred Baker, a grandson
they raised. From left to right in the back row are: Elizabeth,
Joseph Henry, Clara Alice and Mary Ann Baker. James and
Betsy Robinson Baker came from England in 1879 and 1880
and settled in Pennsylvania before moving to Nicholas County.

101

THE JAMES BAKER FAMILY MOVES TO NICHOLAS COUNTY, WEST VIRGINIA

I t is not known what brought James and Betsy Baker to Nicholas County. A land salesman had sold James a small farm, sight unseen, located in the Werth Community. It was to be a farm plus dwelling. One glance and they were aware they were victims of land fraud. The farm was a hillside, and the house was, in their opinion, less than livable. For a while, times were very difficult for the family. However, James was an honest man, so he was determined to meet his part of the bargain in the contract. In later years, coal was discovered on the property, and its value escalated. The Bakers also owned the mineral rights.

While James Baker was doing chores around the farm, he accidentally let the fire he had started get out of control. It burned a neighbor's fence and a few trees. The neighbor assessed him a very high price for the loss. James, being an honest man, went to work in the mines to pay the debt. He had not worked long before he was killed on Oct. 30, 1900.

The first six of the Baker's 10 children were born in England. They were James, Jemima, Bessie "Betsy," Ann Selina, Joseph Henry, and Clara Alice Baker. (More on the family in part three, the conclusion)

James and Betsy Robinson Baker are buried in what used to be known as the Fitzwater Cemetery. It was located behind the original Little Union Baptist Church near Calvin, W.Va. Oren D. Fitzwater, grandfather of Ella V. Cox, donated the entire tract of land for the Little Union Baptist Church and the family cemetery. The original deed indicated it was only to be used for the family and relatives. Mr. Fitzwater had a generous heart, so he permitted the others to lie there, and he never charged anyone. At a much later date, Lou Ann Mullens (sister of Mrs. Cox) and Warren Mullens deeded the cemetery property to the Little Union Baptist Church. They also allowed the original fence to be removed and a single enclosure included the church and cemetery. The church renamed the cemetery Little Union Cemetery. Some Fitzwater family members were sad that the Fitzwater name was dropped. It is interesting that James and Betsy Baker's graves were outside the original fence, because they were not relatives of the Fitzwater Family. Mrs. Ella Cox served as a trustee for the cemetery at one point and recalls this information very clearly.

James Baker (1845-1900) and Betsy Robinson Baker (1845-1928) and son, Joseph Henry Baker (1875-1952) and Lizzie Hanna Baker are buried in the Little Union Baptist Church Cemetery near Calvin. The conclusion of the early Baker Family will be part three.

Note: Family cemeteries are a good source of genealogy information. The Nicholas County Historical and Genealogy Society is doing research on Family Cemeteries to document and map. Any information on Family Cemeteries and locations would be greatly appreciated. Send to: The Nicholas County Historical and Genealogy Society, P.O. Box 443, Summersville, WV 26651.

102
THE JAMES BAKER CHILDREN AND FAMILIES

The children of James and Betsy Baker were: 1. James Baker, born Dec. 23, 1866, died March 3, 1873, age 6 years and three months, in England. 2. Jemima Baker, born June 21, 1868, in England, married William Houser on July 5, 1892. She never moved to West Virginia with the family. 3. Bessie "Betsy" Baker, born Nov. 26, 1871, married C.S. Fleming on April 22, 1891. She did not move to West Virginia. 4. Ann Selina Baker, born Dec. 10, 1873, married Watson Reed Hickman on April 20, 1890. 5. Joseph Henry Baker, born Nov. 8, 1875, married Lizzie M. Hanna on Jan. 8, 1902. 6. Clara Alice Baker, born Aug. 12, 1878, married John Andrew Grose on Dec. 24, 1898. The first six children were born in England.

The next four children were born in the United States after the parents, James and Betsy Baker, came from England. 7. Mary Ann Baker, born June 25, 1881, married Floyd Grose, brother of John Grose, on Dec. 25, 1899. 8. Elizabeth "Lizzie" Baker, born Aug. 17, 1883, married James Isaac White on Nov. 18, 1902. 9. Harry Baker, born Feb. 26, 1887, died 1978, married wife, 1. Chloe Groves and 2. Pearl Flanagan. The last child, William Baker, born Feb. 26, 1889, died the same year.

The families of Ann Selina, Joseph Henry and Clara Alice Baker were raised in Nicholas County. Before Mary Ann Baker

Grose's children were adults, they moved to Parkersburg, W.Va. Harry and Pearl moved to Walkersville, W.Va.

Ann Selina and Reed Hickman's children were Howard, Willie, Bert, Leonard, Alice, Josephine, Bessie Lea (mother of Ella V. Cox), Ada, Cora and Freda.

Howard married Lela Perkins; Leonard married Aleta McKinney; Alice married Londis Bredon, Josephine Hickman married Guy Perkins; Bessie married John Fitzwater; Ada married Bill Lawson and second husband Sam Mellonzi; Cora Hickman married Sterling Milam, and Freda married Raymond Lowry.

Bert H. Hickman was the first soldier to die from Nicholas County to die in World War I. Therefore, the American Legion Post No. 97 in Richwood still bears his name. The Legion offered Ann Selina Hickman a trip to his grave in Europe, but she politely refused. Time had not erased the memories of that trip. The parents desired their son to lie on his native soil, so his body was returned and honored by the American Legion and a host of others. He was originally buried in the family cemetery. When the parents, Ann Selina and Reed Hickman, could no longer care for the cemetery, the bodies of Bert Hickman and other family members were moved to Mountain View Memorial Park near Richwood.

The children of Joseph Henry Baker (1875-1952) were Arnett Baker (1903-1986), married 1. Lela Mae Hutcheson and 2. Edna S. Drennen; Luther Baker Sr., married Vada Maude Groves; Lester Baker; and Walter Baker, married to Lena McClung.

The children of John Andrew and Clara Alice Baker Grose (1878-1977) were: Kermit, Weldon, Frank, Leonard, Joe, Herbert, Zela, Thelma, Lora, Gertrude, Alma, Mary Esther, Roy and Hattie Grose. The last two children died at aged 1 and 4. Mary Esther Grose married Stanton Wiseman. She was born Nov. 12, 1920, and died Feb. 18, 2010, and was the last survivor of 14 children. John and Clara Alice Baker Grose are buried at the Little Union Cemetery near Calvin, W.Va. Daughter, Lora Grose Hanna, took care of her mother, Clara Alice, the last five years of her life. She died in 1977.

John and Clara Alice Grose lived on a 42-acre farm that John and his brother purchased from Robert Curry in 1905. The property joined Reed and Ann Selina Hickman's farm near Calvin. The Grose and Hickman children attended Little Gem School. At one time Nicholas County's former Superintendent of Schools James L. Creasy taught here. Later, in 1937, John and Clara Alice Grose purchased and moved to the Marshall Tyree Farm near Summersville.

The children of Floyd and Mary Ann Baker Grose were: Cecil, Orval Alva, Grace, Eddie, Bert, Lucy, Edith, Junior and Timmy.

The children of Isaac and Elizabeth Baker White were Fred, Bruce, Watson, and Ervin and there may have been others.

Harry and Chloe Baker's children were Carl, Grace and Gertrude. Harry married Pearl Flanagan, and had a daughter, Phyllis Jean Baker.

Carl Lester Baker married Clara Elsa Starting on April 4, 1936.

The James and Betsy Robinson Baker descendants are numerous. Some are residents of Nicholas County, but many located elsewhere. They followed the professions of farming, educators, carpentry and business.

A very special thank you to Ella Cox, Amy Pellegrin and Mary Baker Frazer for sharing Baker Genealogy.

According to W.G. Brown's Nicholas County History Book, Michael Baker who also came from England and settled on Tates Run in 1806, was not related to James Baker and Joseph Baker who came from England to the United States in 1879.

103

ROADSIDE PARKS

After World War II, everyone in the United States was eager to start living and planning for the future. During the days of rationing of food and supplies, there was little left for recreation and very limited transportation.

As cars and gasoline became available, those who could afford it started to travel to visit relatives and to take a vacation to other places. In those days, from the mid-1940s into the 50s, there were no rest areas and fast food restaurants, as we know them.

In some states, small roadside areas were designated as a "Park" where there were a few wooden picnic tables with benches attached, a metal barrel painted blue or green for trash collection and a fire pit or grill for cooking. There were no facilities available.

Those roadside parks brought a lot of pleasures to families and to groups of people who were either traveling or just recreation for local citizens.

Usually, the cooking was roasting wieners (hot dogs) and toasting marshmallows for s'mores, a special treat. Others who preferred an outing away from their home would pack a picnic, find a roadside park, and enjoy the scenery. The children played with whatever nature could provide, such as rocks, sticks or picking up pinecones and wildflowers.

There were many memories made at roadside parks. On Route 41, about two miles north of Summersville, a popular roadside park was established and was used frequently. The State Road

(Dept. of Highways) managed the parks with mowing and trash removal.

Mountain Lake Garden Club established a small roadside park on Route 39, west of Summersville, at a location formerly known as "The Fountain" where spring water was piped from the hillside. A wooden sign was placed there with flowers and shrubs planted around the sign. There was a picnic table with benches for those who desired to picnic in the shaded area. Vandals soon destroyed the lovely park.

When the Interstate Highway System was established, roadside parks soon gave way to large rest areas with big parking lots, a building with facilities and vending machines. The rest areas and welcome centers offer many conveniences to travelers.

The former roadside park on Route 41 was closed. The New River Community and Technical College now occupies the area in Summersville.

NCHS Nine Club Members 1950: left, Mary Sue Taylor, Ann Murphy, Mae Bently and Ruth Piercy at Route 41 Roadside Park.

1950 NCHS Nine Club

NCHS Nine Club Members 1950: front, Lola Malcomb, Joan Sundstrum (teacher), Ruth Piercy, Joey McClung; back, Ann Murphy, Winnie Dotson, Mae Bently Sybil Miller, and Mary Sue Taylor (sponsor).

Mary Sue Taylor and her car at the NCHS Nine Club Members picnic at the Route 41 Roadside Park in Spring 1950.

104

THE CATTLE DRIVE — MAIN STREET, SUMMERSVILLE

"A fine drove of cattle, 226 in number and owned by Arnold McCue of Nicholas County, were driven though Fayette last week on their way to Nicholas.

These steers were two years old or more and all seemed to be in fine condition. At the price at which beef is now selling this drove of cattle represented a small fortune. They were purchased in Raleigh and Wyoming Counties. It is said that Mr. McCue has another drove of about 300 head to bring through.

At Fayette, these cattle all crossed the bridge in a body, being perhaps the greatest weight ever placed on it and although it has been condemned as unsafe for several months, it bore the great weight without any apparent strain ..." Fayette Democrat

This article appeared in the book, Part of Summersville Past by Bonita Bell and Hilda Grose.

Main Street Summersville was not paved until about 1923. It was a dirt and rock street until then.

Many early settlers in Nicholas County farmed cattle, as there was plenty of grazing land.

David McCue Jr. had sons, William D., and Fielding McCue. They were farmers and cattlemen. Fielding McCue had a son, Arnold Mc- Cue, who had the cattle drove in Summersville in 1913.

Charles William Cottle, an early settler in Nicholas County purchased about 800 acres, known as Cottle Glades, where he raised cattle on about 200 acres of meadowland.

There are several cattle farmers today in Nicholas County. Their method of transportation of the cattle is very different in 2010 with specially designed cattle trucks to transport cattle from one place to another location or to market.

The Cattle Drive, Main Street, Summersville, 1913

105

IRA E. HILL

William Hill came from Pocahontas County, settled in the Muddlety Valley, Nicholas County. His sons were James, John and Joseph Hill. Joseph Hill, who lived to be over 100 years old, served as the Nicholas County Court. (Now known as the Nicholas County Commission)

Joseph Hill married Sallie Washington Burr. They were the parents of Ira E. Hill, born in 1882 and served as Nicholas County Clerk from 1933 to 1962, longer than any other clerk. He married Edna B. Herold, Oct. 4, 1904, and died in 1963 in Summersville.

The following is the Recollections of Summersville, West Virginia, by Ira Hill. The date that the story is written was not recorded.

MY RECOLLECTIONS OF SUMMERSVILLE

By Ira Hill (1882-1963)

Summersville was named in honor of Judge Lewis Summers, who introduced the bill in the Virginia Assembly creating Nicholas County in the year 1818.

Summersville's Main Street was laid off due east and west and is located at an elevation of 1894 feet, so marked on the front right-hand corner of the courthouse.

Summersville was originally established in 1824 and was not incorporated until 1860.

The first corporate limits, as I remember, at the west end on Main Street, was at the front of the yard where I now live; the east end was just a little this side of the new Catholic church. The south end was just a little south of the old Burr's Mill. There was no state road leading down by Summersville Lumber Company's Peer parlor, and so on. I do not remember the northern limit.

The main thoroughfare known as the Weston and Gauley Bridge Turnpike coming through the town was also accepted as the Main Street of Summersville. The more substantial sidewalks were constructed of large flat stones that were hauled from the river and placed in front of the business places. There were a few sidewalks constructed of brick since there was a brick plant just below where the Summerville Lumber Company now is that made the brick for a few structures and the flues and chimneys near the town. As to Main Street, it was a wide expanse of mud in the wintertime. The town used much broken stone on the street, which in the summer was very rough. For the purpose of getting across Main Street in the wintertime when mud was 6 to 8 inches deep, the town authorities caused to be quarried from stone quarries near the town, stone about three feet long six inches wide and 10 to 12 inches deep or thick, and placed them in the street with narrow side up, about 30 inches, or a medium step apart with about six inches rising above the street level for the purpose of aiding pedestrians to get across Main Street. These crossings were placed at crossings most used by the public. There were some five or six on Main Street. In the year 1923 the State Road Commission let to contract the hard surfacing of Main Street from the west corporate limits to the east corporate limit. It was a great day for Summersville when it had the first piece of hard surface road in Nicholas County.

Traveling east on Main Street were residences. Up first, to Spruce Street on Main the Baptist Church was on the corner at that time. Leaving Spruce Street and on east there was a home where Clyde Bell now lives and from Bell to where the old garage now is was a large apple orchard and on the right side of Main was the then spacious residence of the late John D. Alderson and at that time a respected Congressman. Within the spacious grounds around the residence I have enjoyed watching the antics of two or three deer.

On the northwest corner of Main Street and Broad Street where Cook Department Store and the Dime Store stood the three-story Summersville Hotel owned and operated by Mrs. Fitzwater. Many people of note have been patrons of this hotel. At one time, a murder was committed within its walls. On the southwest of Main and Broad corner, there stood a very long two-story building, the lower floor being used for a general store and the second floor used for housekeeping and the same corner now occupied by Mobil Gas, Esso Gas etc.

On the southeast corner of Main and Broad there one was located the Alderson House, another hotel owned and operated by L.N. Alderson. Many have had the good dinners and I have ate there for the unheard price of 25 cents.

On the northeast corner of Main and Broad there stands one of the oldest buildings in Summersville and it in all its existence had never been out of the hands of its original ownership and their heirs. A part of the building constructed of logs and is far more than 100 years old.

The next old building, which still stands in the tall two-story building, which has been known during my memory as the Masonic Building, the house of Summersville Masonic Lodge #76 A.F. and A.M. on the second floor until just a few years ago they moved to their new home on South Broad Street, the lower floor is being used by general merchants by the name of Ed Alderson for many years. The building now is owned by a private investor.

The present location of Elizabeth's Shop on the north side of the street was the home of the fist ice cream and soft drink parlor owned and operated by Alfred Groves and his daughters. Mr. Groves had his own icehouse in back of the lot and in wintertime he would stock the icehouse with ice cut and hauled from the river or from ponds nearby. He owned his ice cream freezer of about five or 10-gallon capacity and he would give employment to two nearly blind Wills brothers to turn the crank of the freezer until the cream was complete.

He also made his own lemonade of which he had great sale. The barbershop and the restaurant, which in the beginning was a doctor's office, to which many additions have been annexed, are very early structures. The large brick residence was built by the doctor that built the office on the corner of his lot, his name being Dr. E.J. Rader who moved to Huntington many years ago and has long since been deceased.

I can remember when there was a board fence along the side of the sidewalk from the J.A. Mearns building (the large two-story building just opposite the courthouse) down to the Bell Pool room building. I have seen all the construction in this vicinity. The Farmers and Merchants Bank was organized in January 1909 and first had its home in the front of a residence building that stood where Johnson's Department Store now stands. The property now occupied by the Baby Shop and Stowers Supermarket belonged to the owner of the Mearns Building who also owned and used as a meadow all of the land from the post office, all property served by Lee Street and its tributaries above Water Street. The real estate now occupied by the post office, Mr. Mearns had a large barn for his many horse and cows he kept.

Let's not forget the court square on the south side of Main Street between Church and Court and on the rear by Whortleberry Avenue.

My first recollection of the courthouse was a small square frame structure, which was superseded by the front part of the present building containing the cupola and built of native stone completed in 1896. The annex was built about 1933 or 1934 by W.P.A. Labor and the second floor of the annex being completed for the occupation of the present Circuit Judge.

My recollection goes back to when I used to go into Uncle Billy Grose's saddlery shop, which stood on the corner where the Farmers and Merchants Bank new stands. Uncle Billy wore a long beard and an apron that came down to his knees. He would show me the process of building a man's saddle and also the process of building a lady's sidesaddle, which was all very interesting to me.

Where the Nicholas County Bank now stands there was a blacksmith shop, owned and operated by a man named Alex McMillion. Often I have taken my horse into his shop and he would put shoes on him for me. It was interesting to see the smith heat the metal red hot and lay in on the anvil and begin to apply his hammer, and the sparks would fly and soon he would have the metal to be finished job. Then he would fasten the shoe to the horse's hoof with nails made for that purpose. Later, the blacksmith shop gave way to the Nicholas County Bank, which was organized in 1900, and its first banking home was the present building occupied by the Citizen's Grocery, which was built on the spot where the blacksmith shop stood. Later, the bank outgrew its home, and the building removed where it now stands, and the now spacious Nicholas County Bank building stands where the blacksmith shop once prospered, and the Farmers and Merchants Bank now stands where Uncle Billy Grose's saddlery shop did a lucrative business.

With the advent of the automobile and how crude it was as compared with the automobile of today, came Campbell's Garage as the first one with its expansions. As the industry progressed, more garages sprung up, the old Trent Garage, located just below the Dime Store, being the second one I believe, with the Morris Garage near about the same time.

My education, and what an education it was, outside the one-room country school room was secure at the Summersville Normal School, which stood on the little point where Ralph Kincaid, Festus Drennen and other now live. The Normal was a going concern during the 90s.

I do not think I should close without telling you about Uncle Lewis and Aunt "Sibby" an old colored man that lived near the old ash tree, just back of where Dan Rader lives, on Water Street. I am told that Aunt "Sibby" was an excellent cook and many were the white folks that would go and eat with the colored folks and get an excellent meal for 20 cents. Uncle Lewis made baskets and would tie four or five baskets on his white horse and go out among the farmers and trade his basket to the former for corn to fill the basket.

106

THE FAMILY CEMETERY

The early settlers established a location of the property for a cemetery. The chosen location was usually on top of a knoll or an isolated area that would not be suitable for farming. Often the location would be visible from the house.

The burial ground was used for family and extended family members. A fence enclosed the area to keep animals and cattle from entering and causing damage to the stones or markers.

Many families lost several infants in the early settlements. A stone or a large rock without names or dates often marked those graves. Thus, many graves are unmarked.

More well to do families bought head or footstones with a name, birth and death date. Some grave markers had an interesting statement, which told something of the person. "The Praise of him who sleeps in earth, the pleasant memory of his worth. The hope to meet is past shall cheer the sorrowing soul at last." This is written on the tombstone of Oliver P. Starbuck in the Southern Methodist Cemetery, Summersville, W.Va.

Other words noticed on stones are consort, just sleeping, at rest, or resting, and also many other sayings or words. When visiting cemeteries, one should take note of the different markers, some very unusual in shape and size.

Now that more people are tracing their roots, a visit to a family or a community cemetery can offer important information.

The Nicholas County Historical and Genealogical Society has some information to assist those who are working on genealogy but is also working toward recording family cemeteries and the location. The plan is to assemble all cemeteries into one book.

Your help is needed to assist in the research of hidden family and other cemeteries. Please send any information and location of cemeteries to:

Nicholas County Historical and Genealogical Society, P.O. Box 443, Summersville, WV 26651.

107

SEBERT FAMILY

The Sebert name was first documented in written records in the B. Chronicles of 1320. There are several variations of the German name, such as Seibert, Seybert, Sibert, Seibertz and others. Captain John Jacob came to America in 1738 from Eisleben, Germany, to Pennsylvania in the mountain emigration. He settled in the Philadelphia area and then moved to the Frederick, Md., area where he stayed for about four years. He left for the Wilderness area of Virginia (Pendleton County). He was commissioned Captain of the Militia for Fort Seybert, which he helped to establish on the banks of the Potomac River. He served in the French and Indian War. Captain John Jacob Sebert and wife Maria Theiss, had two sons, Nicholas and Henry Sebert.

Captain John Jacob and wife, Maria Sebert, along with their son, Nicholas, were massacred on April 28, 1758, when Indian Chief Killbuck and a band of Shawnee Braves laid siege to the Fort and burned it. Several others were massacred, and others were taken prisoner. Son, Henry Sebert, was later taken prisoner, escaped and returned. Those killed are buried in one grave. Fort Sebert was located on South Branch, about 12 miles from Franklin.

Henry Sebert's son, Jacob Serbert, moved to the Greenbrier Valley and founded the town of Seebert, located on the Greenbrier River near Hillsboro in Pocahontas County. Jacob's sons, Abraham and Levi Sebert, moved to Nicholas County, purchased land on the head of McKees Creek and Campfork Creek in 1839.

Levi Sebert moved to Illinois about 1840. He married Electa Gillien and they had a son, Samuel Sebert. Levi Sebert received a land grant in Illinois where he and others invested and opened the Algonquin Mutual Insurance Company. He was also a farmer, died in 1886, was buried in Algonquin Cemetery, Algonquin, Ill. There is a Seebert Street and a Seeberts Subdivision where he lived. Son, Samuel Gillilan, returned to Nicholas County.

Abraham Sebert (1797-1871) married Elizabeth Dorney (1804-1870), a Cherokee Indian. They had four sons, John J. Sebert, Samuel E. Sebert, William Sebert and Adam Sebert. Their daughters were: Julia Sebert who married Jerimiah O'Dell, Elizabeth Sebert married John O'Dell and Sarah Sebert married Arron M. Dorsey.

Adam Sebert died without a family. John J. Sebert married Rebecca Bailes, and their sons were Joseph F. Sebert who married May Crawford, and Ellis Sebert who married Lilly Rader. They were farmers in Nicholas County.

William Sebert's sons were Jacob F. Sebert, Abraham Sebert, John Sebert and Samuel Sebert.

Dama Sebert married Gladys Sweeney, Lloyd Sebert married Margaret Hobbs; Lee Sebert married Genevieve Neil and Guy Sebert were the sons of Ellis Sebert and great grandsons of Abraham Sebert (1797-1871).

Kyle Sebert and Hunter Sebert were sons of Samuel Sebert. His daughters were Elsie Sebert and Bertha Sebert who married O.G. Robinson.

Russell Sebert (1904-1996) married Effie Bryant (1905-1953). They were the parents of a son, James Sebert, who married Patricia Painter and are the parents of three daughters. Barbara Sebert, daughter of Russell Sebert, son of Joseph F. Sebert and May Crawford Sebert (1870-1944), was a farmer and served on the Farmers and Merchant's Bank Board of Directors. Later, after wife, Effie Sebert died, Russell Sebert married Iva Mearns, a teacher of Arthur Sebert married Ruth Sweeney.

There are many descendants of Sebert brothers, Abraham and Levi living in the Nicholas County area and other parts of West Virginia.

Each year, the third weekend in September, there is a reenactment at Fort Seybert. The spelling of the Sebert name changed among different families and locations.

Joseph F. Sebert (1871-1947) and wife, May Crawford (1870-1944). Joseph F. was grandson of Abraham Sebert (1797-1871)

Russell Sebert (1904-1996) and wife Effie Bryant Sebert (1905-1953). Russell was a great-grandson of Abraham Sebert (Photo taken in 1949)

Sebert Family Tree

Seyfried Sebert 1500 - 1551	~	Marie Yoder ?
Klaus Sebert 1530 1590	~	Margareth ? 1547 1592
Klaus Sebert II 1560 - 1593	~	Elsie Jung 1570 - 1595
Nickel Sebert 1586 - 1666	~	Mary Mayer 1602 - 1664
Hans Sebert 1639 - 1694	~	Margaret Spangler 1645 - 1699
Christopher Sebert 1682 - 1732	~	Anna Johnetta? 1704 - 1758
Capt. John Jacob Sebert 1720 - 1758	~	Maria Thiess 1721 - 1758
Henry Sebert 1743 - 1795	~	Rachel Trail 1752 - 1840
Jacob Sebert 1776 - 1830	~	Mary Gum 1778 - 1801
Abrahan Sebert 1797 - 1871	~	Elizabeth Dorney 1804 - 1870
Levi Sebert 1809 - 1886	~	Electa Gillien ?

108
NICHOLAS COUNTY CLERKS
AND RECORDERS

T he County of Nicholas was organized at the residence of John Hamilton at Keslers Cross Lanes in April 1818. One of the first orders of business was to elect a Clerk of the County Court. The following have served as County Clerk:

John Given 1818-1820
Strother Bowyer 1820-1823
Noah Davis 1823-1831
Samuel Price 1831-1834
Ro. Hamilton 1834-1842
Samuel Given 1842-1848
Robert Hamilton 1848-1861
Logan Stephenson 1862-1865
James Craig (Recorder) 1865-1870
A.F. Rader (Recorder) 1871-1872
John A. Hamilton 1873-1902
Robert H. Hamilton 1902-1902
Joseph Alderson 1903-1908
P.N. Wiseman 1909-1920
C.E. Stephenson 1921-1932
Ira E. Hill 1933-1962
Spurgeon Hinkle 1963-1980

Tom Blankenship 1981-1988
John Greer 1989-2004
Wanda Hendrickson 2005- present

The Nicholas County Court after the election of County Clerk, which was done by ballot at that time, convened to proceed to business appointments. William Given was appointed as Commissioner of Revenue, with John Bowyer as Assistant Commissioner. Samuel Hutchinson was appointed Surveyor of the County. Several Road Overseers were appointed.

The County laid the levy for taxes, fixed the rates for ferries and set salaries, ordinary rates and fees for all local officers, this controlling the finances of the County.

The early records show a tremendous amount of work done by the County Court, which was done without salary or necessary expenses. It was a high honor to serve as a member of the Nicholas County Court.

The Court also fixed rates of tavern keepers as follows: Breakfast, 25 cents; dinner, 25 cents; Supper, 25 cents; whiskey, one-half pint, 12 and one-half cents; brandy, one-half pint, 17 cents; New England Rum, one-half pint, 37 and one-half cents; West India Rum, one-half pint, 50 cents; cider, one quart, 12 and one-half cents; Madeira wine, one quart, $1.50; common wine, one quart, $1.25; hay to horse, 24 hours, 21 cents; corn, oats, one gallon, 12 and one-half cents; pasturage for day and night, 12 and one-half cents; lodging, 12 and one-half cents. (Note how many things are priced at 12 and one-half cents, including lodging.)

109

ELY-THOMAS LUMBER COMPANY
WERTH, NICHOLAS COUNTY, WV

T he story was told that Ralph H. Ely left home at the age of 13 years and wasn't heard from again until he had become a successful young man.

Mr. Ely owned a band mill in Arlington, Upshur County, as the timber supply was in short supply, he brought his mill to Nicholas County in 1930. Here he and Wellington "Bull" Thomas established the Ely- Thomas Lumber Company at a site that was known as WERTH, a combination of the owners' initials. The operation of the mill started in November 1931.

Money was scarce, wages were low; a few cents per hour paid to the workers. Lumber was trucked to Camden on Gauley and to Hookersville where it was shipped by rail. A three-story mill building was constructed to house all the equipment for the milling operation.

A pond was constructed to clean the logs of mud and debris so the band saw wouldn't be dulled. The saw needed to be sharp to give a good cut and filing a saw required time to sharpen. A good sawyer was required to determine how a log would be cut and how many boards from each log.

Work camps were used to house men who were experts in felling trees. A skilled logger could determine how a tree should be cut and notched to fall in a certain direction. The cut trees were hauled or pulled by strong horses to the loading areas. The work camps were located near a tract of timber until the land was cleared. The men worked long hours after breakfast and went back to the camp for supper. A person or two, usually the camp manager's wife, would be hired to cook for the loggers. Three large meals were prepared from scratch. Potatoes peeled and meat, vegetables and bread all cooked on a wood-burning stove. Dishes and tableware had to be washed by hand and dried three times a day. There was no refrigeration, and food was kept cool if possible. Supplies were purchased in very large amounts.

The men slept in bunkhouses or shanties. The largest building housed the kitchen and dining area. The sleeping quarters were moved to the next location when the camp ran out of timber.

A boarding house was built at Werth where mill workers could stay and have meals. There also was a company-owned house nearby at Werth. The early boarding house rate was about $0.60 per person per day. Through the years, some people were employed by Ely-Thomas Lumber Company to manage the boarding house. They were Gertrude Ramsey, Addie McKisic and Tressie Allman. They had many helpers through the week as some mill workers went home on weekends.

The food supplies were purchased for the boarding house in large quantities, as there could be more than 200 men working. It was important to run good camps and boarding houses in order to entice better loggers. Plenty of well-prepared food ensured a good labor force.

There was also a large company store where employees could purchase most of the necessities such as groceries, furniture, dry goods and clothing with Scrip (a form of money issued by the company).

The logs were hauled by truck and in the 1940's a narrow rail system was constructed to bring logs to the mill. The lumber was neatly stacked so to allow for proper drying before it was shipped to various places.

During World War II, Ely-Thomas Lumber Co. manufactured special lumber for the U.S. Navy in clear oak with no defects for Norfolk, Va., where it was made into landing barges.

The mill blew a whistle four times a day. The whole community of Werth could hear the mill whistle.

The hardwoods of maple, red and white oak, basswood, cherry, gum, poplar and ash were cut into lumber. The small pieces and shavings were used by the mill for steam power.

When the Ely-Thomas Lumber Company mill was running and more timberland acquired, Ralph H. Ely had a rustic home constructed for his family at Werth. He moved his family from Buckhannon to the new home along with the longtime housekeeper, Miss Esta Lewis. The Ely family members were Ralph; wife, Amy Clark Ely; and two sons, Ralph H. Ely Jr. (Sonny) and David Clark Ely.

On Oct. 21, 1959, workers and residents were awakened at 1:20 a.m. by a fire alarm calling the Summersville Volunteer Fire Department to fight the flames at the mill. It was a total loss. The mill was never reopened, which was a tremendous loss to the community and to the county.

110

ELY THOMAS LUMBER COMPANY FENWICK, NICHOLAS COUNTY, W.VA.

After the devastating fire, which destroyed the Ely-Thomas Lumber Mill at Werth, W.Va., in 1959, some of the employees were transferred to the already working mill at Fenwick, Nicholas County, W.Va.

The location of the operation was west of Richwood on Route 39. The history of the mill dates back to the turn of the century when the Fenwick Lumber Company built a band mill. The town of Fenwick sprung up around the mill. It seems that Fenwick Lumber vanished in the 1920s. Pete Eakin's Lumber Company had already cut timber in other areas, built a new steam-powered single-band mill at Fenwick in 1927 or 1928. Eakin logged hardwood along Little Laurel Creek, which flows into Cherry River. The logs were hauled out of the woods on a standard gauge log train powered by a three-truck Shay that became Ely-Thomas Number 3. The rail operation at peak had about 40 miles of track.

Eakin Lumber was finally doomed by the Great Depression. In 1938, the Fenwick Mill and Eakin's Railroad equipment were purchased by lumber barons, Ralph Ely and Willington "Bull" Thomas. It was said that the value of six or seven million board feet of hardwood lumber in the mill yard was sufficient to recoup the price that Ely-Thomas paid for Eakin's entire Fenwick operation.

The standard Shay locomotive continued until the mid-1960s. There were a series of floods crossing Laurel Creek that wiped out bridges. After that happened, trucks brought cut logs on top of a hillside. A loader picked up the logs from the bottom of the hill into flat cars. A Shay locomotive took the logging train to the millpond.

The Shay number 3 went to a Pennsylvania Logging Rail Museum in 1964. Shay number 2 remained in operation until 1965, when a diesel locomotive took the place of a Shay locomotive.

It is sad to note that none of the Shay locomotives remained in West Virginia museums. They were all retired to museums in Pennsylvania, Michigan, New Jersey, North Carolina and Wisconsin.

The Fenwick Mill operation stopped in 1967. The Ely-Thomas Lumber Company was the last logger in West Virginia employing steam locomotives.

After the death of the wife of Ralph Ely, he married again. Later, they built a lovely frame home of the finest wood with a white wooden fence to encase the last home of Ralph Ely in Summersville. The longtime housekeeper Miss Esta Lewis remained with the Elys until she experienced failing health. At that time she returned to Upshur County, where she died. On Saturday afternoons, Miss Lewis would visit with the neighbors. That was her time off duty at the Ely residence.

Logging was and continues to be important to West Virginia. Although wages were small, there was a need for proficient and knowledgeable men. Lumberjacks were skilled in timbering, skidding logs, rolling and stopping logs. It could also be dangerous if a tree or a log went the wrong direction. It is still a big industry in the area, as trucks transport logs on the highways daily, taking logs to the mills or collection yards. The demand for lumber is still great for furniture, building homes and many other uses.

Transporting logs by a river or stream of water to the mill was free, but labor intensive in the process. Chainsaws came about in the late 1940s for cutting timber.

Ralph Hills Ely died Feb. 2, 1966, and his wife, Ruth Cairns Ely, died April 19, 1994. Their final resting place is in the Walker Memorial Cemetery, Summersville.

The logs were hauled out of the woods on a standard gauge log train powered by a three-truck Shay that became Ely-Thomas Number 3. The rail operation at peak had about 40 miles of track.

111

THE OLD SPINNING WHEEL

By John L. Evans

Will you be at my home Thursday? If so, let us visit together. Let us pull up a chair and have a heart to heart talk just talk things over for a little while. Let us talk of the days gone by. Let us recall some of the things of our childhood, father, mother and the old home. These things mean so much to most of us, and we sometimes need to remember or to be reminded of the days gone by.

Does the old spinning wheel still remain in the attic of the old home? There is one in the attic of my old home. It may be dust covered and old, but there is something about it that remains sacred. I recall the hands that used to turn it, and I would give the world if only those hands could reach back across the years and turn it again. Most people today would say that it serves no purpose, but are they right? Who has the heart to dispose of it? I believe that most of whatever is good within me is due to the inspiration and the encouragement I received from the Godly lives of father and mother and the associations with them around the old fireside and the old spinning wheel. It is a priceless heritage, which no one can take away from us and for which we should be thankful.

There are many other things of gone years that I would like to recall, but space permits only a few. Do you remember what a freshly plowed furrow feels like to a barefooted boy's feet? And, oh those flapjacks, which mother used to make swimming in butter and maple syrup, do you remember just how they tasted on a cold, frosty morning? Do you remember how you used to crowd in between two cool white sheets on a summer night and be lulled to sleep by the patter of raindrops on the old clapboard roof and the chirp, chirp of crickets in the old stone and mud chimney? And do you remember on a cold winter night mother would tuck you in your little trundle bed and while the winter wind moaned around the corner of the old house, how warm and secure you felt? I love those memories and am thankful for it all. I would like to live those days over again — "Backward, turn backward oh time in your flight; make me a child again just for tonight." I would like to live again the days when all it took to bind a bargain was only a handshake; when no one argued about guarantees and the word of a man was as good as his bond.

We are not unmindful to our adverse to modern improvements; on the other hand, we are thankful and glad we have all of them — our good roads, automobiles and radios. They are a joy and consolation in that they are bringing the world closer together, figuratively speaking, shrinking the world and making a nation of 130 million people next door neighbors, for this we should be grateful, and in the use of all our modern improvements let us see to it that they are used and employed for the betterment of mankind. But in memory, let us keep a place in the old attic and a place for the old spinning wheel because of all they mean to us.

Note: John L. Evans, born March 2, 1876, in Muddlety, W.Va., lived most of his life in Nicholas County. He was Summersville Postmaster (1920), assistant cashier of Nicholas County Bank, served as Summersville Mayor (1926-27), was a businessman and held other positions during his career. He was married to Nellie Alderson Evans and they were the parents of four children. After the death of his first wife, John L. Evans married Rose Murphy. They resided on Oak Street, Summersville.

Mr. Evans was well liked and respected and wrote many obituaries for families. He was a great storyteller and enjoyed talking to children. He died Sept. 23, 1953. Rose Murphy Evans died June 10, 1995. They both are in a final resting place in Walker Memorial Park Cemetery in Summersville.

John L. Evans (1876-1953) Rose Murphy Evans (1896-1995)

112

NCHS CLASS OF 1950

The Nicholas County High School building opened on Sept. 14, 1914, for the first students to enroll for a high school education. Many students attended and graduated from the native stone building. Classes and teachers were added to the school through the years.

In 1946, following the close of World War II, a large group of 211 freshmen students entered the halls of NCHS for the first time. Most students were transported by school buses while in-town students of Summersville walked, as very few had a vehicle at that time. Many things were still in short supply following the war.

A new vocational building was suggested by Lyle E. Herold, principal at NCHS in 1944. The building was approved by the Board of Education and $65,000 was appropriated. A contractor, Holland from Ripley, and an architect from Charleston were engaged, but due to the war (WWII) and shortage of materials, the building was not completed and ready for use until 1945-46. The building had a cafeteria, chemistry lab, classrooms, home economics department, shop class, a candy store (opened at noon) and storage.

The Nicholas County superintendent was James L. Creasy, serving from 1930 for many years. The high school principal, Lyle E. Herod served from 1942 through 1947. Gladys Herold Vaught served as guidance counselor and taught classes for many years.

There were 25 teachers at NCHS in 1946-47 and two regular substitutes, the Rev. A. F. Gregory and Jenny Bright (Percy). The secretary was Louise Legg.

The NCHS band had a temporary director in 1946. Katherine Drennen served the first semester and Harold Elkins returned to serve as director the second semester.

Football, boys and girls basketball were the major sports at NCHS. The football games were played during school hours as the football field had no lights for night games. Students could attend or go to study hall. Also, a movie was quite often shown in the auditorium during class periods for a small price. Those not attending went to study hall which was usually in the school library. 1947 was the first year for awards presented in citizenship, math and science, commerce, dramatics, home economics and music.

The ballpoint pen was perfected and took the place of the ink well pens in the late 1940s. The class of 1950 tossed aside ink bottles and ink pens for the ballpoint pens. Plastic items, nylon hose and many newer items were available to this class of 1950.

The Class of 1950 graduates had three principals and one acting principal to serve in four years. They were Lyle E. Harold, Harry Straley, and C. P. Wells who came to NCHS in 1949 and served there for many years. Hoyt Dean served as acting principal. The cost annually to educate per student was $500 in 1950.

There were so many outstanding students in the class of 1950. Several attended college by working as scholarships were not offered at that time. Many became teachers as they could attend college summer school and teach the school year and returned to college the following summer until a degree was earned. They had a shortage of teachers following WWII due to other jobs available and many went to college under the GI Bill of Rights for former military people. Following the 1950 graduation, several men served in the military during the Korean Conflict and later in the Vietnam War.

211 Freshmen started in 1946 and 118 seniors graduated May 1950. Class reunions have been held for the class of 1950 in 1970,

1990, 1995, 2000 and 2005. On Sept. 4, 2010, the 60th class reunion was held at the Old Main Building. Tours and visitation were followed by dinner at the Summersville Senior Center.

The Old Main Building in 1946

113

SUMMERSVILLE LIONS CLUB

The Summersville Lions Club organized in 1931 with the following charter members: Joe Alderson, A.N. Breckenridge, Eugene L. Campbell, J.C. Curry, W.G. Brown, J.W. Garrett, William M. Garrison, H.D. Groves, Emmett Horan, Ira E. Hill, George W. King, O.C. Lewis, W.E. McQueen, Shirley Morton, Harry H. Rader, W. Lee Stewart, W.E. Simpson, P.N. Wiseman, Ruskin Wiseman and J.D. Peck.

The active organization has served the community with many worthy projects. They have sponsored many activities throughout the years including the Nicholas County Potato Festival, Annual Easter Egg Hunt and especially Sight Conservation. Many business and professional men have contributed to the Lions Club and served as a Lions Club president. Those who served the first 30 years as President were: O.C. Lewis, Wm. Simpson, Dr. E.S. Brown, A.N. Breckenridge, Ruskin Wiseman, Cecil G. Frantz, B.N. McCutcheon, John B. Breckenridge, J.W. Robinson, Ralph Jones, Arnett Groves, Tom Dotson, B.N. McCutcheon, John B. Breckenridge, J.W. Robinson, Ralph Jones, E.C. McDowell, Jack Waters, Paul Cook and Dan Swartz. For many years, the Lions Club Members met at the Memorial United Methodist Church for dinner meetings, served by the Methodist Women. This was a source of income for the Methodist Women's Society of Christian Service to promote mission projects.

On Oct. 27, 1961, a 30th anniversary of the Summersville Lions Club was held at the Memorial United Methodist Church, Summersville, to honor the Charter Members and Past Presidents. The roster of Lions Club members in 1961 were: President Herbert E. Sundstrom, First Vice President Faber Herbert, Second Vice President Charles H. Howe, Third Vice President John LeRose, Treasurer Dan M. Swartz, Secretary Thomas J. Trent, Director Paul Cook, Director Dr. Hoy Eakle, Director Sam D. Brady III, Lion Tamer Norman Rexrode, Tail Twister Jack Waters. Other members were: Charles A. and Charles N. Adkins, John Breckenridge, Guy Dunn, Charles Eib, the Rev. A.F. Gregory, Edgel Grose, Arnett Groves, Mitchell Haddad, Wally Henderson, Ralph Jones, John McCue, Bernard McCutcheon, E.C. McDowell, Ralph Morris, M.J. Moyer Jr., Lyle Piper, the Rev. Charles Pugh, Dr. James Robinson, Pat Rossano, Glenn Thomas, Robert Wharton, Billy Whitlock and Ruskin Wiseman. Of all of the names listed, it is believed that only three men are still living.

The speakers for the 30th Anniversary Celebration were District Governor James J. Johns, International Director Walter J. Purdy and United States Senator Jennings Randolph.

The summer of 1948, the Summersville Lions Club employed Ann Murphy and Evelyn Huff to sell chances on a 1949 Ford automobile. The vehicle was available through Campbell Brothers Garage and Herbert Campbell, a Lions Club Member. The two young ladies set up on the Courthouse Lawn and at the Ford garage to sell tickets for $1 each. They accompanied Lions Club Members Garold Phillips who drove the 1949 Ford to the West Virginia State Fair where a number of tickets were sold. A local Summersville resident won the 1949 Ford. She did not drive, but her daughter drove the car for many years. This was a big fundraiser for the Lions Club projects in Summersville.

1931 Charter member of the Lions Club A.N. Breckenridge Jr.

1961 Lions Club Member Mitch Haddad

Eugene L. Campbell 1931 Charter member of
the Lions Club and honored in 1961

Ralph Jones, past president of Lions Club,
two times honored in October 1961

Ann Murphy and Evelyn Huff sell chances
on a 1949 Ford in June 1948

114

SHANTIES

Did you ever hear someone talk about a "shanty?" In the early years and during the Depression, workers who were lucky enough to find work in the timbering, railroad track building, road construction or coal mining industries, had to stay in company supplied, rude huts, known as a shanty.

The one, or sometimes two- room, roughly built buildings used for housing, consisted of two or more bunks, chairs or bench, small woodstove for heat and cooking. The men stayed in shanties during the workweek and when able went home on the weekends. A wash basin for hand and face washings was available but no bath or shower arrangements unless there was a nearby creek or stream of water.

The food shanties were sometimes available, especially in logging camps where meals were prepared by cooks employed by the company. The railroad crew's labor camp was made of shanties or rude huts located on the railroad. A dining car was provided for the workers' meals, and sometimes in the winter the dining car would provide coffee during the day when the weather was very cold. The labor crews referred to the "bunk cars" on the railroad. When the track was completed, the bunk cars, dining cars and equipment were moved by rail to the next job. However, there were no phones, CB's, walkie-talkies or communication except by the men in charge. The workers had no contact with families except when they could travel to their home, which wasn't always possible with limited transportation until the job was finished.

Shanties in the coal camp were as uncomfortable as those in the lumber camps. A typical shanty consisted of a kitchen, living room and two bedrooms. They were rented for about $4 per month and an additional charge of about $2 for coal to heat the house and to fire the cook stove. The wages earned were used to buy the necessities at the company-owned store. The wages were paid by the ton of coal mined by hand. The going price was about 10 cents per ton.

Another type of shanty was found on the riverboats, especially during the Depression times when families lacked other means of survival, they took to the river as a source of livelihood. The shanty boat days started back in the 18th century when pioneers began to cross the Appalachian Mountains. The migrants would find someone to build a boat large enough to carry their animals, wagon, supplies and family. Usually the pioneers hired a guide familiar with the rivers to float them downstream for the many hazards of water travel, islands, rocks, sand bars were frightening to newcomers. When the pioneers reached their destinations, they continued to live on the flatboat until land was cleared and a house was built.

The Ohio, Monongahela, Kanawha, Guyandotte and perhaps other rivers were used to transport shanty boats. The living conditions were primitive, with a toilet perched on the rear, which emptied into the river.

After World War II, when people became more prosperous, the need for shanties diminished.

Another type of a shanty was the "picking shanty" known as a place where people who liked to be together to play music assembled. The musicians played the fiddle, violin, banjo, guitars and anything that enhanced the repertory of songs. They learned at an early age from an experienced relative or another musician. The sounds from the "picking shanty" were endless on a Saturday night.

A shanty in a coal mining camp rented for about $4 per month.

115

APRONS, FEED AND FLOUR SACKS

At one time in America, no grandmother, mother or daughter would be found working in the kitchen without an apron. Aprons were simply a part of life. During the last decades of the 20th century, modern life was passing aprons by and the decades old tradition had all but vanished.

The pioneer women always wore an apron to protect the dress and served many uses. Each woman usually had only one or two dresses and laundry was an all-day chore, so the everyday aprons served to also carry vegetables from the garden, gathering eggs and apples, carrying kindling (firewood) and for small children to tug upon for attention or to hide from someone.

The aprons always had one or two big pockets that were handy for small items and of course, to carry the much-needed handkerchief. Young girls wore aprons to protect their few items of clothing as they helped with the chores in the kitchen and about the house.

The Sunday aprons were somewhat special and decorated with hand stitching. The material was of a finer quality if possible. Everyday aprons were made from white flour sacks. Some had the brand name printed on them that remained after many washings. Hostess aprons came later and covered the waist down, made of fancy organza, dotted Swiss or the fancy material that only the more well-to-do could afford.

During the Depression when money, material, food and jobs were scarce, the animal feed in 100- pound sacks was made from off-white cotton or often, printed cotton fabric. The top of the sack was stitched in a manner when pulled loose, the string would unravel in one piece. The cotton string was rolled into a ball for many other uses. Nothing was wasted that could serve a useful purpose.

Feed sacks found many uses in the home. Women and children often chose the bag of feed or flour for the pattern of pretty fabric since they would be wearing the sack made into a nice dress.

Curtains were made from sacks to spruce up the windows. The white sacks were often stenciled with paint or decorated with rickrack braid. Aprons could be decorated the same way.

Men and boys wore shirts made from feed and flour sacks. Undergarments and sleeping garments were also made and worn by all family members.

Dish towels were widely used in the home and were made from both flour and feed sacks. The lasting fabric made into the many items may still be found in homes today.

Aprons were worn by shoe cobblers, butchers, grocery store employees, and gate collectors. "Rosie the Riveter" appeared during WWII in the factories with an apron with long ties around her waist two or three times and tied in the front, as women were smaller than the men.

Grocery stores carried animal feed and made home deliveries after the trucks were available. In Summersville, the following stores carried and sold sacks of feed: Burr's Store and Mill, Citizens Grocery, Stowers Super Market, and Walkers IGA Store and throughout the early years, many other stores sold animal feed in bags.

The store employee wasn't always pleased to see a woman shop for the bags or sacks of feed as she usually chose a bag on the bottom of the pile. Lifting all the bags to get to the bottom was a chore. The men weren't as selective as the women who would imagine a pretty dress made from the fabric bag. The garments, curtains, towels and aprons were all starched and ironed after a good washboard washing and line dried. Permanent press was unknown at that time.

Pieces of leftover feed sacks were made into patchwork or patterned quilts for beds. They were pieced by hand and quilted or tied together.

Aprons tap into our personal memories and remind us of our mothers, grandmothers, and our own pasts. They serve as symbols of home, motherhood, and housewifery from images of colonial women fanning the cooking fire with her log apron to a Civil War nurse wearing her white apron on the battlefield to a country mother during the Depression gathering potatoes in her tattered apron.

The feed and flour sack memories are still recalled by this generation who experienced the Depression and the clothes made from those colorful and floral prints worn as children.

There are museums that display feed sack clothing, quilts, aprons and other items. Today, they are called "textile bags" and not feed or flour sacks, as they were once known.

**Frances Reynolds Murphy (1859-1942)
wore aprons and dust caps.**

Sallie Ann Harlow (1889-1955) with long apron in 1916.

116

ONE ROOM MUSEUM

I n 1830, Nicholas County had seven Commissioners and they reported 18 schools attended by poor children. Of the 150 poor children enumerated, 99 attended school. The average attendance by each child was 52 days, the sum paid for each child was $1.82 and the total expenditure that year for the county was $179.80.

The census of 1850 showed 17 public schools with teachers and 189 pupils. This system for schooling the poor wasn't popular and was denounced "as calculated to create and keep distinctions in society." However, subscription schools flourished as shown by the census of 1850, there being only 52 people in Nicholas County who could neither read nor write.

The Free School Act of 1846 was not adopted in Nicholas County until West Virginia adopted the first constitution of 1863. Teachers were tested and required to keep daily and term records, with 20 days per month for school.

A one room school building was located in most small and rural communities. The land was donated for the school location. The books prescribed by law for use were McGuffey Readers, Ray's Arithmetic, Pinneo's Grammar and Mitchell's Geographies. The McGuffey Readers had been used in Nicholas County prior to the Civil War.

The one room school consisted of a heating stove, desks or seats, a slate board, a water bucket, later a stone water cooler, and an outhouse, or toilet building. The school hand bell was rung for students to return to class, unless some of the students would make the bell disappear for longer recess. The students from the first through seventh or eighth grades learned from each other while a teacher taught lessons to a grade or a subject.

Log cabins were common among the many one room schools. Later, they were replaced with hewn log housed with glass windows and blackboards. The three "R's" were taught and mastered.

Teachers were becoming better educated, newer books introduced, more state government money involved also brought changes in the schools. Taxation provided by levy brought about the "Building Fund" which made providing buildings for schools possible.

One room schools were replaced by larger schools with students transported by bus from rural areas. In 1950, there were 91 one room schools in use. By 1990, there were no one room schools in use. What happened to those one room schools? Often, the building was deeded back to the property owner or sold to an interested party for other uses.

Some one room schools are now one room museums. The Irish Corner School that served students from 1915-1954 was moved to the Nicholas County Veterans Memorial Park and restored. In 1984, it was deeded to the Nicholas County Historical and Genealogical Society by the Draper and Carrie Dotson McClung heirs. Located by the road (Route 19 North of Summersville) at the edge of a woods, it now stands as monument to education of bygone day.

The Irish Corner One Room School Museum is open for tours June through September on Wednesday and Saturdays 2 – 4 p.m. You can wander back in time and see how far the educational system has advanced to date by visiting the museum.

The seats, books, pictures and other museum artifacts will refresh those bygone memories and give insight to those who never had a one room school experience.

Membership is available to the Nicholas County Historical and Genealogical Society for $20 per year or a lifetime membership of $100, which helps support the Historical Hamilton House and the One Room School Museum. (Mail to NCHGS P.O. Box 443, Summersville, WV, 26651.

**Irish Corner School — Dedicated in 1987
as the One Room School Museum**

117

THE WHITMAN FAMILY

The late Edna Groves Campbell, of Summersville, and Homer C. Cooper of Hanover, Mass., researched records, deeds, cemeteries and family Bibles for any information on the origin of the Whitman family in the late 1950s.

Their search took them to the Greenbrier Valley Courthouse records at Lewisburg. There was found evidence of Whitmans in the county before 1800: Andrew Whitman, surety on estate of Martin H. Shoals, June 25, 1793; and Elizabeth Whitman, daughter and heir of John Dunbar will dated April 17, 1794. There appears to have been a sizeable family of Whitmans in Greenbrier County by 1790 – 1800. There were a series of Whitman marriages recorded in Greenbrier County. Among them was George Whitman who married Elizabeth Rogers on May 17, 1804, by minister Josiah Osborne.

Three Whitman brothers came from Greenbrier County to Nicholas County. They were Robert Whitman, born Jan. 15, 1809, married Elizabeth Fleshman who was born April 28, 1818, and Holly Whitman who married Elizabeth Hugart. The third brother's name is unknown.

Robert and Elizabeth F. Whitman married on March 17, 1839, in Greenbrier County and had 10 children: Mike W. Whitman (1841–1905) married Virginia Cottle and (2) Rebecca Morton; George W. Whitman (1843–1857); Virginia Louise Whitman (1845–1924) married George W. Bays on Feb. 1, 1866 and settled in Kentucky District of Nicholas County. They had a large family of 12 children: Nancy A. Whitman (1847–1909) married Mathew Sawyers and they had 11 children; Holly Jackson Whitman (1849–1923) married in 1874 to Amanda C. Cottle; Benjamin Vaught Whitman (1853–1861); Pheobe R. Whitman (1855–1937) married Buren McClung; James D. Whitman (1857–1859); John R. Whitman (1859– ?) married (1) Alice Kessler and (2) Ida Kessler; and Susan E. Whitman (1861– ?) married John Breckinridge Jones (Major).

George West Whitman (1848–1854) and Benjamin Vaught Whitman (1853–1861) died young and are buried in the Whitman Cemetery near Canvas, WV (formerly Earl, WV) along with parents, Robert (1809–1876) and wife, Elizabeth F. Whitman (1818-1898).

Robert Whitman (1809–1876) prospered and reared his large family despite the fact that as a young man he lost his way in the woods, was forced to spend the night without adequate shelter or bedding and had nine of his toes amputated as a result of severe frostbite. He acquired considerable land in the Gauley and Hominy region near Canvas. His holding, the years of acquisition and the conveyors were: 300 acres, 1841, Alexander McClung; 45 acres, 1846, John Brown–Commissioner; 200 acres, 1850, John Cavendish; 600 acres, 1856, Robert Hamilton–Commissioner; 20 acres, 1866, Zacariah Tomlinson; 220 acres, 1866, Zacariah Tomlinson; and 25 acres, 1871, Holly C. Perkins.

Left to right: John Whitman and wife, John (Major) Jones
and wife Susan Whitman Jones, Buren McClung and wife
Pheobe Whitman McClung and Robert Whitman

John Whitman and wife. It is unknown whether the photo
depicts his first wife, Alice Kessler or his second wife, Ida Kessler.

118

GRANDMOTHER'S COVERLETS

everal years ago, we visited the Abby Rockefeller Museum in Williamsburg, Va. At that time, a research project was conducted on Coverlets, which are made by pioneer women. A few were displayed there, and they also wanted to know how many and the location of the coverlet.

A coverlet is a blanket, which is made of wool, dyed and woven on a loom in a particular pattern of two colors. The pioneer women carded the sheared wool from sheep, spun it into yarn and dyed the yarn. The dyes were homemade from either berries, bark, roots or plants. Blue made from indigo was commonly used. Reds and greens were often used as dye colors. The pioneer women learned about the dye process from experience or from a mother or grandmother.

After the yarn was prepared and dyed or left the natural wool color, the loom was set up and a pattern for weaving was established. The woven strips were only as wide as the loom. Two finished strips were sewn or stitched together by hand to make the coverlet wide enough to cover a standard size bed. It must have taken months of preparation to prepare the yarn and a long time to weave the cloth. The edges of the coverlet were neatly folded under and a hem was hand stitched.

The coverlet was quite warm and kept the bed very comfortable in the winter. The log houses with fireplaces for heat were cold at night in the long winter months. Wool blankets and coverlets over a feather tick kept body heat in the bed.

The dyes used in the dyeing process have remained true to color. Blue often fades, but the only blue dye used for coverlets has not shown signs of fading or changing, which is remarkable. The pigment in brown dye seems not to remain true as the other shades or colors, even with today's modern process and dyes. Some coverlets in the picture were carded, spun and woven on the machines at the Starbuck Mill and Campbell Hydroelectric Power Plant located on Muddlety Creek near the town of Summersville by our great-grandmothers.

The darker blue coverlet was made by Rebecca Bays Groves, grandmother of Robert B. Campbell. Mrs. Groves lived on a farm, raised the sheep, carded the wool, spun and made her dye from the indigo plant. It was both enlightening and interesting to hear her story of making her coverlets, which were passed down to grandchildren and greatgrandchildren.

We wonder how many coverlets there may be in Nicholas County today, and we hope that the present owners know of the coverlet history.

The Nicholas County Historical and Genealogical Society has a lovely blue coverlet in good condition on display when the museum is open from June through September each year.

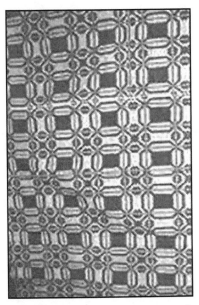

Coverlet made by Rebecca Bays Groves circa late 1890s–1900

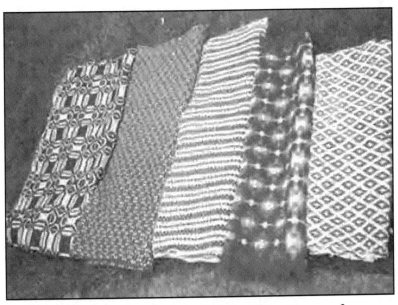

Wool coverlets made by Rebecca Bays Groves of
the Starbuck and Groves Families From left:

1. Blue — made by Starbuck and Campbell Family (from Bessie)

2. Red — made by Sarah Jane Chapman Groves (given by Effie White)

3. Blue — made by Rebecca Bays Groves

4. Red and gray — made by Rebecca Bays Groves

5. Blue — made by Starbuck Family

119

HOME DELIVERIES

In Nicholas County, home deliveries were becoming common after the Depression as people were eager to make a few dollars since work or jobs were scarce.

Few families had refrigeration at that time due to having no electricity in most areas. Rural Electrification brought electricity in more rural areas about 1938-39 and early 1940s. The icebox is designed to keep dairy products and food cool to prevent spoilage. On a weekly basis, a truck would drive in Summersville to make a delivery of a large block of ice. Each house that used an icebox would display a card in the window to indicate the amount of ice wanted. The card would display at the top either 25, 50, 75 or 100 pounds of ice. The "ice man" would pick up the block of ice with large tongs, place the ice in the icebox that was made of oak wood and lined inside with metal. There was a separate door for the ice section with a pan to catch the melted ice. In the summer, it was a real treat to get chips of ice with an ice pick for cold lemonade or iced tea and sometime just to cool the mouth. As refrigerators were more widely used, the icebox was used for storage and now is a desired collectible piece.

If someone was fortunate to have a truck, they often brought truckloads of items to the neighborhood to sell. One man brought a large load of clothespins from Richwood Clothes Pin Factory and sold the clothespins (made of one-piece wood-split) by the bushel or 1/2 bushel. At that time, there was only line drying, as dryers came much later. Many clothespins were needed to hang a family's weekly wash onto a line to dry. It was also fun to play with clothespins. We made many clothespin dolls, and there was a contest for the best-made clothespin dolls sponsored by the Summersville Baptist Church Youth and Children's Program.

Another convenient home delivery was getting farm fresh eggs delivered by Kermit Bailes each week. There was never any concern about salmonella and we often used raw eggs in certain recipes, which we certainly avoid using raw eggs today. We aren't sure about the mass production of eggs.

Getting fresh milk delivered to the house twice a week was most helpful with a young family with high consumption of dairy products. The milk was delivered in glass bottles or jugs. The empty containers were washed and set outside the door for a pickup to be used again by the Groves Dairy. Milk has not tasted as good since it was stored in glass. Also, there was no waste in containers as we know today with paper cartons and plastic.

Another very convenient service was the grocery store deliveries. An order for groceries could be telephoned to either Walker IGA, Stowers Super Market or Citizens Grocery and the items were delivered, carried to the kitchen and the bill either presented to the customer or charged to their account to be paid at the end of each month. Grocery stores also sold animal feed in bags and delivered those as well as groceries. The delivery person often carried the dairy or chicken feed bags to a barn for another customer. Most homemakers had no transportation during the day while the car or truck was used by husband who worked. When the monthly grocery bill was paid, the customer often received a bag of candy or something as a "thank you."

The U.S. Postal Service made mail deliveries to the box near a door or most town homes. That was a convenient service especially in inclement weather but offered lots of walking for a postman. Unless there is a hardship, homes have a mailbox nearby or across the street from the house.

Many people used to "peddle" extra produce or fruit door to door in the growing season. It was nice to be able to buy freshly picked berries, apples, or vegetables without leaving the house. Now it is necessary to drive to a produce place or farmers market for fresh fruits and vegetables.

The most important and common home delivery made was for the birth of a baby at home. Many times, there was only a mid-wife present for the home delivery. Local physicians were willing to travel by horseback, later by car, to make home deliveries and care for the mother and baby. They were not always paid with money; sometimes they received chickens, or a pig, or just an IOU. Dr. Flavius H. Brown Sr. delivered many babies in Nicholas County including the Campbell boys at the Campbell Power Plant and the five Murphy children at home on Duffy Street in Summersville. There are many people living today who were delivered at home.

After World War II, fewer home deliveries of babies were made, and doctors were not available for such deliveries. Hospitals and clinics were used for baby deliveries. Dr. Hoy Eakle made deliveries upstairs over the present Hardmans Hardware building for a brief period of time.

All those home deliveries were convenient, served the intended purpose, but would be more costly by today's economic standards.

Perhaps others will recall home deliveries such as coal, wood and fuel.

120
WORLD WAR II AND USS
TETON (AGC-14)

E very able young man was required to register with a draft
board for a call to serve in the military service during the
early 1940s in the United States. Some men volunteered
for a branch of the service while others awaited notice to report
on a certain date. Many were about to graduate from high school
at the age of 18 or 19 years. Planning for a career or college was
not an option at that time. World War II was spreading.

Upon advice from his older brother, Bill, who was already in
the U. S. Army, Robert, upon receiving a notice, enlisted and was
accepted in the U. S. Navy. Robert graduated from Greenbrier
Military School on June 6, 1944 and reported to the Navy on Sept.
21, 1944 for basic training at the Great Lakes Training Station.

In December 1944, Robert was on leave to Summersville for
a few days. While there, a big snowfall cut off communications
and there was no traffic in or out of town for more than 3 or
4 days. Finally, Robert was able to get a ride to Gauley Bridge
where public transportation was available back to Great Lakes.
On his behalf, the American Red Cross and Selective Service
System, and the local board of Nicholas County wrote letters
to protect his status of being late to report. Those letters were
dated Dec. 14, 1944.

On Dec. 29, 1944, Seaman 2/C Robert B. Campbell went aboard the USS Teton, AGC-14, a 13,910- ton amphibious force flagship built at Wilmington, N.C., and launched February 1944 and transferred to the navy and placed in commission. The Teton was Rear Admiral John L. Hall's flagship during the Okinawa campaign and continued to fly his flag in the Pacific War fighting. The USS Teton sailed on Jan. 12, 1945 from the United States and arrived at Pearl Harbor on Jan. 18, 1945 for a few days before arriving at Marshall Islands on Feb. 5, 1945. Robert kept a daily log of dates, locations and events as they happened.

There had been action big time before the USS Teton got to Leyte on Feb. 21, 1945 and Okinawa on April 3, 1945. The Philippine Islands had been taken back by the United States from the Japanese. Some Japanese soldiers were still hiding in the interior areas. On the daily log was recorded April 3, 1945 "large attack all day – 134 planes brought down." On April 12, 15, 27, 28, 29 and 30, "raids all night." May 3, 1945, "USS Little sunk, Malcomb hit by SS". May 4, 1945, "USS Birmingham hit by SS plane – 125 casualties." The raids continued with losses for some time. The USS Teton left Okinawa on June 11, 1945.

During all this time, each sailor aboard the USS Teton had a duty to perform and a battle station to man. Robert was stationed on the forward 5-inch gun. He cradled ammunition in his arms, passed it on to the platform attendant who in turn placed the ammo in the gun. The gun fired toward enemy planes when the plane was in firing range. The sailors stayed at their station until the attack was over which could last for hours.

When not at battle stations, each returned to regular duty. Robert served on the captain's bridge, and starboard side lookout station scanning with the binoculars the horizon for enemy planes.

One person had to remain alert and stay awake so as to notify the man at each station when being attacked. There were both black and white men aboard the USS Teton. On one occasion, the black sailor kindly served his turn and also Robert's turn at the battle station so Robert could have some much-needed rest time.

The USS Teton AGC -14 (Amphibious Group Command) was a communication ship equipped with radar and sonar. Radar was a large circular screen on top and center of the USS Teton, which rotated constantly and would detect another ship. A special code was extended to the other ship to determine if they were friendly or an enemy. Sonar also aided the detection of other vessels. Since radar was not familiar to enemy ships at that time, they didn't recognize its use.

June 15, 1945, the USS Teton went to Subic Bay, Leyte, part of the Philippines. The men were granted liberty on Grande Island for recreation that included softball, horseshoes and swimming. They left on June 25, 1945 and arrived at Manila Bay where they observed the ruins of 350 Japanese ships that were sunk in Manila Bay.

The USS Teton had a post office. Mail was received only when docked. Outgoing mail was sent at that time. The mail from the sailors couldn't contain any information on activities, location, private codes or any physical or moral conditions. All mail was unsealed and censored. Mailing addresses for those serving the military during World War II was an F.P.O. (Field Post Office) address. Robert Campbell's F.P.O. was San Francisco, California.

Seaman Robert B. Campbell 1944-45

USS Teton at the Mare Island Navy Yard, Jan. 11, 1945

121

USS TETON (AGC- 14) WORLD WAR II – PART TWO

July 7, 1945, the USS Teton left Manila for Subic Bay, arrived July 9 for rest and recreation on Grande Island until July 18, 1945. A change was made on July 19, 1945, when Robert was transferred from First Division to "C" Division to become a radio technician on board the USS Teton. In the training, he was able to repair and set frequency on transmitters and receivers.

Trial firing runs were held July 21 through July 27, 1945 with other ships to assess readiness near Manila where they remained until Aug. 17, 1945.

In July, the American Air Force attacked the main island of Japan with about 250 Mustang Airplane Fighters for three successful days. They also sank seven Japanese vessels off the Japanese Coast. The Japanese guess was that the U.S. was using 11,000 planes for the launch of attack on the homeland. This information was recorded on the U.S. Teton's newspaper The Beacon Press on July 7, 1945. Twenty-five additional miles of runways were added to the airfields of Okinawa, which is 324 miles from the Japanese homeland.

The Japanese populace learned of allied ultimatum outlining the "surrender or else" ultimatum as more than three million leaflets were dropped on Japan by the 20th Air Force. This information was recorded in the Beacon Press on Aug. 5, 1945.

Aug. 6, 1945, US troops dropped an atomic bomb on Hiroshima by B-29 "Enola Gay." An atomic bomb fell on Nagasaki on Aug. 9, 1945. Japan opened peace negotiations on Aug. 10, 1945 and accepted allied surrender terms on Aug. 14, 1945.

The battleship Missouri was anchored in Tokyo Bay where the signing took place. The USS Teton was the fifth ship, the only large ship to tie to a pier in Tokyo Bay, to transmit and receive communication from the signing of the peace treaty on Sept. 2, 1945. The USS Teton had been assigned duty as communication ship for the Supreme Allied Commander, General Douglas MacArthur.

Tokyo Bay: For a while, it looked as though the proceedings would go off with smoothness. The four destroyers carrying dignitaries and correspondents to the formal surrender ceremonies on the battleship Missouri arrived strictly on time. Although every inch of the gun turrets and housings and life rafts above the veranda deck (the place for the signing) was crowded, no one fell off. The ceremonies were on schedule. The early morning sky was overcast, and the wind was chilly. Out to sea as far as the eye could see, lay the gray warships of the American fleet. Overhead, the sky was swept by zooming American fighters.

The Missouri was set for the show and rows of white clad sailors lined the rails. Newsreel men set the cameras grinding. A cluster of microphones and a long table covered with a green cloth had been placed in the center of the deck and on the table laid out big ledger-size white documents of surrender in brown folders.

General MacArthur stepped to the microphones with these words, "We are gathered here, representatives of the major warring powers to conclude a solemn agreement whereby peace can be restored." President Harry Truman proclaimed Sept. 2, as Victory over Japan Day (V J Day).

The USS Teton remained there in Tokyo Bay for a few more days. The sailors were taken on some tours in Tokyo. They saw the Diet Building, the Imperial Palace and other sites. The USS Teton left Japan and headed for Guam, arriving on Sept. 29,

1945. There were about 750 passengers aboard on Oct. 1, 1945 and were transported back to San Francisco on Oct. 16, 1945. They crossed the International Date Line on Oct. 8.

On Oct. 19, 1945, the USS Teton sailed back to Pearl Harbor to bring more troops back to San Diego in the United States. More trips also were made to transport the military to the U.S.

In Dec. 1945, the USS Teton was to go through the Panama Canal to North Carolina for major repairs. The USS Teton took on large amounts of water and was ordered back to San Diego. Some men got liberty to go home for Christmas, and others were eligible for discharge from the Navy. The USS Teton crew complement was 54 officers and 579 enlisted men.

The Teton continued as part of "Magic Carpet Fleet" embarking passengers to the United States until 1946. She became inactivated at San Diego, was decommissioned Aug. 30, 1946, struck from the Navy list on June 1, 1961, and was sold for scrap value in March 1962 to Union Minerals Corporation, New York, NY.

Three years, eight months, and 22 days after Japan bombed Pearl Harbor, World War II ended.

Robert Campbell left the USS Teton and served on the USS Chickadee and USS Pheasant for a short period of time with the decommission of those ships. He received an honorable discharge from the United States Navy on June 6, 1946 at the Great Lakes Naval Station.

The fall of 1946, Robert went to West Virginia University in Morgantown, WV, where he received a college education under the GI Bill, sponsored by the United States Government for the military men and women.

Signing of the Treaty on the USS Missouri in Tokyo
Bay, Sept. 2, 1945, with Japan. President Harry S.
Truman declared September 2 as VJ Day.

122
CHRISTMAS CUSTOMS

C hristmas is observed in many countries in various ways, traditions and on different dates. December 6, St. Nicholas Day, is observed in the Netherlands, Belgium and Luxembourg. St. Thomas Day is observed Dec. 21 in Norway.

The Christmas season lasts from Dec. 16 to Jan. 6 in Mexico where each family looks to the Posada on each of the nine nights before Christmas Day. The Posada is enacted by families in memory of Mary and Joseph's search for a room on the first Christmas Eve.

St. Nicholas served as bishop and was famous for his generosity and people came to believe that any surprise gift came from him. The people of the Netherland chose him as their patron saint of Christmas.

In America, Dec. 25 is observed as Christmas with the belief that Santa Claus entered the house through the chimney, which was an old Norse legend. The roly-poly Santa we know today became a legend in the United States. There are symbols of Christmas with a tree and decorations of evergreens in churches and homes.

The star is a symbol used everywhere as a Christmas symbol. It represents the Star in the east mentioned in the Bible in Matthew 2:1,2. Lights at Christmas represent Christ as the Light of the World. Candles were first used for the light in the window.

People of Ireland believed the candlelight in the window would light the way for the Christ child on Christmas Eve.

Christmas cards or greetings were not exchanged until mid-1860s on a wide scale. They were first printed in London, England and were marketed in the United States about 1875.

Music for Christmas started as musical prayers of the Christian Church. St. Frances of Assisi is known as the father of caroling. Many of the well-known Christmas carols were written in early years. Charles Wesley wrote "Hark the Herald Angels Sing" in 1739. Some of the world's finest music has been written for Christmas. Handel's "Messiah" was first presented in Dublin in 1742.

Christmas celebrations have changed over the years. Now manufacturers begin planning for the Christmas sales for the following Christmas a year or more ahead and the promotions start earlier each year. The sparkle and the dazzle of merchandise is designed to encourage sales for gift giving and for children to request many toys and items from Santa Claus. When the pioneers settled in America, the celebration of Christmas was of religious nature and thankfulness. The time changed as means permitted to allow children to hang a stocking near the chimney so St. Nick could bring them a small gift. As the welfare of settlers improved, there were more possibilities. Getting an orange or a stick of candy or just a new pencil in a stocking was a treat for children many years ago.

Fancy Christmas stockings were available among the more affluent, along with a well-decorated tree. Packages wrapped for gift exchange came about. Santa Claus came after the children were in bed and hopefully asleep. Children usually believed that Santa Claus visited them if they had been good boys and girls all year. On Dec. 24, a letter of request was often left where Santa could read what he or she wanted left under the Christmas tree. Some children believed in Santa Claus longer than others.

In the late 1930s, two sisters had begun to wonder about that jolly man dressed in a red suit with a long white beard. Was he real? How did he know each girl's or boy's wish?

One evening close to Christmas while the mother visited a neighbor, the sisters decided to do some investigating about Santa Claus. They started looking and searching every nook and cranny in the house for Santa's pack. Sure enough, in one location was a doll, in another some house slippers and other things. The sisters kept their findings a secret, but Christmas morning was not exciting for them. Those same things that had been hidden were under the tree. From that time forward, the sisters knew the answers about Santa Claus.

The Spirit of Christmas, learned from giving and receiving in the earlier years, continues through adult years. Merry Christmas has been a greeting for generations, but now seems to give way to Season's Greetings or Happy Holidays. Has Christmas been commercialized so much that the true meaning is being lost? As long as Christ is in Christmas, the Spirit of Christmas will remain in the heart of mankind. The symbols of Christmas will continue to remain all that the birth of Christ Jesus is the true reason to celebrate.

Merry Christmas and Happy New Year with peace for all.

123

CROCKS, CHURNS, AND STONE JARS

The pioneers found many uses for stoneware pottery for food storage. Along the Ohio River where suitable clay was found, creative hands made large and small containers. Large 20-gallon crocks were used in pickling vegetables for later use. They had a small lift handle on opposite sides. Sauerkraut (made from heads of cabbage shredded) was preserved by layers of salted cabbage with a plate weighted firmly to allow fermentation with no air. It is still made by the same method.

The stoneware was fired in a kiln. Some was salt glazed; others are slip glazed. Clay used by Donaghho and Parkersburg Stoneware was of good quality and produced crocks, jugs, jars, earthenware, and flowerpots. Pieces can be located in antique shops, museums, and auctions. Jugs were used for making and storage of vinegar. Once a "mother" is formed, liquids can be added to continue the making of vinegar.

Churns were usually three or four gallons in size. A lid made of wood or pottery with a hole in the middle to accommodate a wooden dasher is moved up and down to separate the cream from milk to make butter and buttermilk. Most rural families had milk cows and a stone churn or two.

Water coolers were used to store drinking water for schools and some businesses. A small faucet or spout located on the lower part of the stone cooler released the water for use. These were used before piped drinking water was available. Students furnished their own metal or tin drinking cups.

Milk pans made from stoneware were used to cool fresh milk and stored in a special milk house or a cellar built into the hillside to keep cool. Canning stoneware jars were widely used before cheaper glass jars were available.

Walker Brothers of Summersville Pottery made churns, jars, and crocks usually after the brick-making season in the fall and winter. The Walker Brothers canning jars had two lids, one to fit the interior of the jar and another lid to hold the first lid in place on the jar.

The Hamilton House Museum has a Walker Brothers churn on display and several other pieces of crocks and stoneware which were used in Nicholas County by pioneer families.

Advanced technology eventually made potteries uncompetitive. Glass containers could be made cheaply and more easily styled. The transparency of glass and its weight offset stoneware durability. Methods for home canning in glass improved and made the traditional preserving and storage of goods in stoneware less attractive. Stoneware preserving was limited to pickled foods such as kraut, beans, corn or cucumber and some fruits.

With further technology, glass containers have given way to plastic containers. A trip to the grocery store is limited mostly to paper or plastic containers in 2010 -2011. To view the changes in containers, a visit to the Nicholas County Historical and Genealogical Museum (Hamilton House Museum) will show the changes.

Pioneers used stone jars, crocks, churns, etc.

Walker Brothers of Summersville canning
jars (made from local clay)

124

WOMEN'S ACCESSORIES

For centuries, it was important for women to cover their head with a cloth, a bonnet, or if it could be afforded, a hat of some kind. Clothing was usually basic for weekdays, but Sunday was known for wearing the best that one had to wear. Along with a dress covered by a long apron, the ladies wore dust caps in the house. When leaving the house for a trip to church or other public places, a bonnet was the head cover of choice. The buggy rides were dusty, with wind blowing around, so a bonnet kept the hair in place and protected the face.

Small girls also wore bonnets for warmth and protection from the weather. Those who could knit made caps from wool for babies and the very young. It was quite a necessity for a young woman to own a hat when financially able to do so. The Millinery Shop, where hats were made and sold, was usually located in towns with other shops. It was a place that every young woman and older women liked to shop for a new hat.

Felt hats were first made in Danbury, Connecticut in 1780. Wool felt has been the choice for fine hat making for both men and women. Fur hats have been made for warmth from rabbit, muskrat, and mink. Felt, straw, and silk hats are made on special molds. Hat factories were big business when the custom required both men and women to wear a hat in public. Some churches required women to wear a head covering. It has become more relaxed in modern times.

As late as the 1950s and 1960s, women wore hats, gloves, and high-heeled shoes when shopping or attending any public event. Even when attending a college ballgame, the women were fully attired with a suit, hat, and gloves.

Shopping for an Easter bonnet or hat was a big event for the young and the older women up to about the 1970s in the United States. Mrs. Marie Bennett, wife of the Rev. Riker Bennett who served the Summersville United Methodist Church from 1958 – 1963, made her beautiful hats. Mrs. Bennett designed her unique hats on hat molds. Others used patterns and made hats from basic materials until it was no longer fashionable to wear hats, except for warmth in the winter.

In the early 1960s, long gloves were made fashionable by Jackie Kennedy, wife of John F. Kennedy. Mrs. Kennedy also introduced the small "pill box" hat she wore, which set the hat trend at the time. Gloves are no longer an accessory for women unless needed for cold weather.

Earlier times in Summersville, there was a hat shop owned and operated by Lydia Duff, wife of attorney Gordie Duff.

Department stores sold hats for both men and women for many years until the fashion was no longer in demand. Groves Department Store in Summersville had a large inventory of lady's hats when hats were a "must have" by women. There was Sybil's Hat Shop on Quarrier Street in Charleston, WV where women traveled many miles to purchase a new hat. It would be nice to see a revival of those lovely hats worn by ladies again. In the present time, women wear visors, ball caps and straw hats in the summer, but usually a hat or a hood attached to a coat or jacket in colder weather.

In some countries, a head covering is still required to be worn by women.

Groves Department Store: Ocie Fulks (clerk)
and customer Sybil Champe Miller

1956: Martha Jane Campbell, 3 1/2 years

Circa 1930, in back of St. Nicholas Hotel, Main Street, Summersville: (l-r) Billy, Joan, Mary E. and Bobby Campbell

125

WASH DAY IN APPALACHIA

The backbreaking job of washing clothes and linens was an all-day chore for families. Finding a water source near a branch or stream of water was most important for the early settlers. Many early settlers took things to be washed to the stream, used stones for pounding to release the soiled item. A line or trough was made from chestnut trees used to direct the water from the "branch" to near the house, so it didn't require buckets to carry the water. Those who didn't have a trough made had to carry the water for the washday.

A big iron pot was placed over a fire to heat the water before the clothes were placed in the pot. Homemade lye soap was rubbed on the soiled clothes or dissolved in the pot. A battling stick with rounded corners made from pine and a paddle were used to stir and lift clothes and linens from the boiling iron pot into a large tub of water for rinsing. The early tubs were made from cutting a wooden barrel into two tubs. Later, zinc or metal tubs were available. Clothes were hung on a fence or a clothesline if available to dry. The washday started early, usually on a clear and dry day and ended late or near suppertime. The food prepared on washday was usually a pot of dry beans cooked with a piece of pork over a wood burning stove.

Flat irons were heated at the fireplace or stove to iron out the wrinkles and the iron remained hot enough to usually iron five pillowcases then reheated. One flat iron, weighing from 5 to 7 pounds, was kept heating all the time. Ironing the clothes and linens required another day of work.

A hand-cranked washing machine came about 1858, patented by Hamilton Smith. When the crank was hand turned, paddles moved inside the tub, pushing clothes through the water to force out the dirt.

The washboard was used in a tub of water by soaping and hand rubbing against the ridges on the board. The washboards were used for a long time, especially to release heavily soiled farm or work clothes. Some washboards were made from glass but mostly of tin or metal. They were especially hard on knuckles and fingers.

The wooden hand-cranked rollers were made to help wring out the excess water from the hand washing or pot boiling method. This was a time-consuming process, but removed more water than hand wringing. In the early 1900s, a wooden tub with a wheel and a food pedal was introduced. About 1910, the electrically powered machine was invented by Alva J. Fisher and manufactured by Hurly Machine Company of Chicago, Ill.

Not everyone had electricity until much later so a gasoline-powered machine was made available. The machine had a starting step-pedal that required much effort to connect to the motor. Those gas-powered machines were very loud and could be heard for a long way. If the machine ran out of gas, a refill of gas from a can was required and the machine had to be started again. A load of white or light- colored clothes was washed in the same water in the machine. Water was scarce and it took much effort to keep a supply of water for washday.

A conventional machine came about in the 1930s and 1940s with a wringer with rollers to hand feed the clothes and linens for wringing out the water and placing to a tub of rinse water. Sometimes, a finger or hand or a person's hair got caught in the wringer. There was a release on the side of the roller that when pressed would release whatever was caught. It was a great invention when used with caution.

The greatest washer invention was the automatic washer with a control that started the process of filling the tub with an agitator to a selected water temperature and level, through the various cycles of washing, spinning, rinsing, and spinning to almost dry. After World War II, many manufacturers offered automatic washers and dryers that took the workload from those who had been in charge of the washday.

Commercial laundries have been around for a long time, especially in the cities.

Those who recall the pot boiling, washboard and water-heating day have much appreciation for the automatic laundry facilities that the modern day offers. Some may consider those earlier washdays as "plain living." Others may not consider the automatic laundry as a luxury but an important necessity.

In many countries, the early pioneer way of the washday is still being practiced.

126

CORN COB PIPES, TOBACCO, AND ASH TRAYS

Tobacco was important to early pioneers for pleasure, a trading commodity and for profit. Growing tobacco has been one of the leading industries of the Americas. Many products are manufactured from tobacco leaves and the plant. There have been many brands of cigarettes, cigars, snuff, chewing and pipe tobacco and useful chemical products to kill insects. Also, some medicine is derived from tobacco.

Growing tobacco was part of the crops grown by pioneers. They selected the plants, cut them when ready for harvest and hung the plants to dry and cure. Special log barns were built near the growing fields for the purpose of curing. Aging the tobacco for a year or more provided a more mellow-flavored product.

The first shipment of tobacco from Jamestown, Va., was sent to England in 1613. From that time, growing and manufacturing of tobacco products has been a leading industry in the United States. The United States has led the tobacco production with China in close behind. North Carolina and Kentucky lead the U.S. in tobacco growing and production of products.

In the days of radio, many tobacco companies sponsored the popular radio programs. You may remember some brands such as Lucky Strikes, Phillip Morris, Camels, and other companies who received radio advertisements as sponsors.

Television shows were sponsored by many cigarette brands and other forms of tobacco products. Many adults started smoking at an early age and believed that it was the accepted thing to do with no thought of harm to health.

Smoking was done in most homes and public places. There were ashtrays or dishes conveniently placed. Many businesses gave away ashtrays with a name or service printed on them. Receptacles were also placed in lobbies of public buildings, at doorways and other places for smokers to leave cigarettes.

The United States Government placed packages of cigarettes in the C-Ration packages for the military personnel during and after World War II and other conflicts. The smoking habit was widespread around the world from the 1940s forward.

Pipe and cigar smoking were the gentleman's way of smoking tobacco. Smoking rooms and smoker's jackets were fashionable. Pipes were made from various roots, shaped and priced accordingly. The corncob pipe was widely used in Appalachia by men and women, as the pipe was cheap and available. The more affluent were smoking expensive pipes and tobacco. Meerschaum and Briar pipes were more costly. When in Charleston, W.Va., to shop before Christmas one year, a friend asked us to shop for a Meerschaum pipe for her husband's Christmas gift. That was our only pipe shopping experience. The price would have bought a nice outfit of clothing.

The American Indian introduced the pleasure of smoking to white men. A pipe was sent to Sir Walter Raleigh by Sir Ralph Lane of Virginia. The legend is when a servant saw his master smoking a pipe, water was thrown on Sir Walter Raleigh as he believed Sir Walter to be on fire.

Cigars were smoked mostly by men until a smaller slender cigar was made available for women to smoke. We recall seeing many businessmen dressed in a suit and hat with a cigar in hand or mouth. Imported cigars could be very expensive.

Ashtrays were everywhere inside and outside of public buildings. In the homes, there were lovely glass ashtrays conveniently placed. Non-smokers displayed ashtrays or dishes for the smoker who visited in the home. Many years ago, we, as non-smokers, decided that our home would be smoke-free. All of the colorful ashtrays were gathered, placed in a box, and labeled. They could have been destroyed, but who knows, someday the ashtrays or dishes may be among collectables of "days gone by."

With the Surgeon General's report on the health effect of smoking and tobacco use, we should know that tobacco products are hazardous to the health of everyone.

Those who have used tobacco for centuries did not have the knowledge of the harmful tobacco use that we have today in 2011. It was an acceptable behavior for them during their lifetime.

127

BEIRNE AND MURPHY FAMILIES

March 25, 1810, Charles Henry Beirne was born in Ireland. He married Margaret Matilda Burke, born Dec. 13, 1817, in Ireland. Two of their six children were also born in Ireland. Betty Beirne, born June 3, 1839, and Patrick Beirne, born in 1842, came to America with their parents. Four of the children were born in the United States. Henry and Ann Beirne, twins, were born Nov. 13, 1849, in Monroe County, Virginia. John Beirne, born May 1852 and Robert R. Beirne, born June 13, 1854, in Nicholas County, Virginia. They were of the Catholic faith. Henry Beirne married Mariposa Wyatt in 1875, and Ann Beirne married John Leonard in 1874. Charles Henry Beirne died at Hughes Creek and is buried in St. John's Cemetery, Summersville.

Bertha Betty Beirne married Robert Ferguson Reynolds on June 6, 1853. Robert Ferguson Reynolds was born Jan. 30, 1826, the son of Thomas J. Reynolds and Sarah Honaker Reynolds, in Monroe County, Virginia. They lived on the Thomas Newton Farm in Malden District, Kanawha County. In 1862, Robert F. Reynolds rented a farm from Billy Dickison. Later Robert F. Reynolds purchased about 50 acres of the farm on which the large brick house stood. During the Civil War, the soldiers of both armies passed through this section and Mr. Reynolds suffered the loss of his fences. In 1863, he opened his store and when General Grant became president of the United States, Robert Ferguson

Reynolds was made postmaster. When the railroad was built to this point, he was again appointed postmaster by the late President Harrison and served officially until his death on July 21, 1911. The large brick house remains in what is known as Belle, WV, and after his death, daughter, Cathryn Reynolds Gardner served as postmistress from the brick house.

The Reynolds were parents of six children: Mary Cathryn Reynolds, born Feb. 23, 1858, in Nicholas County Virginia. She married Charles E. Gardner; John B. Reynolds, born July 1860 in Nicholas County, Virginia, married Roberta Salmons; Sarah M. Reynolds, born July 1861 and died a month later; Fannie Reynolds married James Salmons; Charles William Reynolds, 1867 – 1950, married Susan Stepto Keeny (1870 – 1957); and Belle Reynolds, born about 1867 – 68, married James Hill. She was the youngest child born to Robert Ferguson and Betty B. Reynolds. The name of the town, which was Reynolds was changed to Belle, West Virginia in honor of Belle Reynolds. The name of Belle, West Virginia remains today.

Charles John and Mary Jane Murphy Beirne were united in marriage Feb. 4, 1884. He was 29 years old and she was 19 years old. They resided in the Irish Corner of Summersville where they raised a family of six children. Annie Mary Beirne, born May 2, 1885, married Leslie McCutcheon, who was a schoolteacher at one-room schools. They were parents of two daughters, Ida Pearl and Mary Elizabeth; and seven sons, Beirne, Glen, Dana, Otis, James, Loyd and Boyd (twins).

Betty Beirne, born 1888, married Robert Emmett Horan in 1908. They were the parents of Edith Agnes, Bernice Maxine, and Mary Blanch Horan. Mother, Betty Horan, died March 25, 1915.

Margaret "Maggie" Beirne, born June 18, 1893, married Robert Tallman. Maggie died May 20, 1979, in Hamilton County, Ohio.

Charles R. Beirne, born Jan. 26, 1896, in Nicholas County, died in 1922 from a slate fall in the Barren Creek Colliery Company's mine at Barren Creek. He and his brother, John Cornelius Beirne, were cutting coal with an electric machine and no other help was near. John Cornelius Beirne was caught and slightly injured in one leg, but was unable to extricate his brother, Charles, from the pile of slate. Thirty minutes later, help arrived. He was 26 years old, and laid to rest in St. John's Cemetery, beside his mother, Mary Jane Murphy Beirne Sweeney.

John Cornelius Beirne was born March 8, 1891, in Nicholas County to Charles John and Mary Jane Murphy Beirne. John Cornelius married Stella Walker, May 29, 1916. (Their family story will be in part 2).

On Oct. 27, 1895, Charles John Beirne died after a long illness. He was 43 years old. He was reared in Nicholas County on a farm where he lived until his death. He was the father of five small children at that time. His widow, Mary Jane Murphy Beirne, cared for the children and later married Charles Patrick Sweeney in about 1900. They were the parents of James Bernard Sweeney, born March 16, 1901, married Marie Snyder in 1924, and he died Dec. 1978 in Kanawha County, W.Va.; daughter, Anna Gladys Sweeney, born Dec. 17, 1902, married Charles Dana Sebert on June 14, 1924. She died January 1987; Ruth Marie Sweeney, born July 8, 1904, married Arthur V. Sebert. Ruth died Oct. 17, 1978; Michael Sweeney, born Feb. 18, 1907 and died May 25, 2907. The mother, Mary Jane Murphy Beirne Sweeney, died at her home of pneumonia on Nov. 12, 1918. She is buried in St. John's Catholic Cemetery in Summersville.

Charles Patrick Sweeney and Mary Jane Sweeney lived on Main Street, Summersville, for some years. It was a large frame, two-story house with a porch situated across the street from the present Community Trust Bank drive-through. "Charlie Pat," as he was known, died Jun 11, 1951, in Cabell County, W.Va.

A Beirne – Murphy reunion was held August 2010 in Summersville with more than 50 relatives in attendance. Plans are being made for a second Beirne – Murphy reunion Aug. 12 and 13, 2011.

Much appreciation and thanks to Maria Beirne Yeager for her research of the genealogy of the Beirne and Murphy families.

Mary Jane Murphy Beirne Sweeney (1866–1918)

179 DuPont W. — Belle, W.Va., Robert F. Reynolds,
Betty Beirne Reynolds, others unknown

Main Street home of C.P. and Mary Jane Sweeney
in Summersville: Murphy – Sweeney family

128

JOHN CORNELIUS BEIRNE AND FAMILY

A son, John Cornelius Beirne, was born March 8, 1891, to parents Charles John Beirne and Mary Jane Murphy Beirne in Nicholas County. He was one of six children born to this union. At a young age, Charles John died on Oct. 27, 1895, at his home after a long illness. He and the family lived on his father, Charles H. Beirne's farm on Irish Corner near Summersville.

The widow, Mary Jane Murphy Beirne, later married Charles Patrick Sweeney. Four children were born to this union. James Bernard Sweeney (1901–1978), Anna Gladys Sweeney Sebert (1902–1987), Ruth Marie Sweeney (Arthur) 1904–1978) and Michael Sweeney (1907–1907).

The young son, John Cornelius Beirne, age 4 years when his father died, was raised by his mother, Mary Jane and stepfather, Charles Patrick Sweeney.

At the age of 25 years, John Cornelius Beirne married Stella Patricia Walker, age 21 years, of Paintsville, Ky., on May 29, 1916, in Kanawha County. They resided in Fayette County when daughter, Betty Lee Beirne was born Aug. 6, 1916, and son, John Pete Beirne born March 10, 1918.

Mary Frances Beirne, born Feb. 20, 1920, at Barren Creek, W.Va. Margaret Jane Beirne was born March 22, 1922, at Barren

Creek. The next six children were born while John Cornelius and Stella W. Beirne lived at Queen Shoals, W.Va.: Robert Michael Beirne, born July 16, 1924; Jimmie Cornelius Beirne born Oct. 17, 1926; Ruth Aline Beirne born Feb. 5, 1928; Elizabeth Ann Beirne was born March 16, 1931; William Ray Beirne born April 25, 1933. Barbara Ann Beirne, a grandchild, was born July 9, 1953, and raised by Stella Beirne.

John Cornelius Beirne, 51, was killed at Quinwood while attempting to fix the dump-bed of his truck, which was loaded with sand. He was lying under the truck fixing the hoist when the truck bed fell on him. He had hauled sand for several mines in the vicinity of Summersville. His death on July 6, 1942, left his widow, Stella Walker Beirne, and 10 children, seven still living at their home. The service was held at St. John's Catholic Church and burial in the Catholic Cemetery in Summersville. There was much sadness among family and friends of the Irish Corner.

Stella Beirne went to work as a cook at the Summersville Elementary School to help support her family. She worked for many years as a cook and also raised a grandchild. Stella Walker Beirne died at 78 on June 5, 1976. She was a Methodist and is buried in the Walker Memorial Park, Summersville.

A son, Thomas David Beirne, born Sept. 20, 1937, the only surviving child, resides in Texas. There are several grandchildren and other descendants living.

John Cornelius Beirne (1891–1942)

129
CHILDREN'S GAMES

G ames through the years do not change much, that is, for the past generations. Hopscotch was played by the Roman children. The numbers are in blocks for the jumper to hop on one foot to up a ringer of some kind and return to finish without stepping on a line. Other games sung in rhyme, such as Farmer in the Dell and London Bridge are still played the same way by children in the United States and other countries.

Follow the Leader can be played by any number of children who are in line behind a leader and must do all the same motions. There are many Tag game variations. Cat and the Mouse is a tag game. Drop the Handkerchief is another tag game played by a large number of players in a circle with a designated "It" to drop the hankie behind a player who attempts to tag the "It" player. This has been a popular recess game among school children for generations. The Mulberry Bush was also a popular game. Most of the above-mentioned games were played by younger children outside in the fresh air and sunshine.

Older children enjoyed games like Hide and Seek, Tug of War, Fox and Geese, and Leap Frog. Races such as the Sack Race, Three-Legged Race, and The Egg and Spoon Race all require some skill but offer lots of fun.

A sure sign of spring was indicated when young boys brought a sack of marbles to school for a game of marbles at noon and recess. Marbles is an old game of skill played by children of ancient

Egypt and Greece. A ring was marked by string, mark in the soil, or a chalk line with marbles placed in the center. Each player had a choice marble with which to direct a hit to the marbles. Much skill was required to be a winner in the game. Boys played marbles on their knees with signs of the earth displayed on the trousers or bare knees. The marbles of many patterns and colors were made of glass, mostly in West Virginia at marble factories in Clarksburg and St. Mary's, West Virginia. Aggies, marbles made of agate, a variety of quartz, are produced in Germany.

There are rules and terms in marble games. A shooter is larger and is the attacking marble in a game of marbles. Ringer, one of the most popular marble games, is played on a 10-foot circle with two to six players. Marble tournaments are played nationally each year by boys and girls. They advance through elimination.

There are board games and card games for young and older persons. Chinese checkers, a favorite, is played by moving marbles on a board. There are other checkers, which are played by young and adults.

Rope jumping has been a very good exercise for many generations among girls. There are several rhymes called for the jumpers while a person is on each end of the long rope to turn slowly or faster as the case may be. Individuals also turn a shorter rope for themselves and may add fancy steps while jumping as the rope turns.

Croquet has been a family favorite sport or game for many generations. In the early 1900s in the Irish Corner area, there were Sunday afternoon croquet among the young and older family members and neighbors. Friends from in town (Summersville) would visit in the Irish settlement and play croquet. In the town of Summersville where the streets were paved, you could see children playing games, riding scooters or bikes and often rolling a hoop. Those who had bikes or scooters, or hoops would share them with those who had none. Sharing was a common practice among the children.

Games and creative play have given way to modern technology, games on the computer, and other electronic devices, which are individually played in the home or while traveling in a vehicle. Group participation and comradery among younger generations seems less, except in organized sports.

What on earth will the younger generation tell their children what they didn't have and how they spent the "growing up years?" Memories of playing children's games and those friendships still linger among many adults.

130

EARLY HISTORY OF QUILTING AND PATCHWORK

The history of quilting and patchwork is a fascinating evolution of the techniques from their simple beginnings to their incredibly varied use today. A trip through time and following quilting and patchwork as they evolve from Far Eastern beginnings to become an American tradition.

Quilting could be Chinese in origin or Egyptian or wherever, but it did begin a long time ago, born of necessity for sure. The bitter cold of winter and damp chill made warmth a matter of life and death. Discovered in the Holy Land, quilting rode across the Mediterranean into Europe beneath the heavy armor of battle-weary Crusaders. Such padding protected their bodies from devastating winters in the 14th century, the coldest in Western Europe in the memory of man. Great rivers froze during these years, and the quilted bedcover was established as a necessity.

Quilting frames and tools were devised. The women used anything they could find for filling. Lamb's wool, moss, feather and grass were sewn into quilts for warmth. Large one-piece material was used for top and bottom. The stitching was very simple in the beginning of quilting but became more elaborate and decorative. In the countries of southern Europe, where the winters were less severe, quilting was regarded as a means of embellishment rather than a necessity.

The art of quilting was spread, to a great extent, by the inter-marriage of European royal families. Quilting in the north became necessary as a means of protection against the weather. Quilting evolved into a sort of cottage industry in Britain and Holland. Quilts or "bed furniture" as they were called, rose to such levels of artistry and craftsmanship that upon the death of their owners, they were bequeathed to deserving relatives as prized possessions. They were generally whole pieces of cloth intricately quilted with an overall design or appliqué with embroidery as the decoration, but they were all alike in that the material for quilts was of one piece of fabric. They were not pieced in a pattern as we know them.

Many customs and superstitions grew from the practice of quilting. At a tender age, girls were taught by mothers to quilt, aiming for a full dowry chest on the eve of marriage. The bridal quilt was not begun until the woman was formally engaged as to begin before engagement was to invite bad fortune. Relatives and friends would often help to finish the quilt. This custom, along with many others, emigrated from the Old World to the New. Each pilgrim family departing the shores of Europe had in their possession complete sets of bed furniture (quilts) in preparation for the many hardships ahead. Ill prepared men and women struggled through terrible winters and wearying labor to build new lives. So poor were the settlers and so isolated from European conveniences that everything was re-used and re-used again including quilts. When worn, they were repaired with scraps of old clothing, gradually appearing as a patchwork top. These tops were not as beautiful as the patchwork that we know, for the materials used by the pilgrims were "sad colors," sturdy dark reds, blues and browns.

This was the beginning of beautiful piecework patterns of 1700s and 1800s, designs of originality that chronicled the history of settling of North America. Eventually, the Eastern coast of America was settled. Shipping lines carrying goods for the settlers were established, making it possible for the housewife to obtain precious bolts of imported cloth. She was more fortunate than her inland sister who depended on her own hard work to spin, dye and weave flax or wool into useable lengths of fabric.

Quilts became chronicles of a way of life but also left an impression on the structure of our social life. Quilting bees grew to be great social events. After the last stitch was taken and the frame put away, the men would appear, and a rousing good-natured evening would begin.

Quilt making continued to be a popular home art until the advent of machine-made goods marked the end of quilting as a common household activity. For several decades, quilting and patchwork were sporadically resumed and ignored until in the 1960s, quilt making, along with other handcrafts, was recognized for its unique qualities and revived.

Today, quilt making, and patchwork are practiced by housewife and artist alike, both appreciative of the techniques and qualities and heritage inherent in the patchwork quilt. Patchwork quilts are often referred to as Memory Quilts. Family members would make decorative stitches or some embroidery to embellish a particular piece. Also, the better part of a garment was cut to fit on the quilt or patchwork. Material was not to be wasted by our ancestors.

Batting used between fabrics was cotton batting until about 1960 when Dacron batting was made available for quilting. Cotton batting separated when washed, requiring close stitching to hold together. The early experienced quilter was a much better fine-stitch quilter.

Quilt shops, numerous patterns, tools, batting and widespread interest in quilt making is very popular and available. Memory quilts and handmade quilts are treasured by many families.

Memory Quilt (1907 – 09) made by Rebecca Bays
Groves and sisters for daughter, Lottie Groves Eakin

Crazy or Memory Quilt – 1900 (circa) made by Rebecca
Bays Groves daughter, Edna Groves Campbell

131

ALLEN EDWARD DORSEY

Allen Edward Dorsey, or perhaps better known as "Dick" Dorsey was a fourth-generation descendant of the Nicholas County Family. His great grandfather, John Dorsey, was married on Sept. 28, 1791, to Airy Stocksdale in Baltimore County, Md. The family came to Greenbrier, VA, in 1800 and to Twenty Mile Creek, which in about 1815 was part of Kanawha County. The grandfather of A.E. was Benjamin B. Dorsey who married Jane Neil on Feb. 9, 1819, and settled on Panther Mountain (Nicholas County). Benjamin and Jane Dorsey had nine children, the second of whom was John Basil Dorsey, Allen Edward Dorsey's father, who was born July 10, 1822. John Basil Dorsey was married to Margaret Ann Summers, to whom 10 children were born. The second wife of John Basil Dorsey was Rebecca Walker Neil. Rebecca was the daughter of Hiram and Fannie Legg Walker. Allen Edward (A.E.) Dorsey was the first born of four children to this union, having been born Dec. 25, 1868, at Tates Run near Drennen. A.E. Dorsey married Cora Belle Robinson on Sept. 2, 1891.

A.E. Dorsey served three terms as Deputy Assessor of Nicholas County, served as clerk of the Summersville Water Board and two terms from 1930–1934 as mayor of Summersville. A. E. and Cora Dorsey were members of Summersville Baptist Church where he served as Sunday school superintendent for 10 years.

They were the parents of 12 children as follows: 1. Grace born June 9, 1892, married Otis H. Milam, died April 1978; 2. Lela, born Nov. 8, 1893, married Frank Biggers, died Aug. 27, 1930; 3. Carl, born Nov. 10 1895, died 1919; 4. Haymond, born Jan. 27, 1897, died Oct. 8, 1930; 5. Gladys, born Sept 2, 1899, married Guy S. Dooley (nine children), died Nov. 18, 1984; 6. Hattie, Born Feb. 25, 1901, married Carl. D. Johnson (10 children), died 1971; 7. Goldie Mae, born Dec. 31, 1903, married Wm. Wyant; 8. Edward Allen, born Jan. 22, 1905; 9. William J. born Jan. 12, 1907, died 1966; 10. Margaret L., born Jan. 26, 1910, married John Sims (one child); 11. Robert W. born Oct. 5, 1912, died Dec. 26, 1932; and 12. Dana R. born Aug. 12, 1915, married Naomi Scragg (nine children).

A.E. Dorsey was known and appreciated in Nicholas County for his gift of poetry, which was published in newspapers and magazines. In 1963, the family published in his memory a book of Mr. Dorsey's poems for the family members.

Allen Edward Dorsey died Oct. 18, 1950 and Cora Dorsey died Dec. 24, 1953.

The poem about the Morris children, the last victims of Indian treachery in West Virginia, dated Feb. 3, 1927, follows:

"Morris Children"
By A. E. Dorsey
In seventeen hundred and ninety-two
Settlers here were very few
Ere Nicholas County had been formed
A few brave men the wilds had stormed
And ventured out to settle here
To chase the panther, bear and deer.
Simon Girty, and Indians too,
Were often seen as they passed through
Chasing the bear or fleeting deer
Or spying on those who had settled here.
A Mr. Morris, I've understood,
Had built his home at now Lockwood.

A famous dog he then did own
Desire for him the Red had shown.
Simon Girty, the renegade,
To the dog, a plan was laid.
They stayed o'er night with this pioneer
Ere break of day did disappear
And with them too, the dog did go,
And Mr. Morris quite well did know
What had happened; He took his gun,
And followed them till set of sun,
Secured the dog and then returned;
Revenge within their bosoms burned.
Two daughters dear did bless this home;
Around the place they oft did roam.
They brought the cows from glade and glen,
Were not afraid of Indians then.
Betsy and Peggy for this trip did yearn,
They went one day, did not return.
Their piercing cries did fill the air
As they ran homeward in despair,
But swifter still was Indian's speed,
For scalps they'll come, this was their greed.
The fleeing girls they did slay
And scalped them both just where they lay.
Tradition tells this gruesome tale,
The fate of these we do bewail
A church now stands right near the spot
Where this deed was by Indians wrought
Some crude gravestones now mark the place
Where they both fell – did lose the race
A statelier monument lifts its head
On our courthouse lawn to these dead,
Placed there by hands that should be blest,
G. H. Alderson's name should lead the rest.
We owe to those who thus have died
The just demands of civic pride.

Allen Edward Dorsey 1868 – 1950

132

PANTHER MOUNTAIN HISTORY

The following story of how this community got its name has been handed down from generation to generation.

A hunter went into the mountains near what is known as High Rocks and succeeded in killing two deer. He couldn't carry both of them to his cabin as he went that evening, so he bent down a sapling and hung one of the deer on it thinking that it would be safe until the next day. He took the other deer with him to the cabin.

Upon his return the next day, two panthers were feasting upon the deer that he had left the previous evening. He promptly shot one panther and the other was so enraged that it rushed upon him before he got his gun loaded again so he threw gun powder in the eyes of the panther which caused the panther to retreat to a safe distance until he got the gun loaded and shot the panther.

From this incident, it is said the name of Panther Mountain was applied to the entire community in Jefferson District, Nicholas County, West Virginia lying between the mountains and Gauley River. Some say that Captain George Fitzwater was the hero of this story. Others attribute it to another pioneer.

It is also said that Captain George Fitzwater camped for two weeks under a rock just above Pine Grove Schoolhouse with nothing but venison (deer) to eat. He was hiding from the Indians. Dirt has washed under this rock now so there is not much space. Once there was considerable space under this particular rock, enough for shelter. Captain George Fitzwater was one of the first white men to visit this part of the country since we find that he took upon 100 acres of land by authority of land warrant, number 20196, issued Oct. 28, 1783, survey made Dec. 14, 1798, and patent issued June 13, 1801, by James Monroe, Governor of Virginia.

' These 100 acres is considered as cornering upon another tract of land owned by said George Fitzwater as he got a patent for 250 acres on Jan. 14, 1800. This land was sold to Charles W. King and conveyed to him by deed dated June 4, 1801. It is believed that this Captain George Fitzwater was a soldier of the Revolution since he held a land warrant dated 1783 and the land was not claimed until Dec. 4, 1798. This Captain George Fitzwater may still have ancestors living in Nicholas County. The oldest mark that was found in the early 1900s in the community are some hieroglyphics cut on a beech tree just over the brink from Arnette Church with the date 1797.

According to Campbell's reminiscence, Charles W. King moved from Wythe County, Virginia in 1810 and made a clearing on the land purchased from Captain Fitzwater. He had taken up land on Patterson's Branch in 1798. He purchased the 250 acres from Fitzwater in 1801. So it seems that Charles W. King was here and took up land about 12 years before he moved his family here.

In 1822, Charles W. King got a patent for 130 acres of land now occupied by Orbin Cavendish and others. In the course of time, Charles W. King died and was buried in the cemetery on the 250 acres purchased from Captain Fitzwater.

In a very early day, Jonathan Dunbar settled on land on Backus Branch. It is though that his house stood on land now owned by H. E. Backus. We do not know the exact date of his settling here but the court records show that he had part in the first circuit court so we must conclude that the Browns and Dunbars both came to this community prior to the year of 1818.

Alexander Brown lived on Laurel Creek on the farm later owned and occupied by Mrs. J. W. Backus. This is just outside the Panther Mountain Community, but Alexander Brown had a son, Dr. William Brown, who lived at the head of Backus Branch on the farm later known as the Burdette place. He was a farmer and a doctor of good repute and a man of considerable influence in the community. He was a staunch Union man during the Civil War and while he was too far advanced in years to join the Federal Army, he did not let an opportunity to aid the federal cause pass without doing what he could for the advancement of what he advocated. His son, William H. Brown, settled in the community and raised a family of useful citizens of whom W. G. Brown of Summersville was the eldest. His other son, Wesley Brown, moved to the West soon after the Civil War. One of Dr. William Brown's daughters, Martha A. Brown, married William A. Burdette and they settled on the home place, lived and died there, leaving a family known and respected by the entire community.

It is not known the exact date in which Joseph Backus came to the community. He married a daughter of Alexander Brown and lived in a house on Backus Branch. It was a log house, noted for the nice true work done on the hewing of the logs and building of the walls.

Joseph Backus had a reputation of being a very careful workman and he was also noted for his promptness at church. He had a certain place to sit at church and if he was not on hand in time to get his place, it was pretty strong evidence that there was something wrong at Uncle Joe Backus' home. Joseph Backus left four sons, Benjamin F., Henry, Alexander and Isaack; and two daughters, Mrs. Dempsy Baker and Mrs. Levi Nutter. Benjamin F. (known as Frank Backus) married Caroline Grose, a daughter of William Grose, and settled on the home place. His father and mother moved to a house on the hill but in sight of the home place. There was born to this union five children: Clark, Alexander A., Bloomfield, and Rufus G. Backus. The only daughter, Lucy, died of flux when she was only 8 years old. The mother also died of this dread disease.

Rufus G. Backus, youngest son of the family, grew up, entered the ministry, joined the West Virginia Conference of the

Methodist Episcopal Church, rose rapidly until he became district superintendent which position he held for a number of years, and remained active minister in the West Virginia Conference.

Henry Backus, second son of Joseph Sr., married Mary Ann Grose, a daughter of William Grose. They settled on Backus Branch, raised a family of four sons, Weldon W., George W., William P., and Henry E. Backus. Henry Backus had the reputation of being a very careful farmer and orchardist. He subscribed for and read the American Agriculturist, the only agricultural paper that came into the community at this early date. He was skilled in grafting and introduced many new varieties of apples among his neighbors by grafting them upon native stocks. He knew most standard varieties of apples by name and could identify them at sight. He died in the prime of his life of a disease. His wife lived to be 84 years old.

133

HISTORY OF PANTHER MOUNTAIN – PART TWO

Not much is known of Jonathan Dunbar who settled on Backus Branch, except that he raised a family. One son, Jonathan, lived on the head of the Mason Branch above the Charles W. King property. He married a daughter of William Legg who lived on Laurel Creek. They raised a large family of daughters. The two sons died of tuberculosis when young. One daughter, Mary, married Clark Grose and settled in the community. Another daughter, Talitha A., married John Cavendish, lived in the community for a number of years, but finally moved to Montgomery, W.Va. The other daughters married but finally left the community. Jonathan Dunbar Sr. died at about the close of the Civil War. A daughter of Jonathan Dunbar Sr. married Dr. William Krown who lived on the Backus Branch. The other members of the Jonathan Dunbar Sr. family moved out of the community.

John M. Mason came from Virginia and married Elizabeth King, daughter of Charles W. King at an early date. It is not known the exact date of his settlement in the community, but it was probably around 1825. He settled on the land that Charles W. King purchased from Captain George Fitzwater and lived on this property until his death a few years after the war. His wife lived until she was very old. Of this family there were three sons and two daughters. The two daughters both died young. Henry, the oldest son, married Caroline Walkup from Fayette County. John Marion, the second son, married Jane Sparks and settled on a part of the home place. Their children were known by all the community. Charles, D., Augustus L., and Omar W., sons of John M. Mason, lived in the community and were honest, law abiding, and useful citizens. John M. Mason lived in the community until he was well along in life when he moved to Mason County, W.Va., where he died.

Thomas Legg, one of three brothers who came from Monroe County, VA, now West Virginia, settled on the farm known as the Renick place early in the history of the community. He was a good citizen but unfortunately he risked too much to help another person. He became surety for another, had the debt to pay, lost his home, and moved to Fayette County where he reared a large family, all who became useful citizens. His grandson, Charles H. Legg, returned to the community in the year 1860, and married Harriet J. Gross. They settled in the community and lived there for the remainder of their lives. His wife died in the year 1865, leaving a family of eight children. He afterwards married Serena Hull who died in 1910 of measles, leaving seven children. Charles H. Legg died April 5, 1929 at the advanced age of 90 years.

After Thomas Legg left the community, Willis Martin moved to the farm he had left and lived there for a number of years. He got into trouble and moved to Illinois, leaving the farm to his stepson, James A. Renick, who married Margaret Grose, daughter of William Grose. They lived on this farm, except for a few years during the Civil War, until their death, both living to be quite old. They raised a large family. All were dead by 1929 except Margaret Harrah of St. Albans, WV. Henry Hess took up 100 acres of land, the land on which Albion Post Office was located. The patent of this land is dated Nov. 17, 1820 and signed by Thomas M. Randolph, Governor of Virginia. Hess lived on this land for a number of years but in the course of time, sold his farm to William Grose and moved to Fayette County.

It is not known when William Grose moved to the community, but he first settled on a tract of 50 acres taken up by a man named Foster, a find that he made survey of and got a patent for 140 acres adjoining this land in September 1832. His father had moved to Line Creek in 1815. William married Susan Koontz of near Keslers Cross Lanes, so it is concluded that they settled in the community prior to the year 1832.

William Grose was born in the year 1799 and came from Bath County, VA, to this county. He and his wife were industrious, good citizens. They accumulated considerable property. They bought the Henry Hess farm, moved to it, and lived there until their deaths. They both lived to be old. They reared 11 children. William Grose was a leader in his church. He and his wife belonged to the Methodist Episcopal Church. He was a licensed exhorter and was an earnest and forceful speaker. Some of his friends asked him to obtain license to preach but he thought that this was out of his line of work, so he preferred to remain as an exhorter and local worker in the church. His oldest son, A. J. Grose, moved to Cooper County, Missouri. His second son, Franklin Grose, married Sarah Keenan. They had one son, A. D. Grose. While he was yet a little child, his mother died in the year 1848 and was buried in the Grose Cemetery.

A. D. Grose (Andy as he was called) grew up at his grandfather Grose's home and married Estaline Harrah. They settled on his father's farm, which adjoined the William Grose farm and was the place where William Grose first settled in the community. Franklin Grose lived with them until his death in 1880. He was somewhat of an invalid and spent much of his time caring for the children.

George Richmond Grose was the eldest son of A. D. Grose's family. The second child was a daughter who afterward became the wife of State Auditor Arnold C. Scherr. The second son, Wesley, died at 3 and was buried in the Grose Cemetery beside his Grandmother Grose. The next son of A.D. Grose's family, Arthur Grose, was a practicing attorney in Columbus, Ohio.

A.D. Grose moved from the community when his son, George Richmond, was 13.

George R. Grose taught school for a few years in Fayette County, WV., then went to Ohio Wesleyan University where he graduated with a degree of A. B. 1894, and received the degree of M. A. and S.T.D. in 1908 and L.L.D. in 1916. He married Lucy Dickerson of Cadiz, Ohio, on June 28, 1894. He was an ordained minister of the Methodist Episcopal Church in 1896 and served as pastor of church in Leichester, Mass., for three years, then went to Boston where he preached for three years. Then he went to Newton, Mass., for five years. He served at Lynn for three years and from there he went to Grace Church, Baltimore, for five years. From there, he was called to the Presidency of De Paw University at Greencastle, Ind., in 1912, where he served as president for 11 years. He left his work to become bishop of the Methodist Episcopal Church to which position he was elected in 1924. He later resided in Peking, China. He was the author of the following books: "Religion and the Mine," The Outlook for Religion," "Life of James Whitford Ashford," "The New Soul of China," and "Edward Rector."

134

HISTORY OF PANTHER MOUNTAIN – PART THREE

Covington Grose, third son of William Grose, married Nancy Walker. They had three sons: George, Clark, and Joseph T. Grose. The mother died and was buried at the Walker Cemetery on Laurel Creek. Covington Grose married again but soon left the community. George Grose was a very studious boy and reached manhood at just about the time that the free school system was established in the community. He taught his first school in the area and afterward taught school in the wintertime and attended summer schools until he obtained a good education. He was reputed one of the best, if not the best, educated man in the county in the early days of the free school system. He perhaps exercised a greater influence in the community and its surroundings than any other person. Especially was this the case among the younger people. He died in 1916 and was buried in the Grose Cemetery.

Clark Grose, second son of Covington Grose, married Mary Dunbar and settled in the community. He was a leader in the church, was honest and industrious. He took pride in having the best stock on his farm that he could get. He served one term as a member of the Board of Education, died at the age of 46 years, and was buried in the Grose Cemetery. He left his farm in good condition and had one daughter, Mrs. Emma Mason, still living in the community. His son, Edward A. Grose, lived at Fairmont, West Virginia.

Joseph T. Grose moved to Fayette County in early manhood where he lived and taught school. He was elected county superintendent in 1887. Served one term then worked as a bookkeeper for William Beury Cooper and Company for a few years. He was elected county clerk in 1896. He served in this office for six years. He then organized the Bank of Fayette and became its cashier. He also helped to organize other banks and business institutions. He had accumulated considerable property and lived at Fayetteville, West Virginia.

William Grose, fourth son of William Grose Sr., married Becky Anne Stephenson and lived in the community. Then they moved to Hutchinson's Creek where he became owner of more than 1,000 acres of land. He was the father of Rev. Logan S. Grose and Professor Walter R. Grose of Buckhannon. His second son, B. F. Grose, resided on the farm owned by his father. He was successful farmer and businessman.

Socrates Wesley Grose, youngest son of William Grose Sr. lived with his parents until they died and became the owner of the farm. He was an earnest church worker, a licensed exhorter in the church, and was class leader in the church for years. He died in the fall of 1887 and was buried in the Grose Cemetery.

Benjamin Dorsey, the first settler on the Samuel Neil land, was one of the first settlers of the community. We do not know the exact date of his arrival there. It must have been some time before 1830. He cleared out a farm and raised a family of five sons and three daughters whose names were John B., Robert L., Socrates, Samuel, Andrew, Benjamin, Sarah, Elizabeth and Talitha Dorsey. Samuel died in early manhood and Socrates moved to Iowa.

John B. Dorsey married Margaret Summers and settled on lands adjoining his father. They raised a large family but while the younger members of the family were still small, Mrs. Dorsey died. Their children were Lorenzo, William W., Rensselare Vaught, Lydia (who married Lewis Walker and moved to Illinois), Jennie (who married a Mr. Bell and moved from the area. She was the mother of C. W. Bell of Zela, WV) Evermont, Clark, Lizzie (who became the wife of M. B. Mason), Viola, and Catherine (the last two named both died young). John B. Dorsey afterward married a Mrs. Neil, daughter of Hiram Walker. One son was living at that time and served as office deputy assessor Nicholas County for several years. His name was A. E. Dorsey. All of John B. Dorsey's family moved from the community.

Rensselare Vaught Dorsey was born Dec. 16, 1854. He attended the schools of the time and afterward a school taught by P. D. Horon. He obtained a teacher's certificate and taught two terms of school in Nicholas County after which he went to Illinois where he taught one term of school and then returned to West Virginia. He married Victoria C. Neil in 1879 to which union four children were born. He moved to Hurricane, West Virginia where he engaged in mercantile business for about 20 years. He was elected sheriff of Putnam County, West Virginia in 1896 and again in 1904. He owned an interest in two tobacco warehouses, was a stockholder in Twentieth Street Bank of Huntington and a director of Putnam County Bank. He had extensive oil and gas investments and owned a 400-acre farm near his home at Hurricane. He was a member of the Baptist church.

Robert Dorsey married Alice Cavendish and settled on the home place. To this union were born two children. Henceford Dorsey, the oldest and Mrs. Dorsey died in a few years and Robert Dorsey married Margaret Kincaid. There were several children born to this union, all who are now dead. Robert and his wife both died in 1877.

Sarah Dorsey married Alexander Cavendish and they settled on land adjoining John B. Dorsey. They reared a family of seven sons and one daughter. They were Samuel, John, Andy, Robert, Joseph, Clark, Benjamin, and Jane Cavendish. Benjamin Cavendish died at the age of 49 years. Joseph F. Cavendish, the youngest son who married Ermina J. Legg, settled in the community while the others moved from the community. Joseph died at the age of 69 years leaving a wife and nine children. Orbin

Cavendish lived with his mother and served as commissioner of the Board of Education. Two daughters, Vina and Letha, were teachers. Both held diplomas from Marshall College. Alex Cavendish (1812 – 1899) and Sarah settled in Nicholas County near Wood's Ferry in a territory known as Buck Lick where they reared their family and died.

Back: Emma Grose Mason and Omer W. Mason
Front: J. Howard Mason and Ethel M. Mason

**Pioneer family of Panther Mountain,
Clark and Mary Dunbar Grose**

135

HISTORY OF PANTHER MOUNTAIN – PART FOUR

Franklin Crookshanks was an easygoing, honest citizen who married a Miss Rose. The family consisted of four sons and two daughters. The two older sons, William and Robert, were just old enough to appreciate the advantages of free public schools at the time that the system was adopted by the new state of West Virginia. They were both good-natured boys. William was a great boy for having fun that sometimes led him into trouble with the teacher who as a rule was pretty strict and arbitrary. The teachers of those days had not learned any better method of controlling delinquent boys than by using the rod of correction freely. These boys attended school regularly and grew up to early manhood with sufficient education that they passed the teachers examination successfully and both taught school in the county for many years. William allied himself with the Republican party though his father was a Democrat and the Democratic party was in a majority in the county. His party was several hundred votes in the minority but when the votes were counted, it was found that William Crookshanks was elected circuit clerk of the county by a safe majority. After serving the people for a term of six years, with credit to himself and to the people who elected him he moved to the town of Richwood where he was twice elected justice of the peace.

After teaching several terms of school, Charles Robert Crookshanks attended college at Richmond, Virginia, and a theological seminary at Louisville, Kentucky and became a licensed preacher in the Missionary Baptist Church. He preached to several different churches. He was located at White Stone, Virginia where he preached to a congregation for more than eight years. A number of his schoolmates who attended the Backus School remained in the community and were proud of the success of the life of Rev. Charles Robert Crookshanks (Cruikshanks - new spelling) of White Stone, Virginia.

The social relationships of the community remained with those who stayed while those who had pursuits in life after leaving the community. It does not seem that the people took much interest in politics prior to the Civil War though most of them were opposed to human slavery and as far as was known that there was not a colored slave owned in the community.

The Brown family, Backus family, Mason family, Renick family and the Grose family were all adherents to the Methodist Episcopal Church. The Dunbars and Dorseys held to the Methodist Episcopal South, and the Cavendish family was Baptist. There were no organized churches in the community prior to the Civil War, but all active members of the Methodist Episcopal Church held membership at Bethel Church on Laurel Creek. The Methodist circuit rider had a regular appointment to preach in William Grose's house. As William Grose's home was a regular stopping place for the preacher, his children took advantage of this and they used him both as preacher and teacher. The Grose family accumulated the largest private library in the community, and they took advantage of every available means of getting an education. There were crude schoolhouses in the community before the war. One of these schoolhouses stood up the hollow back of where O. W. Mason lived. It was a log house with puncheon floors and a log cut out of one side for a window. It was told that a greased paper was pasted over this opening.

The early schoolteachers of the community were Marshall Keenan, Franklin Grose and others. Isaac C. Cavendish taught a school in one of the Dorsey dwelling houses. William Renick taught the first free school in the community in the winter of 1867 – 1868 in Franklin Backus' kitchen. The second term of school was taught by George Grose, his first experience in teaching, during the winter of 1868 – 1869 in a dwelling house used for preaching services and vacated by A. J. Grose. The house stood where Orbin Cavendish's house was. Some of the pupils walked for three or four miles to attend school. He had a large school of pupils whose ages ranged from 5 – 24 years.

Later, two schoolhouses were built: one for the upper part of the community and one for the lower part. The board of education arranged to have four months of school each year, but the school was to be kept in these houses alternately. George Grose taught the first school in each of these houses. In a few years, the board decided to have school in each of the houses every year. The teachers in the upper school, called the Backus School, who taught in the early days of the free school system were George Grose, James Koontz, Alfred Grose, Rev. Joseph L. Smith (who later became county superintendent of schools), W. W. King (who afterwards was a distinguished preacher in St. Louis, Missouri) and John McCutcheon (who afterward also became a prominent preacher and president of a theological seminary.

In the early years of the lower school, George Grose taught the school most of the time. There were several persons who came from other places to attend his schools. Among those was J. C. Hull from Fayette County, who afterward attended college and attained the degree of D. D. He rose to a high position both as a preacher and lecturer and exercised a wide influence in the church, but unfortunately lost his mind before he hardly reached middle age and died in an asylum for the insane. J. T. Grose taught this school for a term or two. He then went to Fayette County where he served as county superintendent of schools and was elected county clerk.

The other school in the community was known as the Dorsey School and was situated in the lower part of the community. It was also called the Panther Mountain School. It was usually a small school, but some very good teachers were employed, and the students took interest in the work.

When the Civil War broke out, a large majority of the people of the community favored the union cause. Benjamin Dorsey Jr. joined the Confederate Army and was severely wounded at the Battle of Droop Mountain. C. H. Legg joined Captain Isaac Brown's company of state soldiers and wore the federal uniform until the company was disbanded. He received an honorable discharge.

136

HISTORY OF PANTHER
MOUNTAIN – PART FIVE

There were some incidents of the Civil War that occurred in the Panther Mountain Community. While Gen. John C. Floyd was camped at Carnifex Ferry, some Confederate scouts came into the community. They took several horses from the people and as they passed the first small drain, Mud Hollow west of where Arnette Church stands, they were fired on by Captain Ramsey and a few of his men who were concealed in a laurel thicket. One Confederate soldier was wounded. Ramsey and his men escaped unhurt across Gauley River. John M. Mason, passing along the road late that evening, picked up a sword lost by a Confederate officer.

Just after the battle of Cross Lanes, three soldiers from Colonel Tyler's army had escaped to the woods. They went to James A. Renick's home and hid under a cliff until it was safe for them to return or travel. One of these, a Mr. Coneit visited the Renick family two or three times after the war.

The day after the Battle of Cross Lanes, Major Andrews and 17 other Union soldiers wandered into William Grose's place where they were fed and given rations to take with them. They traveled on down the river and reached the Union camp at Gauley Bridge. Edwin Spriggs, a Union solder from Ohio who belonged to General Rosecrans' army with two other soldiers were crossing the river and their boat capsized. All were drowned. Sometime thereafter, Sprigg's body was found just below the Edz Ferry near where Albion post office was located on the Nicholas side by William Kincaid, a boy living just across in Fayette County. John B. Dorsey, Franklin Grose, C. H. Legg and perhaps a few others buried the body, which later was raised and identified by a Union scout named Carpenter. It was afterward taken up by his brother, aided by John Dorsey, Alex Cavendish, C. H. Legg, and others and removed to his old home in Ohio. C. H. Legg had built a cabin and moved to a new clearing about one-fourth of a mile back from the public road. Near the close of the war, a Mr. Legg, Franklin Grose his son A. D. Grose, Lieutenant Samuel B. Koontz, who had recently returned from the Richmond Rebel Prison and C. H. Legg were near the road just about where Pine Grove School House was located. Shooting and men running their horses was heard. Mrs. C. H. Legg was scared so leaving a daughter and son at the house, she hastened to see what had happened. She found Grandfather Legg and Franklin Grose had been taken prisoners by the Confederate Captain Holstead and a party of his men. Samuel B. Koontz, A.D. Grose and C. H. Legg had escaped to the cliffs.

The soldiers also had Dr. William Brown with them as a prisoner. They would not allow Mrs. C. H. Legg to return to her home until they had gone within a mile of the ferry. The Confederates seemed to be fearful of Union soldiers in the community so they were afraid to let Mrs. Legg return for fear that she could carry news to their enemies. This was the last incident of the Civil War that occurred in the community. A. J. Legg was the son who remembered the incident that happened to his parents.

James A. Renick, Covington Grose and A. J. Grose moved their families to Ohio during the early part of the war. Soon after the war, Covington Grose, and James A. Renick moved back to their farms, but A. J. Grose moved to Missouri and never returned. He lived and died near Clifton City, Mo., at the ripe old age of 89.

After the close of the Civil War everything was in a rather disorganized condition. The free school system had never been introduced into the state. There had been no schools of any kind in the community during the war and church services were of rare occurrences. The majority of the people held to the Methodist Episcopal Church though there were a few Missionary Baptists and a family or two of Methodist Episcopal Church South. The Methodist Episcopal preacher, Benjamin Darlington, had a reputation of being a faithful servant of the Lord and a true servant of his church. After the war, he was assigned the Nicholas Circuit with A. D. Perry, a young preacher as his assistant. After him, the Rev. L. H. Jordan preached for three years. Then a preacher named Rhodes was assigned to the work, but he made only one trip and gave up the work, which fell to the Rev. George C. Wilding, an enthusiastic Welshman, who had just entered the ministry. He traveled over the circuit and preached his third sermon at an old house used for worship, which stood where Orbin Cavendish's house stood. After one year's service, he was assigned work near his home at Point Pleasant. He afterward became a noted preacher and lecturer. He died in Jersey City, N.J.

After the Rev. George C. Wilding, Rev. H. C. Berkley, a Confederate captain, served as preacher for three years. Then came Rev. F. H. J. King for another three years who was followed by Clark Grose, J. E. Renick, and Ira W. Legg.

The Methodist Episcopal Church had kept up an organization and had regular preaching in the community for many years, first in a dwelling house then in a school. In the course of time, they decided to build a church and in May 1903, Arnette Church was completed and dedicated. Since that time, the church has been kept up and the other people have had a church building of their own in which to meet together for worship.

Of the other persons who moved to the community, lived for a number of years, and took an active part in the community work was Leonard Crookshanks, who lived for a number of just over the line from Grant district. He was class leader of M. E. Church, South, at Tipton, but took an active part in Sunday school at the upper schoolhouse of the community. His wife died before he moved to the community. His family consisted of two daughters, Ada and Flora, who both married and moved away. The father died some time before the family moved to the community.

B. F. Legg moved to the Jonathan Dunbar place and lived there for a number of years then moved with his family, except for two of his sons, Gordon, and Newman, to Virginia where he died. B. F. Legg and his wife were Baptists, but they worked with other churches in the Sunday school work and the community prayer meetings.

Joseph F. Harrah married Margaret Renick and lived in the community for a number of years. He was an industrious and enterprising citizen. He took great interest in schools and the church work. After a residence of about 15 years, he and his family moved to Roane County and then to St. Albans, W.Va.

137
HISTORY OF PANTHER
MOUNTAIN - PART SIX

D uring World War I, the Panther Mountain Community furnished the following soldiers: Wiley Mason, who was wounded in action; James H. Burdett, who spent more than a year overseas; Lawrence Legg, who went overseas; Clarence and Francis Legg, each of whom spent considerable time at camp and were just ready to go overseas when peace was declared; Roy and Herbert Legg, over-sea soldiers (Roy Legg was gassed and almost lost his life but partially recovered from injury) both of whom grew up in the community but moved to another community; Oliver and Ote Cavendish, both served overseas; and their younger brother, Orbin, who was called to camp but sent home after a few days stay in camp because of a foot injury sustained in childhood.

There was an interest in higher education and the following persons who at the time of their graduation were residents of the Panther Mountain Community, attended colleges and Normal Schools and attained the degrees indicated: W. G. Brown, B.S.; E. Brown, B.S.; W. T. Burdette, B. S.; and Theodore A. Cavendish Jr., A. B. Vina and Letha Cavendish hold standard Normal Certificates. A. Legg, Ethel Mason, and Ethel Legg held short-term Normal certificates. Norine Backus, Audrey Legg and Carl Legg held high school diplomas. Edward A. Grose, Theodore

Cavendish, Ote Cavendish, Leora Cavendish are graduates of business college. Wiley Mason, Lawrence Legg, Ivy Frances Legg, and Leona Cavendish are also graduates of business colleges.

Audrey Legg was a student at New River State School and several students attended Nicholas County High School at the time of this writing in 1930. They were Mary Keenan, Maisie Legg, Bonnie Lee Legg, and Robert Johnson.

There are many unmarked pioneer graves in the Grose Cemetery at Albion, and as a matter of records for those who want to check up at some future time, we are listing those who are buried there. Beginning first row at the southwest corner the graves in rotation are: Covington Grose; Franklin Grose and his wife, Sara Grose; Wesley Grose (second son of A. D. Grose); Bertie Copeland; Aggie Copeland Dunlay; Viola Grose; a Baber child not known; Hezikiah Copeland; and Mary F. Copeland.

The second row beginning at the south: Mrs. Henry Martin, John S. Nutter, Elisha Williams, Mrs. Pritt, a vacant space, Walter Pierson, infant child of Wellington Grose, James A. Renick, Margaret Renick, and George Grose.

Third row beginning at south: Rebecca Serena Legg, Charles H. Legg, Harriet J. Legg, Caroline Backus, Lucy Backus, William Grose, Susan Grose, Jerusha Nutter, Clark Grose, Mary C. Grose, and Eva Bobbitt.

Fourth row beginning at south: the youngest child of Clark and Mary C. Grose, Thomas O. Harrah, a grave not known for certain, Socrates W. Grose, vacant space, Harry Cavendish, and Joseph F. Cavendish.

Fifth row beginning at the south: Myrtle Mason, infant child of A. L. and E. S. Mason, infant child of Iris W. and Mary Legg, vacant space, infant child of B. B. and Mary Cavendish, and Benjamin B. Cavendish.

Sixth row beginning at south: Mary A. Legg and Arvin P. Legg.
There were 42 graves in the cemetery on Jan. 2, 1930.

In submitting this brief narrative the writer has made considerable effort to obtain the actual facts and to briefly record the most important events that have occurred in the community and to give due credit to those who endured so many hardships and much sacrifice to establish a community with the advantages of church and public schools. We hope that our account of those who have acted their part so well in the past will be an inspiration to the present generation and if they perform their part as well as their predecessors that someone else will take up the work I have begun and give credit to whom credit belongs. A. J. Legg

* * *

Note: This account of Panther Mountain history by A. J. Legg, written in 1930, was of special interest to us and we hope it will be to many of the Nicholas Chronicle readers. How remarkable that many pioneers settled in such a remote area of Nicholas County, West Virginia and built a community with many good and useful citizens. Education and churches were of great importance to the pioneer families. There remains very little of the structures or families living in that area, but the heritage continues among the many descendants still in Nicholas County and other places. Panther Mountain is located off Route 129 west in Nicholas County. This concludes the Mountain history of pioneers who settled Panther Mountain.

138

ONE HUNDRED YEARS CELEBRATION ORDER OF THE EASTERN STAR WAKOMA CHAPTER #52

1 911 - 2011 History On May 27, 1911, petitioners assembled in the Summersville Masonic Hall to establish a local Order of Eastern Star. Following the explanation of the purpose of the meeting by OES member Cecil Alderson, Nettie Groves of Buckhannon Chapter #18 was elected temporary chairman. Officers were then elected pending certification, and it was ordered the Grand Officers be requested to institute the chapter and to have installation of officers on Wednesday, June 7, 1911 at 7 p.m. It was at this meeting the name Wakoma was adopted as the name for the chapter and the meetings were scheduled twice a month on the first Tuesday at 7 p.m. and the third Saturday. On June 10, 1911 (the date being changed from June 7 at the request of the Grand Patron, Wakoma Chapter, U. D. Order of the Eastern Star was instituted. Its members have relatively close ties to members of the Masonic Order, but it is a separate organization.

The following charter members were duly initiated and declared members.

Charter Members: Mrs. Sabina Alderson, Miss Jennie Alderson, Miss Mary Alderson, Miss Lola Brock, Miss Laura

Brown, Miss Byrna Carden, Miss Lillie Craig, Mrs. Malinda Duff, Mrs. Emma Fleger, Mrs. Maud Graves, Miss Bonnie Mae Groves, Miss May Groves, Miss Florence Grose, Mrs. Eva Hamilton, Mrs. Strauss Herold, Mrs. Mary Patton Kincaid, Miss Mary Louise Kincaid, Miss Ethel McQueen, Miss Nellie McClung, Miss Grace McCutcheon, Miss Virgie Neil, Mrs. Dorothy Rader, Mrs. Birdie Stephenson, Mrs. Goodbridge Skaggs, Mrs. Lula Summers, Miss Zetta Stanard, Mrs. Mertie Woods, Mr. George H. Alderson, Mr. Dan Brock, Mr. Henry Dorsey, Mr. Forrrest Groves, Mr. A. A. Hamilton, Mr. R. A. Kincaid, Mr. O. C. Lewis, Mr. Marshall McClung, Mr. John Neil, Mr. George A. Rader, Mr. John S. Rader, Mr. J. C. Summers, and Mr. C. W. Alderson.

Deputy Grand Patron Debendarfer; assisted by EOS members from the Weston Chapter #40; then installed the following: Mrs. Mary Patton Kincaid, Worthy Matron; O.C. Lewis, Worthy Patron; Miss Vergie Neil, Associate Matron; Miss Bonnie Mae Groves, secretary; Miss Zetta Standard, treasurer; Mrs. Lula Summers, conductress; Mrs. Goodridge Skaggs, associate conductress; Mrs. Eva Hamilton, Adah; Miss Laura Brown, Ruth; Miss Lillie Craig, Esther; Miss Jeannette Alderson, Martha; Miss Grace McCutcheon, Electa; Miss Lola Brock, Chaplain; Miss May Groves, Marshal; Mrs. Maud Groves, Warder; and A.A. Hamilton Sentinel. Trustees elected were Mrs. Straus Herold, Mr. C. W. Alderson, and Miss Camilla Craig. On Sept. 5, 1911, Mary Louise Kincaid was elected to complete the year as secretary. On Oct. 21, 1911, the charter was read designating Wakoma Chapter as #52.

In the 1940s, public installation of officers of the Order of the Eastern Star was held in the old Nicholas County gym which was a big event for the community. The gym was decorated with Doctor Van Fleet roses that were plentiful and very fragrant. The ladies were dressed in long white dresses and the men who were installed as officers wore suits. I (Ann) recall attending the OES Installation in 1949 for the first time. Robert was a member and was busy assisting in the event. After the installation, and the social was over, he took me home as we had just started dating. I, Ann, joined OES in 1952.

The Masonic Hall was erected on Main Street, Summersville, WV in 1877. The land was secured from James A. Mearns and Art Peck and was valued at $100 at the time. The frame timber was hewed and cut out in the forest on land then owned by James S. Craig estate. The second floor was used as the Masonic Hall and the first level was used as a store and had many other uses through the years.

In 1956, the Masonic Lodge, A.F. & A. M. No 76 built a new home and permitted Wakoma Chapter #52 to meet there also. The upstairs in the new building had a hall, a well-equipped kitchen and dining area. The last meeting in the old Masonic Hall was Dec. 7, 1956. The meetings were held on the first and third Fridays of each month at the Summersville Masonic Hall.

The Worthy Matrons who have served Wakoma Chapter #52: Mary P. Kincaid, Goodridge Skaggs, Lula Summers, Eva Hamilton, Merta Brock, Maude Groves, Mary Louise Kincaid, Mertie Woods, Malinda Duff, Jenny Rader, Hattie Alderson, Sarah Dixon, Gertrude King, Maggie Cox, Berta Fitzwater, Eva McMillion, Maurine Summers, Margaret Alderson, Ethel Mearns Echols, Florence Starbuck Campbell, Edna Groves Campbell, Dainty Igelmann, Catherine Damron Campbell, Louise Chandler, Mary E. Batron, Iva Tinnell, Mintie McMillion, Ada Hughes, Ida May Dorsey, Maude Craig, Sarah Hamilton, Dessa Wiseman, Myrtle M. McDowell, Thelma Roop Harper, Blanche Summers, Margaret Hinkle, Merze Williams, Mary Lunter, Altie Carter, Ferne Simpson, Margaret Evans, Ruby Groves, Deva Phillips, Chessie Chapman, Gay Grose, Pauline Dooley, Myrtle Chapman, Orpha Morrison, Annice Damron, Russie Perkins, Aurelia Phillips, Dorothy Dobson Bobbitt, Josephine Bryant, Betty McHenry, Martha Shelton, Louise Hamilton, Maude Ballew, Marie Facemire, June Worlledge, Margaret Turner, Ruth Chapman, Dottie Fields, Norma Brown, Lind Hayes, Shirley Huffman, Wanda Hendrickson, Patty Louk, Janice Gum, Barbara Bell, Deloris Fox, Jessie Facemire, Bonnie Stephenson, Joyce

Bennett, Eunice Wood, Betty Beam, Donna Malcolm, Drema Young, Debbie Simpson, Annie Groves, Angela Myers, Modena Workman, Marie Facemire Farland, Aileen McKinney, Brenda Dempsey and Jackie Groves.

Worthy Patrons who have served Wakoma Chapter #52: O. C. Lewis, Paris Herold, Wallace Kincaid, C. W. Alderson, T. W. Ayers, E. W. Skaggs, L. O. Bobbitt, J. J. Summers, James C. Cox, Arnett Groves, N. C. Stephenson, J. D. Peck, O. E. Batron, Curtis Chandler, Hammond Summers, Verner White, Howard Campbell, Rev. A. F. Gregory, Roy Alderson, James S. King, Porter Groves, Robert B. Campbell, Carl Morrison, Wallace Henderson, Rodney Facemire, Strawn Brown, Charles F. Gum, Wayne Bennett, Joe Bell, Larry Board, John Beam, Don Malcolm, Joe Simpson, Joe Groves, Elmer McFarland, Lester Dempsey and Herbie Groves.

According to the minutes of the Masonic Lodge A. F. & A. M. #76, the order was given in late 1879 to order supplies to build a new building. The article in the 1930 Nicholas Chronicle give the building date as 1877.

One Hundred Years Celebration of the OES Wakoma Chapter #52 was scheduled for Saturday, June 11, 2011 at 2 p.m. at the Masonic Hall, Summersville, WV with Worthy Matron and Worthy Patron Jackie and Herbie Groves and Secretary Patty Louk.

An OES Social followed the January 1952 Initiation Ceremony for members and guests in the upstairs hall. (r-l) Merze Williams, May Lunter, Grandwothy matron – Etta Scott, Izora Bashaw (2 men unknown) and Lovell King

Order of Eastern Star, Wakoma Chapter #52, January
1952 were guests (left) unknown, Grand Worthy Matron –
Etta Scott, and Grand Worthy Patron – Ira Halstead

New OES members taken into membership of Wakoma
Chapter #52 in January 1952 (l) Anna L. Campbell and
Gerrie Boley (r) with Grand Worthy Matron Etta Scott.
Lodge Hall located 604 Main Street, Summersville, WV

First Masonic Lodge, built circa 1880, 604 Main
St., Summersville, WV. (Oct. 2001 photo)

1950 Wakoma Chapter #52 Order of Eastern Star. Front
(l-r) _____, _____, Sarah Hamilton, Marjenny Bickle
Middle (l-r) Edna Campbell, Verna Cody, Myrtle McDowell,
_____, Catherine Campbell. Back: Howard Campbell,
_____, Catherine Freeman, Frances Jacobson, Gay Grose,
Roy Alderson, Hattie Alderson, and Deva Phillips

139

THE TWIN CHURCHES

Beulah Baptist Church was established May 10, 1873 with I. C. Cavendish, the preacher who delivered the first sermon. His text was taken from Matthew 16:18. The church completed their first building in 1884 and was located just back of where the present building stands. The Methodist Church South was built over next to the creek from it. They were known as the Twin Churches until the 1950s when the Methodist Church moved. The Beulah Baptist Church as it is known at this time was built in 1849 while Homer Piercy was pastor and rebuilt in 1972 while Don Walker was pastor.

The Muddlety Methodist Church started with a deed recorded in Nicholas County Courthouse, dated March 10, 1825, between Thomas and Elizabeth Callahan, first part and Jacob Hutchinson, David Murphy, George Cutlip, Robert Kelly and Enoch Hamrick second part in Nicholas County, Virginia on Muddlety Creek. A log church was built on this lot in 1834 and called Armstrong Chapel. Later a frame church was built and called Anthony Chapel. Leaders were Jacob Hutchinson, David Murphy, George Cutlip, Enoch Hamrick, Anthony McClung, Peter Craig, George Craig, and others. Anthony McClung camped on the ground and kiln dried the lumber for the building.

After the division of the Methodist Episcopal Church in 1844, a Methodist Episcopal Church South was built in 1859 at Hookersville and named Pierce Chapel after Bishop Pierce.

In 1895, a new church was built and destroyed by fire in 1941. The leaders of this church were Jacob Hutchinson, John Tyree, William O. Grose, Benjamin Pierson, and David Eagle. When the branches of the Methodism reunited in 1939 the church was named Muddlety Methodist Church and was moved from the old site on Rt. 19 at Hookersville on Sept. 9, 1960 with a new addition built in 1961.

There is an interesting story submitted by James Dyer Stanard of Hurricane, W.Va., about the Twin Churches which follows:

"The story of the Twin Churches located on Muddlety Creek not far from the Dyer Herold Property. A Baptist Church and a Methodist church were built side by side and up on a hill in sight of them was another Methodist church.

One Sunday morning, they were all having services at the same time. It was said that the Baptist church was singing "Will there be any stars in my crown?" while the Methodist church was singing "No not one" and the church on the hill was singing, "That will be glory for me."

Stanard recalled attending a service at the Baptist church with his parents as a young boy. He lived his early years in Nicholas County.

140
TUSCARORA INN

I t is an interesting picture with the Model T Ford cars, the dirt road, and the electric wire poles. The picture may have been taken circa 1915-20 with four Model Ts in one place. The Model T Ford invented by Henry Ford was produced about 1912-1913, which made the car available for the average income.

With affordable transportation, families started traveling and touring the country. More inns and eating places were in demand.

The Tuscarora Inn, Smith Bros. Property, Tuscarora Summit, US Ele 2240 on Lincoln Way is listed on the picture that is owned by Mrs. Louise Hamilton of Summersville. She is curious as to the location of the inn. Does anyone know anything about the Tuscarora Inn and the location? The picture belonged to Mrs. Hamilton's mother who has passed away.

NOTE: Art Anderson, of Summersville, later called with the information that Tuscarora Inn was located on Rt. 30 near Gettysburg, Pa. Mr. and Mrs. Anderson spent their honeymoon at the location in 1949. Thank you, Mr. Anderson.

141
FAMILY REUNION

L ittle did the ancestors know that when they settled and raised a family in Nicholas County would a reunion of descendants bring together relatives meeting for the first time. Such was the case August 12 and 13, 2011, in Nicholas County, WV.

Michael and Barbara Baldwin Murphy settled near Runa and raised a family of seven children. Michael, born in County Cork, Ireland, arrived in America with other family members in 1850.

Charles H. Beirne and Margaret Burke Beirne, both born in Ireland, arrived in the United States, and settled in Nicholas County, and raised a family of six children. The Beirne family owned land in the Irish Corner. Farming many acres in that section of the county was the way of life in the mid-1800s until about the mid-1900s.

John and Emily M. Sweeney had a family who settled in the Irish Corner area during that time period. The three families, Beirne, Murphy and Sweeney members married into the families and many settled in the Irish Corner and raised their families there. Later, the families moved to other areas for work or military services. Many members of those three families returned to the reunion from Texas, North and South Carolina, Kentucky, Florida, Massachusetts, and many areas of West Virginia.

Story telling was an important pastime for the family elders of the pioneer families. Those stories surfaced at the recent reunion of the three families who lived so many years ago. The stories shed some light upon an individual's life and character. One of the stories told by a family member follows:

"Some relatives went to the man's home, knocked on the door several times with no response at the door. After a brief wait, several knocks were made on the door. Again, no one came to answer the knocks. After the third attempt at the door, the man of the house opened the door and stated, "I've told you not to disturb me when I am praying!" This experience indicated the dedication to prayer by the man.

It was a good and friendly reunion with more than 100 relatives from the three families getting together for two days to share genealogy, stories, laughter, and delicious meals.

A special event took place when two siblings met for the first time at the reunion. They had been raised by different families in separate locations. They were excited and happy and had lots of questions to have answered. A great ending to a delightful reunion was shared by many relatives and guests.

Two cousins, Barbara Beirne Fennell and Maria Beirne Yeager planned and executed the second Beirne, Murphy and Sweeney Reunion at the Good Evening Ranch, Canvas, near Summersville. A special thank you to Barbara and Maria for making the event a big success.

142

THE MODEL A FORD

The Model T Ford brought about changes in affordable transportation about 1908 when mass production started. That lasted until 1927 when the Model T boom in sales ended. With prosperity at hand, the average car buyer was willing to pay for the extras promoted on competitive makes of cars. The plain Model T didn't stand a chance with models that offered paint schemes in place of solid black, nickel trim and speedy engines.

On May 26, 1928, Henry Ford ordered Model T production stopped with the 15 millionth unit, closing the plants to plan for a new car. Enormous business was lost while Ford shut down. Suppliers suffered, workers laid off, and only the strongest dealers remained in business by selling used cars, parts and service. The Ford marketing system wiped off, giving competing makes advantage of the sales market.

Edsel ordered drawings of a variety of open and closed body types and selected new color and trim schemes for a new model. Developed under a veil of secrecy, public curiosity intensified, the Model A was unveiled at dealer's showrooms on Dec. 2, 1927, by far the biggest introduction in the history of the automobile. It is estimated that in the first two days, 10 million Americans stood in line to see it. Thousands of cash deposits for cars were taken on the spot, even though it would be weeks before production could fill all the orders.

Demand for the low-priced fashionable car was so great that sales boomed for the next four years, despite the grip of Depression. By the end of 1931, five million Model A cars had been produced. Each year, just enough model distinction to be different from the previous year. Thus, began a new model from year to year. The Model A was a popular car in Nicholas County. Herbert and Howard Campbell purchased a garage from A. C. Brock in 1916 at Summersville, where they established Campbell Brothers Ford Garage. They offered sales and service and remained in business until Howard B. Campbell died in 1970. Hebert Campbell died in 1954.

In the mid-1930s, James Ralph Murphy purchased a Model A Ford, which was driven by him until about 1949. That Model A Ford was transportation for the parents and five children. About 1938, the Model A Ford was driven by Mr. Murphy who took his family of then three children to Kentucky to spend Christmas with Aunt Annie. It was a long day of travel to reach the destination. After a cold day wrapped in blankets to keep warm, tired and cold travelers were welcomed to a warm house, food, and hot cocoa for the children. It was an exciting Christmas. Santa Claus delivered the requested presents there. The three children were surprised to find presents for them away from home. The return trip back to the Murphy home was again a long day of travel. The family was thankful for a safe trip over the less desirable roads.

Finally, in 1949, Mr. Murphy sold the well-used Model A Ford, purchased another vehicle and recalled the memories of the wonderful Model A Ford.

The Model A Ford

143

A SPECIAL TREE

Almost everyone from early childhood has a memory of a tree that held a tree house or was fun to climb the lower limbs or simply a shade tree that made the hot summer days enjoyable.

Trees come in many shapes, varieties and sizes and are harvested for the valuable wood. Some trees bear fruit. Others are used in landscapes and for shade. However, there are diseases which destroy some trees. In the 1930s, the Dutch elm disease and phloem necrosis killed many or most American elm trees. Phloem necrosis is caused by a virus carried by the leafhopper. An infected tree cannot be recognized until its leaves begin to turn yellow and fall. The Dutch elm disease, also carried by insects, the American bark beetle which spread the disease from tree to tree. It is so called Dutch elm disease because the Dutch first noticed it in Holland in 1919. The disease first started in New York and spread to many states and far west in the United States.

The American elm tree was valued for its lumber and for shade. Elm trees often reach a height of 75 to 100 feet. Some healthy elm trees have lived for more than 200 years. Elm wood is tough, hard and light brown and does not split easily and was used for making wagon wheels and farm implements.

Famous elm trees were the "Washington Elm" which stood in Cambridge, Mass., in 1775 and the Elm Tree at the White House in Washington, DC which was featured on a bill of money. We believe it was on the 20-dollar bill. That tree has been removed from the White House location.

In 1938, Eugene L. Campbell planted an American broadleaf elm tree on his property in Summersville for shade. That same tree survives, measures 15 feet in circumference and has been pruned by professional tree experts three times in the past 35 years. The tree is fast growing, makes wonderful shade, but drops tons of leaves in the fall. Only one tree from the American elm roots, has been planted and still survives. It is not known if there are other American elm trees in the state as it is rare that any survived the dreaded Dutch elm disease.

An interesting story happened to a young friend who prepared a booklet on leaf collection and identification for a class assignment. The young friend visited our property to collect leaves. Among the collection was an American broadleaf elm leaf. When the young student turned in the assignment, the teacher told the student that the leaf was not an American elm leaf as all those trees were gone due to a disease. The young friend replied to the teacher, "I am sure that it is an American Elm leaf as Mr. Campbell told me so."

The American broadleaf elm tree was reported with the Elm Research Institute, Harrisville, NH in 1984. Research continues to produce disease resistant elm trees.

The American broadleaf tree is our special tree as it is a survivor and offers wonderful shade in the summer.

**American broadleaf elm tree. Planted in 1938
and measures 15 feet in circumference.**

144

GARDEN CLUBS PLAN LANDSCAPING FOR SUMMERSVILLE CONVALESCENT HOSPITAL

THE GARDEN CLUBS OF SUMMERSVILLE, WV

June 1938, Mt. Azalea Garden Club of Summersville was organized and chartered. A constitution was adopted with Articles I to V. The object of the club shall be mutual improvement of the members intellectually, beautification of the home and city and social enjoyment. The officers (president, vice president, secretary and treasurer) will hold offices for two years. Amendments were added as necessary to the constitution. Garden clubs are part of national, state and district organizations.

Standing committees were usually civic, finance, flower show, flower arrangement, membership, programs and yearbook, publicity, project, and scrapbook. Telephone and hospitality committees were added.

Learning the proper techniques of flower arrangement was done in workshops and programs conducted by experienced and accredited arrangers. The monthly meetings were held in homes of members and in church fellowship halls. Requirements for a standard garden club were an active organization, a systematic course of study, at least one flower show each year, one garden pilgrimage a year, one or more club projects and an authoritative speaker for one meeting.

A spring banquet was held and for several years when hats were fashionable to wear; the ladies made their hats from fresh plant material. Prizes were awarded for the most creative and other categories.

Many civic projects throughout the years were completed by members for beautification such as flowerbeds, landscaping to entrances of public property, and clean-up projects to public areas such as roadside parks and roadways.

Attending district and state meetings in the spring or fall was a big social event, meeting, reporting on projects and learning new ideas enhanced the club members interest in garden clubs. Conservation of natural resources was encouraged in the 1960s and 1970s.

By the mid-1960s, Mt. Azalea Garden Club had increased membership to more than 50 members. It was suggested and voted upon to form another club to meet in the afternoon while Mt. Azalea continued to hold evening meetings. Members were given a choice to remain or to form a new club. A chapter was applied for, granted and received at a West Virginia State Garden Club convention in Parkersburg by Mrs. Hoy Eakle (Nancy) and Mrs. Robert B. Campbell (Ann). (Note: the name of the husband was used).

Both garden clubs were active in the community, doing beautification projects, staging flower shows, and promoting and sponsoring young people to conservation camp. In 1970, a nature tour of the area was conducted by Mountain Lake Garden Club.

Both Mt. Azalea and Mountain Lake Garden Clubs planned and executed the landscaping of the Summersville Convalescent Hospital in 1969. The community tree planting in Summersville was a large pilot project in 1968 in conjunction with the city, Mt. Azalea and Mountain Lake Garden Clubs, Monongahela Power Company Conservationist Norman Rexrode, extension agent. Trees were of the tailored variety from Scanton Nursery of Ohio to keep low growth under power lines. Trees selected for particular areas were Little Leaf Linden, Shakespeare Crab, Flowering Cherry, Cleveland Maple, Kafugen Cherry and Chanticleer Pear. An award of $300 was given by Monongahela Power Company to both garden clubs in recognition of the successful completion of their pilot street tree demonstration project. Both clubs remained active for the next several years until many members started a career in the workplace and could no longer participate.

Met at St. Nicholas Hotel in 1968. Front row: Peggy Cline, Norman Rexrode and Ella Fulton. Back row: Grace Wells, Lena Dotson, Eva Herold, Maysel Groves, Nancy Eakle, Ann Campbell, Nancy Hopson, Nina Herold and Helen Safreed

145

HANDWRITTEN LETTERS AND CARDS

When did you last receive a hand- written letter or card? According to the U. S. Post Office, it is estimated only once in seven or more weeks does one receive handwritten mail in this modern time with the latest technology of computers, phones, iPad, Email, and texting. The typewriter of early years has been replaced with other tools of communication.

The written word has been used to communicate with each other for centuries. The ability to write effectively has a great deal to do with what you want to say about a subject, what your feelings are and how you are going to present it to others.

When families moved far away for better opportunities, sending a post card (costing one cent) was a common practice to inform the others that all was well or not and the location of the new settlement. That was the only method of communication when distance was involved. It would take weeks or longer before the delivery of a handwritten message was completed.

Penmanship was practiced in school until the letters were mastered by young children in each grade throughout grade school (elementary). It was taught in the eighth grade in the 1940s by teacher Miss Corile Hill who believed the importance of fine handwriting. The cursive handwriting was taught in the early grades. Now children learn to print first.

Early documents in the United States were handwritten before the printing press and were copied by scribes. Deeds were handwritten and recorded in county courthouses where they are available to read or make copies of them. When reading earlier obituaries, you will find them to have been handwritten and often a person in a community displayed skill for composing and writing for those who weren't as skilled. In genealogy research, it is often signed by a writer of the obituary.

Receiving a card or letter in the years past was a treasure to keep and read many times. It is a wonderful experience to read letters handwritten long ago from a relative or ancestor. It gives us an insight to the time period, what was significant to them and, of course, the weather was often mentioned as well as the hardships experienced. It was good to finally receive a copy of a letter written in 1868 from a brother who walked from Massachusetts to try to find a brother who settled in West Virginia. The trip was not completed, but the letter revealed the struggles and problems in making such a long trip on foot. (He stated the shoes were worn out.) The handwritten letter finally reached my great-grandfather, and someone thoughtfully typed a copy with some words omitted which were not clear. That letter is a treasure to have in our genealogy information. For various reasons, not everyone can read or write. It was not always compulsory to attend school until the age of 16 years. Some only attended one or two years of school. Those who couldn't write would sign an "X" for the name and someone would write the name for them. This was the case of many immigrants to the U.S. in the earlier years.

A handwritten card or letter still is considered very special to receive. A person took the letter written by the parents before the marriage in 1923, put them in a booklet, made copies for family members. The handwritten letters, along with the stamped and addressed envelopes reveal how the times, weather affected the courtship which usually took place by meeting at church on Sunday. The early letters also displayed the more formal greetings and later to the terms of endearment for the couple. What a treasure to learn about the times, communication only handwritten account of the friendship. Often, the letters states, "I'll see you on Sunday if the creek doesn't rise." (they traveled by horse or by walking.)

Will the art of handwritten cards and letters disappear with all the technology known at this time?

146
BARNS

When early pioneer settlers came to the area, they had little or no means in equipment to settle a piece of land. The tools were very primitive and limited. He went into the wilderness with a rifle, ax, and fire to clear the fields. To build a cabin, an ax, large auger, and broadax were needed. The hardship prevailed for those who started empty handed. Those who were more well to do brought better tools along for building. A cabin was the first necessity for early settlers. Food and clothing were also important.

Animals such a flock of sheep need protected from wolves and panthers by being penned at night. The men were busy planting and harvesting crops, making farm implements, yokes for oxen, sleds, rakes, and other necessities. They needed a building to protect the animals and to house equipment, storage for grain and animal feed. So, a barn was built for such purposes. The design was very simple from logs for early barns. As more and better tools and sawmills to cut the logs into boards were available, barns were built with lumber. A loft was added for hay storage, and partitions were added for animal stalls for cattle and horses to protect them from predators and the cold winter weather.

Neighbors would often help to build and when the "barn raising" took place, the women prepared food for all to celebrate the accomplishment. Barns became more elaborate with features to accommodate more comfort and convenience. Horse barns today have music, automated water systems and special clean outs. Tobacco barns were designed for drying and storage of tobacco plants.

Round barns are very interesting to see but have no idea of their advantages. Barns have been used for advertisements of tobacco products and other commercial ads. Barns are frequently photographed and painted by artists.

100-year-old barn built from lumber milled at the Starbuck Mill on Muddlety Creek in the early 1900s

147

FAIRING BOXES AND PINS

Fairings are small charming china objects that were purchased or given away as prizes at English fairs in the 19th century. They were also made in Germany. Fairings depicted amusing scenes of courtship, children, or animals on the top. The early examples (1860–1870) were of better quality than later ones.

Match strikers' boxes and trinket boxes were similar. Most boxes are round, oblong, or square and measure three to four inches tall and wide. They were generally unsigned but may carry impressed numbers beneath the lids or bases.

During the Victorian period, sewing was a necessity. Fancy sewing was regarded as an elegant and often artistic female accomplishment. Sewing tools were treasured and a pretty box in which to store pins brought great pleasure. Some box lids represented a stove or farm animals or royal emblems such as a crown, sword, or scepter.

A small daughter delighted in owning a pin box with Riding Hood and the Wicked Wolf or animals peering in a mirror. The girl's mother was likely to keep her pins in a fairing adorned with a child or angel. The safekeeping of pins dates from medieval times when pins were luxuries. In England during those years, law limited sale of pins to the first two days of January. Husbands and fathers gave wives and daughters money enough for a year's supply of pins (a practice from which the term "Pin Money" is derived.) These pins were treasured and stored in pin cases.

Victorian women, much occupied with sewing enjoyed having pins stored in fairings made for this purpose.

While women cherished pin boxes (fairings), men admired and often bought matchboxes. The rectangular boxes had a roughened and ribbed surface beneath the lid to use as a striker. Matchboxes were a decorative addition to the parlor, displayed on a mantel, shelf or a tabletop.

Pretty little fairing trinket boxes were likely found on bureaus or dressing tables in bedrooms to conveniently store lockets, brooches, rings, or other jewelry. Trinket boxes, still popular, are purchased in many shapes and sizes and are adorned in many ways. The collectors are interested in the older china or porcelain fairings found in antique stores or markets. The early fairings were a joy at fairs, free or sold for a few pence, but now if available, may sell for many dollars if in good condition.

Pins once considered a luxury are now plentiful, available any day of the month for a few cents. Fairings may still be in use for storage, but pincushions are more in use at this time.

148

WORLD WAR II EXPERIENCES
OF GERALD M. CUMMINGS

M r. Gerald M. Cummings was a well-known and respected educator in Nicholas County from 1946 until his retirement. He served as a teaching principal, general supervisor, assistant supervisor, assistant superintendent of Nicholas County, and served as superintendent of Nicholas County Schools from 1962 to 1972. His teaching career was interrupted by World War II where he served in the 82nd Airborne Division attaining the rank of Master Sergeant and was the recipient of the Bronze Star.

Before Mr. Cummings passed away June 22, 2006, he copied his World War II experiences and shared his writing with those who may be interested. He wanted his story to be told and read. For the next several weeks, we shall share his World War II experiences from his account in the Passage of Time.

To: The Reader

From: Gerald M. Cummings.

The following pages describe my experiences as a soldier during World War II. The account is based on letters written to my fiancée and a log I kept of activities overseas.

Most of this is written from the perspective of a clerk in Regimental Headquarters, for that was my assignment most of my military career. Although not on the front lines slugging it out with the enemy, I was in the combat echelon, which means that every time my regiment entered the combat zone, I went with it. Sometimes that meant landing in a glider behind enemy lines, and sometimes I was alerted to go into the line of combat if the situation didn't improve.

Hopefully, this account will be of interest to some of my fellow soldiers and any others who may be interviewed in knowing what life was like in the 325th Glider Infantry during World War II.

Part VII – The War Years

When I was a boy, I felt very fortunate that I was growing up at a time when I would very probably never be called upon to go to war. If I did have to go to war, I wanted to do my fighting on foreign soil so that these United States would not see the destruction of her cities and countryside.

Oct. 16, 1940, 30 days after the Selective Service Act was adopted, I registered at Mt. Lebanon School. B. E. (Bert) Summers was the registrar.

On. Jan. 23, 1941, my father died, and I felt that if the United States became embroiled in the war then raging in Europe, I would be exempt, as we had a farm and I was the only man on it. I was teaching though, and as my mother drew a small insurance check ($13.99) each month, it could not be said that she was dependent upon me.

On Oct. 14, 1941, I went to Spencer for my screening examination. Dr. C. W. Shafer was the examining physician, and nine days later I received my classification card marked 1-A. Two weeks later, I went to the draft board and asked for reclassification. However, I failed to get it.

On Dec. 7, 1941, I heard by radio that our ships at Pearl Harbor had been attacked. I felt sure that Uncle Sam would be calling soon for more draftees and that I was likely to be one of them.

On Jan. 7, 1942, I received orders to go to Parkersburg on the 13th for my final examination. On the 13th I drove to Spencer and joined a group of fellows who also had orders to take their final examinations. We went via Greyhound bus to Parkersburg.

I passed. Four days later, I heard a rumor that I would get my call Feb. 16.

On Jan. 24, Mom disclosed the fact that she had written to President Roosevelt requesting that I not be called to the service. I tried to convince Mom that every man is born with the obligation to defend his country if called upon. Five days later, I received notification from the draft board to report on Feb. 3 for induction. I filed an appeal.

On Feb. 9, the United Stated went on War Time. In effect, everyone started to work an hour earlier.

On Feb. 27, I heard from the Appeal Board. I was still 1-A. On March 7, I talked with Grover Hedges, Appeal Agent or some similar title, about appealing my classification to the President of the United States. Mr. Hedges would not permit me to do so.

On March 17, I received my call to report for induction on March 28, so I made my plans accordingly.

On March 28, I got up early and drove to Spencer. I left my car at Ray Conley's Esso Station for Cleo Berry to pick up and return to my garage.

Thirty-nine of us left Spencer on a Greyhound bus at 8:30. We switched to a C&O train in Charleston, leaving there at 11:00. We went through Huntington, Ashland, Russell, and Maysville and picked up draftees at most of those places. It was my first real train ride, and I enjoyed it. (I had ridden from Elkview to Charleston when 3 or 4 years old, and I had ridden a local from Dundon to Widen while in high school.) We switched to buses at Newport and were escorted by a motorcycle cop to Fort Thomas.

Upon arriving at Fort Thomas, we went directly to the recruiting office and signed two papers when our names were called. We stripped and were given a brief checking over. Then we went through some more "red tape," were fingerprinted, sworn in, and marched to Company D barracks. We were fed and allowed to wander out until 11:00 if we wanted to. Three of us took a little walk but returned in time to go to bed at 9:00.

The next morning, we were given two tests. One was a general test and the other was a mechanical aptitude test. I wanted to make 110 on the former one to make me eligible for officers' training school if the opportunity presented itself. There were 150 questions on the test, and I answered 138. I thought I answered most of the vocabulary test correctly, but much of the test consisted of counting boxes stacked in various shaped piles. I couldn't figure many of them out, so I did some guessing. The mechanical aptitude test also consisted of 150 questions. I thought I worked all 45 arithmetic problems correctly, but the pulley, cogwheel, driver, etc., questions stumped me.

After dinner, we were taken to the supply house for our outfits. They made me really feel "big" by putting size 9 shoes, pants two inches larger than I normally wore, and a shirt one-half size too large for me. Then they put a size 37 coat on me and a size 36 overcoat on me — to shrink me I suppose. I was given two wool shirts, a pair of wool pants, a wool coat, an overcoat, work coat, work hat, work pants, two brown shirts, brown tie, black tie, two suits of cotton underwear, one suit of "longhandled" underwear, four handkerchiefs, three pairs of socks, a pair of wool gloves, a pair of leggings, a belt and a cap. (Each of us had been given a raincoat, three towels, shaving brush, toothbrush, soap, mess kit containing knife, fork and spoon, and a water canteen the day before).

They were very particular about the way we made our beds. We had double-decker bunks similar to those found in a college dormitory. We had to watch our dress. Some officers spoke rather harshly and profanely.

The food was good. For dinner we had chicken and gravy, mashed potatoes, lima beans, pineapple, pickles, cake, coffee, and milk. They didn't ration sugar — they just didn't serve it.

Rumor had it that we would only be stationed at Fort Thomas two or three days and then we would move on. We would probably undergo training from 9 to 13 weeks and then be sent where we could be of benefit to the government.

On March 30 we received our shots for smallpox and typhoid. We just slid down a bench and by the time we reached the end of it, we had been vaccinated. We also received our dog tags, which made me feel like a sissy wearing them, since I had never worn a necklace before. In case a soldier is killed, one tag is clipped off and the other is left on the body for identification purposes.

We also received our test scores on March 30. I scored 153 on the general test and 152 on the mechanical aptitude test. Since there weren't as many questions on the test as my score, I assume that each answer was worth more than one point. I signed up for $3,000 worth of insurance at a cost of $2.07 per month. Later, I hoped to raise the amount to $10,000.

We rolled out of bed at 5 o'clock and most of us had to work. We had the silliest looking work clothes that made us look like convicts.

I thought the government furnished everything in the army, but I was mistaken. Some doggone corporal was trying to sell us something all the time. They even sold holes. We had five holes punched in our caps and coats so that we could fasten our insignia correctly. Each hole costs 4 cents. Fifteen busloads of men left on the afternoon of the 29th and 550 new men came in on the 30th.

The next day, March 31, it was out of bed at 4:00, breakfast at 6:45 and to work at 8:00. Eight of us were assigned to a quartermaster truck. The first thing we did was unload 232 cases of Pet Milk. Then we moved a sergeant to Dayton, Kentucky. On the way back we picked up 6,000 pounds of coffee, which we delivered to the commissary. Then we moved a captain from one part of town to another.

I'd rather work than loaf. We weren't allowed to sit on our bunks until after 11:00 and no one was allowed to smoke in the barracks until after that hour. We had a few "smart alecs" who didn't care for work or anything and before the day was over one was in the guardhouse. For my part, I wanted to get off to a good start. The corporal told us that most of us would be leaving the next day. I was anxious to be on my way and anxious to hear from my fiancée.

On April 1, we spent most of the day loafing and waiting to move out. Although they called the names of those of us who were leaving Ft. Thomas early in the morning, it was 8:00 before we "fell out." After half an hour wait, we boarded buses to Newport and boarded a train. Military police were as thick as flies. We were not supposed to leave the car to which we were assigned. There were 365 in our group. The porter told us we were going south but he didn't know where. I went to sleep and awakened as we were crossing the Ohio River. I knew we were heading north. We stopped in Cincinnati a long time then went west along the Ohio. The moonlight lent a romantic atmosphere to the river.

On the morning of April 2 when I awoke, I thought we were in Arkansas or Missouri. The porter told us we were in Kentucky. Most of us had been asleep when we re-crossed the Ohio and thoroughly confused.

Our train consisted of 10 Pullman cars and two kitchen cars. The kitchen stoves were fired with wood. Some of the fellows were drafted for KP. One fellow asked the sergeant if he would like to go down on Big Sandy. The sergeant asked him his name and told him to report to the kitchen saying it pays to keep quiet.

Later in the day, a sergeant came though asking for fellows with a college education. I spoke up, then thought that I would get a KP assignment. He told me to go to Car 1 and report to the major. I, along with four or five others, did so. The major started talking about KP and said that just about took men with a college education to work in the kitchen. I thought that we were in for it. Then he told us why he wanted us. The army keeps a big card for each soldier and the major wanted the cards for the men in our group sorted.

The major interviewed each of us and he sent me outside to wait. He called me back and said that the lawyer in the group would be in charge and that as one fellow had a BS degree and I had a BA, he would rate the BS the higher degree and that the holder of same could work and I could go through the train and see how many artists I could find. Everyone thought the artist hunt was a gag to get someone on KP and only one boy admitted that he was an artist. He was not the type of artist the major was looking for.

A little later, an orderly came to me and told me that I was to report to the major again to help with the classification cards. I found that soldiers were divided into five groups according to the scores made on the Army General Classification Test. Group I is made up of men who have scored 130 or more points; Group II, 110 to 129 points; Group III, 90 to 109 points; Group IV, 70 to 89 points; and Group V, below 70 points. Men in Groups I and II may be eligible for officers' candidate school. The average soldier is Class III, and those in Groups IV and V slower but necessary.

I found the work with the record cards to be very interesting. Although there were only three teachers in our group, they ranked high on the test. When the major asked those of us who were working what our individual scores were, and I told him mine was 153, he said, "My God, here's the genius among us." My head started swelling. I had the highest score of the bunch. A general clerk scored 151, a salesclerk scored 133, and a stenographer scored 130.

We arrived at Camp Claiborne, Louisiana, about 11:00 on April 3. We were immediately taken to a gymnasium and divided into groups. Then my group was taken to another building and subdivided. I would up in 3rd Battalion Headquarters Detachment, 325th Infantry, 82nd Division. Out of the 365 men who came down on the train, I was the lone man assigned to 3rd Battalion Headquarters. It was the first time since I started to grade school that I found myself in a group where I knew no one.

Camp Clairborne consisted of acres of tents. Fortunately, the tents had wood floors and were sided up about three feet. From there up they were screened. There were six of us to a tent, and most of us were from West Virginia.

Gerald M. Cummings

149

WORLD WAR II EXPERIENCES
OF GERALD M. CUMMINGS
– PART TWO

L uckily, the lieutenant in charge of our group was a patient
fellow who didn't cuss and rave like most of the Ft. Thomas
guys. He took us over to the camp theatre for some instruc-
tional movies. We tried to march, but as we had no training in
that, we looked very ragged. After our return, we received some
instruction in coming to "attention" and doing "right dress". I
paid my first visit to the Post Exchange, commonly referred to
as the PX. One could buy just about anything there. I also got
my first military haircut.

April 5 was Easter. Three services were held – 9:00, 10:00,
and 11:00. I went to the 11:00 service. The chapel was nice, and
the sermon so-so. Dinner was good, but we were so crowded that
we had to keep our elbows close to ours sides.

As April 6 was Army Day, we thought we wouldn't have
anything to do, but we were mistaken. We stood reveille at 6:20,
ate breakfast, policed up around our tents, and marched about
a mile to the dispensary to get our second typhoid shots. After
waiting two hours, we were told to come back at 9:45 the next
day. After lunch, we drilled a while and were told to memorize
11 rules pertaining to guard duty for the next day. (These rules

are called General Orders). Then we were given a lecture on military courtesy.

By this time, our detachment had grown to 40 men. (The T/O called for 48). We were assigned to specific sections, and I landed in what was known as the Ammunition and Pioneer squad. The latest rumor had us beginning rigorous training on the 13th for a period of 13 weeks.

Odds and ends: There were some illustrious men in the Army. I saw Jesse James at Ft. Thomas and I heard John Hancock's name called. Moved to another tent. The wind blew sand over most everything. Laundry rates were $1.50 per week. We wore fatigue clothes when we drilled.

On April 7, postage became free for servicemen. We went to the dispensary as directed and they had no slip for me. That meant that I had to start over and take four shots instead of three. We listened to lectures on health and military courtesy and then were called up by twos to come to "attention" and give the hand salute. Someone told about a soldier who, when he saw officers coming on both sides of the street, saluted with both hands.

On April 8, I got acquainted with a Louisiana rain. As the supply tent leaked, they took our tent to cover it and we were forced to move. I ended up back at the first tent to which I was assigned after I got to Clairborne. We marched to the dispensary through the rain, waited in the rain, had our blood typed, and marched back through the rain. (My blood type is A).

I heard about two fellows with similar names who reported to the dental clinic. One of them was supposed to have a certain tooth extracted. The other's trouble I did not know. Anyway, when the first fellow's name was called the second fellow walked in and found himself minus a tooth before he knew what was happening.

On April 9, a photographer took a picture of our outfit, even though we were not up to authorized strength. Those in the picture are listed as follows: Walker, Thomas, Mel Adkins, Marvin Hulvey, Craig, Harrison Vickers, 1st Lt. George Richardson, S. Sgt. Robert J. Maxwell, Earl Blevins, Couch, Barger, Elmer K.

Western, Corp Smith, Corp Cooper, Morgan H. Rose, Roush, Mason, John Richards, Brown, James R. Hogan, James Blevins, Whitte, Thobin, Svellinger, Hynds, Bradley, Eugene Moore of Richwood WV, Samuel Vieth, Rhodes, Ralph Dempsey, Hixon, Donald Coleman, Hoffman, Carshell Shamblin, Ruppert, Gilbert Sill, Browsky, Tipton, W. Adkins, Jones, Horkevy, Edwin T. Thornhill, Willshire, Frazier, and one man I cannot identify. First Sgt. Hedrick and drill Sgt. Herbert Scalf were not in the picture.

On this day, we drilled a while, then some of us were picked to go up front and take charge of the detachment for commands. My voice wasn't strong enough to be heard without yelling. It didn't matter much what one said on the command of execution, but the preparatory command had to be sharp and clear. They put a new top on our tent, so it was move again. The Alexandria paper said we had 5.51 inches of rain during the two-day period. I received my first mail since being in the army – a letter from my fiancée.

Observations about the army: A lot of time was wasted. They always detailed more men that were needed for a job and seemingly didn't know from one minute to the next just what they were going to do. I noticed a good bit of rivalry among the different companies of the regiment which indicated that a good spirit would be developed.

We ate at Company M mess hall. They had a sign above their door that read: "The best damned men in this regiment come through these doors."

I was given the cutest little entrenching mattock. I'm sure the folks in Nicholas would have liked to have one for the ramp patch.

On April 11, I received news that Grandmother Cummings had passed away on March 30. She was very ill when I was inducted, and I had been expecting the bad news. On this day, the lieutenant inspected our tents and was greatly disappointed with ours. He climbed upon a bed, put his hand on the plate at the top of the tent and found some dust. Then he looked through the grate in the top of our stove and found some dirt, so he growled about that. We didn't have clothes racks, and we didn't have a paper posted showing whose bunk was there. The Lt told us that our training would be 17 weeks.

On April 12, I served as room orderly and had a new experience. Actually, I didn't do much except clean headquarters, answer the telephone, and run a few errands. I signed the payroll so that I could draw some pay when payday rolled around.

The next day, we got down to business. We marched out to our training area, which was about a mile away, trained awhile and marched back. We did that both in the morning and afternoon. We had calisthenics for half an hour, practiced the hand salute for half an hour, did closer order drill for an hour, and listened to a lecture on the parts of a rifle and a lecture on the care of equipment. Then we assembled with the rest of the regiment for an orientation speech. After supper, I helped clean the cosmolene out of 46 rifles. The next day, we each got to the "Hup, two, three, four" of the leader. My section would be involved in building and repairing roads, blasting bridges, building tank traps, unloading ammunition, etc.

Some notes about the fellows as taken from my diary: "Our detachment commander is Lt. Richardson. He attended Texas University, but you would never know it to hear him talk. He mispronounces words and uses poor grammar. He is sarcastic. Our drill sergeant is Robert J. Maxwell. He is Irish, regular Army, swears, has a sense of humor, is tough but understanding. Hebert Scalf, buck sergeant, also drills us. Is young and carefree. Hogan, a tentmate, is 35 and a griper. Blevins, a tentmate, is young and unsettled. Hulvey, a tentmate, has been in 38 states and almost as many jails. Is a habitual drunkard and undependable. Craig is the awkward man in the detachment. He can't even do a "right face."

On April 15, the new skills we worked on were the manual of arms and the stacking of rifles. Lectures were about protection from chemical warfare interior guard duty. My section repaired some dummies for bayonet practice. After supper, I made a First Aid chart for Lt. Richardson.

A word about pay. At that time, privates were paid $21 per month for the first four months, then $30; private first class received $6 more than privates; corporals received $54; sergeants received $60; staff sergeants received $72; first sergeants and technical sergeants received $84; master sergeants received $126; and generals were paid $8,000 per year.

The next day, we learned that the motto or our regiment was "Let's Go!" Our regimental commander, Colonel Claudius M. Easley, trying to build up a fighting spirit, gave us a pep talk. For failing to get us to one of the colonel's lectures and for getting us to another lecture 10 minutes late, our lieutenant was restricted to our area. Lectures were about first aid and protection from air and mechanized attacks. We practiced hiding and being hunted. Our fatigue suits blended so well with the surroundings that it was hard to see a man if he kept his head down. Although other sections quit working at 4:30, the Pioneer Section had no definite quitting time. We worked until 6 o'clock on a bayonet course.

The next day, April 17, we had the usual calisthenics, some rifle drill, and some practice in hiding and advancing on the enemy. We took our first three-mile hike and I had some trouble keeping in step. At the conclusion on the march, we had foot inspection. It was important that our feet be kept in good condition in order to take all the walking we had to do.

The next day was inspection day and we got through it in good shape. The officer even bragged about our tent. We had had a time keeping the tent clean until inspection time. Sand stuck to our shoes so badly that every time someone came in, he tracked sand in with him. I asked a corporal who was not wearing his stripes to clean his feet before he came into the tent and he didn't like it very well.

All of us who had been in camp two weeks received passes to go to Alexandria that afternoon. I did not take advantage of my pass.

The next three days were pretty much routine. We had preparatory marksmanship, extended close order drill, and ran the obstacle course which consisted of logs, ditches, wire, ladders, hurdles, etc. We were supposed to be able to run the course in 3:05 carrying a full field pack. We carried nothing and made it in 2:10. We had lectures on the Philippine Islands and the use of the bayonet. The sergeant who demonstrated the use of the bayonet told us that a bayonet fight must be fought well, or a guy will never fight but one.

On April 23, we took part in our first retreat parade, and we were lousy. We were issued foot lockers to put our clothes in and I was issued more clothes, a gas mask and a bayonet. I had received a new pair of shoes, some socks, and a fatigue jacket the day before. Rumor: our 17-week training period would be cut to 13 weeks. My address was changed to APO #82, the APO standing for Army Post Office.

April 25 was inspection day again. Everything went along pretty well except the inspecting officer found some dust on my rifle. Browskey and Hulvey went on sick call to skip the inspection but Browskey returned too early. I went on pass to Alexandria that afternoon. Round trip bus fare was 55¢. Alexandria had a population of about 40,000 and was filled with soldiers on a Saturday afternoon.

On April 28, I started my second month in the Army. I had tetanus and typhoid shots, did a little close order drill, listened to lectures on hand grenades and chemical warfare, and did some work in the supply room. I helped check out sheets and pillowcases and took in the men's laundry.

An interesting incident happened at the breakfast table that morning. A fellow near the end of the table called for the sugar. The fellow beside me had it but passed it back the other way. The fellow who had asked for it called again rather loudly. The fellow beside me said, "I'll pass you the bowl!" the top sergeant told the fellow who yelled to leave the mess hall.

On April 29, ten of us listened to a colonel explain how to sit when firing a gun and how to squeeze the trigger. Then we went out to our drill area and coached the others. I used muscles that morning that I didn't know I had. I was already sore, but I got sorer. That afternoon we had to lie as flat as we could and dig "fox holes". Then we spent an hour and a half digging trenches for hand grenade practice.

150
WORLD WAR II EXPERIENCES
OF GERALD M. CUMMINGS
– PART THREE

The next day, I was the runner and I did a bit of running. I missed a battalion hike, but I didn't mind. I did quite a bit of dusting around headquarters. One could dust the furniture every 30 minutes and it would still be dusty.

We started the month of May off by getting up at 5. Then we drilled from 8–12 and I then worked in the supply tent until 10 o'clock that night. We had to check everything in the tent and then sweep and mop the place. The next day we stood inspection wearing cartridge belts with bayonets attached. We also carried our rifles. I think I was the only man in the regiment who wasn't "gigged." Sgt. Maxwell said, "You look good Cummings. You look like a soldier." Then we went to our tents for quarters' inspection. We had to have our beds made just so, have our hat on our pillow, cartridge belt below the fold in the sheet and the blanket, and our gun lying in the middle of the bed. The lieutenant said that we had a nice tent.

The next two days I spent part of my time drilling and part of my time in the supply tent. Supply work wasn't difficult, but I preferred drilling because of the long hours and the aggravating situations we sometimes got into. We did a lot of "dry running" with the 03 rifle, but heard we would use the Garland MI for actual firing. On the 5th, I received my first pay, which amounted to $16.18 in cash.

On May 7, we were up at 4 and left at 6 for the firing range. Each man fired 50 rounds of ammunition from prone, sitting, kneeling, and standing positions – slow fire. The highest score was 243, the average was 213, and I scored 229. (This was not for record). After returning to camp, we cleaned up and marched to division headquarters where we listened to Sgt. Alvin C. York, hero of World War I and a member of the 82nd Division, make a speech. The first 15 minutes of his speed were broadcast by CBS.

On May 10, Cpl. Western and I spent most of the morning taking rifles back to 1st Battalion. We took a truckload of them and they wouldn't accept them. We reported to our top sergeant, he called 1st Bn Hq, and then told us to take the rifles back. Battalion could either notify its companies to pick up the rifles or we could leave them in the street. Company supply sergeants finally came and picked out their rifles.

The next day the Pioneer Section of which I was a member worked in the target pits. We raised and lowered targets, pasted paper over bullet holes, and signaled to firers what their success had been. A white marker signaled 5, red 4, cross 3, black 2 and a red flag was waved if the target was missed. From the pits some of the bullets sounded like angry bees and others weren't even audible. Occasionally someone would shoot too low and we would get a shower of dirt.

On May 11, Svellinger and I took the laundry to the laundry and were bawled out by an officer because we left our truck while we waited for our turn to unload. We returned too late for regular chow and Sgt. Hedrick had to make special arrangements for us to eat. The truck we were to ride to the rifle range had already gone, so we decided to walk. We were told that a truck was coming. We waited and then were told that it wasn't coming. I worked in the supply tent until 2:30, then the Sgt. decided I should do some shooting. Svellinger, Tobin and I headed for a truck. The lieutenant came along and I rode with him. I was on the range about 15 minutes when I was sent back to get a broken rifle. I couldn't find it, and I learned that it was already on the range. I rode back to the range, scored 38 out of a possible 40, rode back to camp and ate supper at 8:20.

Each man had a coach while firing. The gunner turned his head and the coach loaded the rifle. The gunner aimed and the coach pulled the trigger on the first three live shots. Several dummy shells were used, and the gunner never knew whether or not the gun would fire until he pulled the trigger. A man wasn't allowed to shoot a live round until he got to where he wouldn't bat and eye or flinch when the trigger was pulled.

One of our fellows always frowned — even when he laughed. He had trouble keeping in step when we marched. One day the sergeant said, "Get in step, Craig." He replied, "I am. I'm setting one down every time that fellow does."

During the next five days I was up from 18 to 19 hours each day. We were on the firing range. I qualified with a score of 165 out of a possible 220. (147 points rated Marksman, 184 Sharpshooter and 195 Expert.) I scored 13 out of 20 standing, 17 of 20 kneeling, and 18 of 20 sitting. I got mixed up on rapid fire and only scored 116 out of 160.

Rumor department: Mason and Brown have been recommended for medical discharges. Craig is going to be shipped. Sgt. Maxwell is slated to leave in about 60 days as part of a cadre to form a new division. The 82nd may finish its training in Indiana. I may be transferred from the Pioneer to the Communications section.

On May 17, I called my sweetheart and was thrilled to hear her voice. I worked in the supply tent until time to go to church. After lunch, Western and I went back to the supply tent and worked until 7. We were listing everything that belonged to our detachment. The next day, we spent most of our time on the miniature anti-aircraft range, firing 22s at moving targets that were about 8 inches long and 2 inches wide.

I spent May 20 in the supply tent. Some goofy-looking guy came to the tent to get a "pie stretcher" for Company G. Then two or three of our fellows came in to see a new "flexible rifle."

On May 23, I was "gigged" on my rifle during inspection. Our regimental commander made a talk in which he said we would have to be tough enough to march 60 miles in two days.

I spent May 25 through 29 in Pioneer school. We played with barbed wire, observed tank traps, and laid dummy antitank mines. Then a tank came along and ran over them to give us an idea as to how they worked. We built a splinter-proof shelter and repaired a bridge and built some road. I picked up quite a terrible sunburn in the process. I went after the laundry after 11 o'clock on the night of the 28th and didn't get back until 1 o'clock. Then I rolled out at 5:30 for a full day's work.

On May 30 our regiment paraded while the other regiments in our division took it easy. Although the parade was not very long, it certainly seemed long. One of the fellows who was pretty well filled with firewater did his best to cheer me up. He said, "What the H--- are you best fitted to do?" I told him I didn't know but that I would try anything they wanted me to do. He said I was behind the 8-ball as long as I was in the Pioneer Section.

Working in the supply room wasn't so bad. It kept me from being runner, waiting tables, and going out to work details after quitting times.

On June 1, I had the first formal drill I had had in three weeks. We had half an hour of calisthenics, some close order drill, and two and a half hours of bayonet drill. Then we practiced squad tactics. One squad took up a defensive position while the other squad tried to find where the first squad was hidden. I think I crawled a quarter of a mile through grass and poison ivy and then I was "killed". While I was on defense, I shared a hole with some lizards.

On the bayonet course they taught us one method, changed to another method, then switched back to the original. On June 4 we were up at 5 o'clock, ate breakfast, and headed for the bayonet course. The course was 100 yards long and had to be run in 40 seconds with a score of 58 to pass. We had to start from the prone position, run 20 yards, parry left and make a long thrust into a target about six inches wide, run to some six other targets using thrusts, jabs and butt strokes, then run 20 yards farther, stop and fire two shots. I ran the course in 37 seconds and made a perfect score (66). The fastest man made it in 30 seconds.

Later in the day we were paid. I received $16.73 and felt like I earned every cent of it. It didn't take long for some of the fellows to get a poker game going.

One of our gang, Hogan, was a continual griper. Marches burned him up. He griped about the food at the Company K and I bragged about it. While marching we saw two poor ponies, and Hogan said they must eat at Company K.

On June 6, Western, Hoffman and I went to Alexandria on pass. We ate banana splits and sundaes and took in two movies while in town. There were soldiers everywhere we looked and everywhere we went. We heard someone say that Roosevelt and Hitler were fighting over a woman named Pearl Harbor.

On the night of June 8, we saw an interesting demonstration. We saw matches struck at different distances from us and it surprised me that one could see the flame of a match so plainly at a distance of 1,000 yards. A lot of different sounds were made at different distances and we were asked to identify them. They fired machine guns and mortars so that we would be able to identify them in the future. "Tracer" bullets intrigued me. They looked like red balls considerably larger than bullets.

On the afternoon of June 9, we practiced rolling packs. This consisted of rolling our shelter half, blanket, tent pole, and pegs into a roll about the size of a joint stove pipe – a short joint that is. The next morning, we were up at 4:55 and Western and I had to roll officers' bedrolls. As we hadn't been shown how to do this, it took some time for us to get them rolled. We finally caught up with our gang and waited an hour before we began our hike. We found that carrying a full pack wasn't much fun. It made my shoulders sore and I broke out with heat rash. We ate dinner at 3:30 and arrived at our destination, Castor Plunge, at 6.

We went to bed at 9 o'clock and as the bedsprings weren't what I had been used to, I didn't sleep so well. We spread our raincoats on the ground and then put a blanket on them. We slept with our clothes on, shoes and all. I slept under a mosquito net and wasn't bothered by mosquitoes. However, some of the fellows complained about them. About 9:30 an airplane flew over us and dropped some flares.

The next day I was lucky enough to get a ride back to camp. It rained nearly all day and was a miserable time to be out. Eight of us Pioneers left on a road repair detail about 7:15, filled some holes on the way in, and arrived in camp at 10:15. The poor fellows who walked arrived about 4 o'clock.

On June 12, Lt. Col. Fisher, commander of our battalion, was transferred to a camp in Tennessee. Brown and Mason were transferred from our detachment to another part of camp. The next day we moved to a spot some 300 yards away from where we had been staying. We were up early and packed our stuff in readiness for the move. We had quite a time putting up tents and getting our things inside. Our tent used the ground for a floor. Art Ward, an acquaintance from Spencer, visited with me for two hours.

On the night of June 15, we started hiking about 9 o'clock with orders to be quiet and to neither talk nor smoke. We hiked about 50 minutes without lights and then put up our tents without lights. Hulvey and I worked together on the edge of a swamp where the bills of the mosquitoes were very sharp. We tore our tent down and rolled our packs in the dark. We were told that eventually we should be able to tear our tents down, roll our packs and be ready to go in two minutes.

We divided into two squads for the return hike. Each squad was given an azimuth to follow. We got into a big swamp and had quite a time finding our way out. We were in mud to the tops of our shoes several times. As it was pitch dark in the swamp, a few flashlights were used, and someone started singing, "Lord, lift me up to higher ground." We reached camp at 1:30 and were served coffee and cakes.

151

WORLD WAR II EXPERIENCES OF GERALD M. CUMMINGS – PART FOUR

T he next morning, I rolled out at 5:30 and worked on the laundry detail. Lots of rumors were afloat that day: 68 men from the division were to be chosen to attend officers training school; we would be moving closer to home; one fellow had received a letter which said that the writer had seen a sign at another camp which said, "Welcome 82nd Division". On this day, I also noticed that many of our soldiers were becoming "sissies". They were using fingernail polish to kill chiggers. Fingernail polish is also good to polish buttons and buckles. I read about a note that a girl received from a censor. It read, "Your boyfriend still loves you, but he talks too much." The censor had confiscated the entire letter.

At 9 o'clock on the night of June 17 we left on a hike. I got very hot but managed to pull through. We pitched our tents about 11 o'clock and tried to sleep until 3. We were back in camp about 5:20, cleaned up, ate breakfast, slept an hour, and went to work. I worked in the supply room some and spent a little time laying anti-tank mines. Thoben received a commission in the Navy, so he left us on this day. I filled out an application to attend the Infantry Officers Candidate School although my commanding officer recommended that I try for Adjutant General's School.

On June 19, one rumor came true. I was promoted to Private First Class. That meant $54 per month compared to the $50 I was receiving as a private. That morning, we had some tough calisthenics and rifle marksmanship. That afternoon, we hiked 7 or 8 miles. Several of the fellows fell out, but I managed to make it through. By the time the hike was over, I wasn't enjoying walking one bit. I had a big blister on the back of one heal and a big one on the bottom of the other one. On June 22, Willshire and I enrolled in gas school. Since the other boys went on a long hike that night, we were glad we were in school. As it was, we spend about 80 minutes walking to and from school. Some of our lectures sounded a lot like John R. Wagner's at Glenville State. Some of the poisonous gases have big names, but their nicknames were more appealing to me. "Hot Stuff," "Enemy's Delight", "Choky Gas", "Dope and Choke", "Cry Now", and "Cry Always" were some of the nicknames used.

The next day, we moved from our tents to "baby hutments. Since Willshire and I didn't have a chance to move, someone moved our stuff for us. We were told we would be moving again in about two days. Willshire and I had our first encounter with tear gas that day. We walked into a gas chamber, put our masks on then took them off before we left the chamber. That stuff really made us cry.

On June 24 we were up at 3:55. With the exception of four of us, the rest of us of the detachment left at 5:10 on a 15-mile hike. They were supposed to "double time' six minutes out of every hour, wear their gas masks an hour, and then run the obstacle course when they returned. All but two of the fellows made it.

We listened to more lectures and had an hour of gas mask drill. Our goal was to get our gas masks on within six seconds of the command to do so. On this day, the engineers demolished a barbed wire entanglement by exploding 50 sticks of dynamite in a piece of piping. We were some distance away and the instructor said over a loudspeaker, "If you listen carefully, you can probably hear it." And did we hear it! It nearly knocked us off our feet.

General Omar Bradley, Division Commander, gave his farewell address to the division that afternoon. I missed the parade because the laundry truck came, and I had to go to the camp laundry. I signed my application for OCS, noticing that my detachment commander had given me a good recommendation. The next two days were filled with lectures, smoke screen demonstrations, review, and practice in leading troops around areas contaminated with mustard gas (simulated, of course). Our final test at Gas School wasn't as rough as the colonel had led us to believe.

I spent most of June 27–30 in the supply room. Sergeant Hedrick said he was going to make a supply sergeant out of me. Horkavi left us for Glider Pilot School and the word was out that several others from our regiment would also be going to this school.

On July 3, I became a member of the Communications Section, having been transferred from the Pioneers Section. I spent part of the day in the supply room and part of the day in the field, the first day I had drilled in two weeks. I heard a new mosquito story. One flew into an airplane hangar not far from camp and an attendant pumped 40 gallons of gasoline into it before he discovered that it wasn't an airplane.

On July 4 I scored 90 out of a possible 100 on the grenade range. The next day, orders came down on furloughs which stated that we might get a 10-day furlough after our firing was over if we had reason for one. However, not more than 10 percent of us could go on furlough at any one time.

Things were more or less routine for me during the period of July 6 through July 8. I got up about 4:30, hurried around, waited, sat around the supply room, typed some statements of charges, and went to the laundry. Another Louisiana mosquito story: A soldier at Camp Polk was ill and needed a blood transfusion. There was no one near who had the same type of blood and it looked as though the soldier wouldn't get well. A mosquito happened to hear of the man's plight and flew out and bit a man having the same type of blood. He then flew back, bit the soldier, and pumped the blood into him. Needless to say, the soldier got well, but when he tried to talk, he could only make a buzzing sound.

Definition of a jeep: "A jeep is a sort of pogo stick on wheels. Or, one might say, a galvanized go cart. It has three speeds – first, second, and hang on boys, here we go. It does 18 miles an hour in neutral, and will do anything but stand at ease."

Thornhill was the first man from our detachment to go on furlough on July 10. Four days later, I was on my way home on a 10-day furlough plus two days travel time. It took me 44 hours to go from Alexandria to Charleston. I traveled by train – Texas and Pacific to Texarkana, Missouri Pacific to ST. Louis where I had a long wait, New York Central to Cincinnati where I had a two-hour wait, and the Chesapeake and Ohio to Charleston, My fiancée came to my home for a brief visit and I went to her home, then to Charleston by bus. The return trip from Charleston took 38 1/2 hours. The C&O train was the only one that ran on schedule.

Upon my return from furlough, I found that our detachment had been changed to a company and a fellow by the name of Peck was our commander. Since we were going to have our own mess, Sgt. Western and I counted a lot of dishes. And since Western was on a cadre that was starting a new division, Lt. Peck said I should then be supply sergeant. However, that never worked out.

The last three days of July were routine. I worked in the supply room, made out reports, went to the RSO and waited, picked up 82 heavy comforters even though the weather was unbearably hot, got up at 11:30 one night and went after the laundry, got out of making a long hike. I decided that there was no danger of getting that rare malady known as "toomuchsleep" in the army.

The first three days of August were hot with the temperature reaching 101 in the shade. More men were coming into our company and by the 3rd we had 67 men. We ordered dishes, pots and pans necessary to set up our own mess. One of the fellows on furlough whose family owned an electrical appliance store in Columbus, Ohio sent us 51 light bulbs. There was a rumor afloat that we would soon be getting a new type of training.

During the period of Aug. 4 through 6 I picked up 139 mosquito bars from the RSO, got bawled out by a sergeant for not making a report I had already submitted, and was mildly "chewed" by a lieutenant and a major. I missed getting paid but managed to collect $12 from the fellows who had borrowed from me. I slept so late one morning that I fell out for Reveille without any socks and with my shoes unlaced. Luckily, it was so dark that the sergeant didn't notice. We always policed our area following Reveille and by this time of year it was so dark that matchsticks would have to be as large as handspikes before we could see them.

The headline in the August 6 paper said "CLAIRBORNE TROOPS WILL MOVE TO BATTLE BY AIR". The article said that there would be two divisions formed each containing 8,000 men (a regular division contained about 15,000 men). These divisions were to be trained to fight on deserts, in the mountains or any place and would travel entirely by glider and airplane. Although the paper didn't say so, rumor had us going to Montana where we would train with Canadians. Only men in the best physical condition would be chosen.

I heard about a sailor who applied at the Shreveport sugar-rationing office for a sugar-rationing card. "Have you any excess sugar?" asked the clerk. "Yes, about 110 pounds, but I can't register her," was the quick retort.

This record of my military experience would not be complete without including a copy of "General Orders".

To take charge of this post and all government property in view.

To walk my post in a military manner, keeping always on the alert, and observing everything that takes place within sight or hearing.

To report all violations of orders I am instructed to enforce.

To report all calls from posts more distant from the guardhouse than my own. To quit my post only when properly relieved.

To receive, obey and pass on to the sentinel who relieves me all orders of the officer of the day, or officers and noncommissioned officers of the guard only.

To talk to no one except in line of duty.

To give the alarm in case of fire or disorder.

To call the corporal of the guard in any case not covered by instructions.

To salute all officers, and all standards and colors not cased.

To be especially watchful at night, and during the time for challenging to challenge all persons on or near my post and to allow no one to pass without proper authority.

Mess Hall General Orders

To take charge of this meal and all spuds in view.

To watch my plate in a military manner, keeping always on the alert for any dessert that comes within sight or smell.

To report any bread sliced too thin to the Mess Sergeant.

To repeat all calls for seconds.

To quit the table only when satisfied that there is nothing good left to eat.

To receive, but not pass on to the next person, tapioca or beans left by the cooks.

To talk to no one when I am busy eating.

To allow no one to steal anything in the line of chow.

To call the mess sergeant in any case not covered by instructions.

To salute all chickens, steak, pork chops, ham and eggs, and liver.

To be especially watchful at the table and during the time of eating, to challenge anyone who seems to be getting more to eat than myself.

On Aug. 7 while I was at the RSO the regimental commander visited our supply room and threw quite a fit.

152

WORLD WAR II EXPERIENCES
OF GERALD M. CUMMINGS
– PART FIVE

When I came back, nearly everything was out in the street. Ruppert and Mell Adkins had worked most of the day on a new filing cabinet and the colonel ordered it thrown out too. However, we sneaked it back into the orderly room.

The next day, we had a field inspection. We put our tents up and they had to be exactly in line. We then laid our equipment out in a prescribed manner and the major walked through hurriedly and inspected things. Later in the day, he inspected our supply room, but the colonel never came as expected. We heard that "brass hats" were coming from Fourth Corps Area Headquarters to see if we were as good as reported.

Another story: One time some fellows went fishing and their luck was particularly good. One decided that they should mark the place so that they would know where to fish the next time. He made a big X in the bottom of the boat. About the time they got home, one of the men started worrying about the possibility of not being able to find the fishing spot again. Another spoke up and said, "That's right. We might not have the same boat next time."

About August 10, I was transferred from Message Center Section to Headquarters Section. However, my work didn't change. A lieutenant from corps visited our supply and room and was noncommittal, neither criticizing nor bragging. I missed the inspection of Gas NCOs by being on the laundry detail at the time of inspection.

On August 12, cadre men were relieved of their duties at noon. Then began the task of receiving equipment they were supposed to turn in to the supply room. I found that the hardest items to get turned in were the division insignia. I received orders to draw "tin hats" from RSO the next day. Our division sign was changed to read "82nd Air-Borne Division". It was officially announced that 125 Company L men would be in the 101st Division and would move to Fort Bragg, NC. Rumors were afloat to the effect that we would be moving to Montana, Michigan, Monroe LA or Indiana. As this was my fiancée's birthday, you can guess where my thoughts were.

The next day, the major and Lt. Chapman inspected our supply room and cussed about how we were running things. After they left, our lieutenant cussed about the way they wanted things done. Our "tin hats" came in that day and furloughs were canceled until further notice.

On either Aug. 14 or 15, the name of our regiment was changed to 325th Airborne Infantry. On the 17th, it was changed to 325th Glider Infantry. Lt. Chapman told us to start saving boxes to pack things, as we would be going to Fort Bragg about Sept. 1 for further training. We heard rumors about the strength of our company – 130, then 175, and then 143. Although the division was to be made up of 8,000 men, it was supposed to have firepower equal to a regular division of 15,000.

The next week was pretty much routine except that I went on a hike one day that started at 11:20 p.m. and ended at 4:35 the next morning. Since I hadn't been on a hike for some time, I ended up with tired, aching, sore feet and blisters on the bottoms of both heels. Nearly everyone I saw was limping. Field telephones were used for communication even though our battalion and company headquarters were only 100 and 150 feet apart. We used the phone any time we had anything to communicate. One time I call Frazier, and since he didn't know how to operate the switch on his transmitter, he stuck his head out the window and yelled back.

I ran into a little item called "The Rise and Decline of Man: Six months – all lungs; age 5 – all ears; age 14 – all hands and feet; age 21 – all muscle; age 45 – all paunch; age 90 – all in!"

During the period of Aug. 27 – 29, I got out of a 58-mile hike (one day out, overnight camp, return next night) but I caught a lot of CQ. I don't think I had to answer the telephone more than a dozen times.

A note on mess halls: At Company K, we lined up and had our plates filled as we passed the counter and we began eating as soon as we reached the table. At Company M we waited until all the men that a table would accommodate got around it before anyone sat down. At Company C we sat down when we wanted to, but no one turned his plate over until the command "Eat" was given.

About the first of September, we were told that everyone had to hike for an hour five days a week. A day or two later the major refused to sign our ammunition report because I, and no officer, had signed it. He finally said that if regimental supply would accept my signature, Sgt. Maxwell would sign for him. Regulations required that I sign it and the battalion commander, not the sergeant, was also required to sign it. A few days later, Dempsey, the major's driver, told me that the major wanted to know who Pfc. Cummings was and he raved because I signed the report. Then the major said, "Whoever he is, he did a good job."

In early September the 3rd Battalion became the 1st Battalion. We were told that we would be getting 55 new men and that we would be taking on new responsibilities. Up to this point, we had not been required to pull guard duty, but we would soon take our turn with the rifle companies.

We had some peculiar names in our outfit: Alesiak, Boots, Clodfelter, Dowdy, Gaa, Krawetz, Midtlien, Schauss, Shimko, Sladovnik, Stelzel, Van der May, and Weinzapfel.

On the night of Sept. 8, we took a 19- mile hike. We started at 10 o'clock and traveled very slowly for three hours. We were in the woods and swamps and couldn't see each other even when we were almost against each other. We went through swamps and a creek that was knee deep. Twice part of the gang got lost. I actually did some walking while I was asleep. We made it back to camp at 6:30 a.m.

On Sept. 11 (?) we began operating our own mess hall. The sergeant from Company 1 became our supply sergeant and I was one of his helpers. We were told that we were supposed to put our serial number in our return address on envelopes, and if we spent a night at a hotel, we were not go disclose our camp address. We were either to give our home address or just say U.S. Army.

The rest of September was pretty much routine, waiting to move. We would usually take a 3-mile hike in the morning. I drilled in the field with the rest of the fellows, thus making my day seem shorter. The drawback to being in the field was that made me likely to pull KP or guard duty. During this period, I saw an organizational chart that listed me as a scout, and Lt. Kelstrom was trying to get me into Intelligence School. I figured that scouting would be a great life for an ex-schoolteacher. We also did a lot of "dry running" with our rifles. Sometimes breakfast was almost a dry run too. The night was beginning to cool down, reminding me of the weather in West Virginia about a month earlier.

One more Louisiana mosquito story: It seems that two mosquitoes picked a soldier up and flew away with him. One said to the other, "We must be careful and not fly over that swamp because one of those big mosquitoes might take him away from us."

On Oct. 1, we ate sandwiches for dinner at 10 o'clock, changed clothes, and fell out ready to move at 10:45. We stood and sat in the sun until 1, marched to the train, and were on our way at 1. The train proceeded north to Monroe, then turned east. From

Monroe we went through Jackson and Meridian, MS and then into Alabama and Birmingham. I pulled guard duty from midnight until 2 a.m. Scenery wasn't much along the way – cotton, dead ripe corn still standing, negroes, and dilapidated buildings.

I awakened in Augusta, Georgia on the morning of Oct. 3, having gone through Cuba, Alabama and Denmark, Georgia. We reached our area at Fort Bragg just after 5 o'clock in the afternoon. A band met us at the train – just as one gave us a send-off from Camp Clairborne. We walked five fast miles from the train to camp.

The barracks at Fort Bragg were red-roofed frame structures heated by coal furnaces. They were built for 50-some each but there were more than 70 in ours. Surroundings were nicer than at Camp Clairborne. Once could look out and see some hills and trees.

On Oct. 5, fifty of us loaded into trucks at 3:30 and went to unload a train that was expected at 6 o'clock that morning. It came at 6 that evening and we spent two hours unloading trucks, jeeps, anti-tank guns, ambulances, etc. They came on flatcars and we had to cut wires loose and pry chocks off the floor. Then the vehicles were driven off the flatcars and onto a big platform.

On Oct. 6, I spent three hours cleaning a carbine. I was assigned to the supply section of headquarters platoon, thus switching the kind of weapon I would carry from M-1 to carbine. To impress upon us the necessity of obeying an officer, one of our officers read to us an account of a member of our regiment who had been sentenced to Leavenworth for 20 years because he had refused to obey an officer.

Mornings were really chilly at this time of year. Anything we put on to keep us warm had to be put on under our uniforms, not over them. The sky was blue. Someone said, "The sky is so blue I wish I could wear it."

On Oct. 10, we had a division parade. We had expected the general to visit our area the day before, but he never came. Our company commander told us that conditions would get tougher and tougher, but anyone who could sing in Louisiana should be able to sing in North Carolina. He told us that from then on, we would double time to and from our training area.

The formality of things got overwhelming about this time. Everywhere we went we were told to keep in step – even when we double times. When we walked in to get our pay, we had to do a left face, salute sharply, take our pay envelope, step back one step, salute, do a right face, and step off. (Yepko received 87 one-dollar bills in his pay envelope.)

On Oct. 13, we switched from cotton to wool uniforms. We received some instruction on "Unarmed Defense for the Soldier". A sergeant demonstrated how to take a rifle and bayonet away from a man. There are some various holds to get on a man whereby one can break his arms or knock him out. This type of training is not very sissy-like.

The old sergeants tried to give me every break, and the new ones piled the work on me. One of them would say they wanted me for an instructor, and another would say there was no rating for me. One would say he would get me on a cadre, and another would promise to get me on another cadre. Looking back, my greatest break came about the middle of October. Sgt. Hedrick asked me to report to the supply room, and when I got there, he asked me to substitute as battalion clerk while Morgan Rose, the regular clerk, was on furlough. The next step was to regimental headquarters, which I shall relate later.

We had two telephone systems in camp, our own private system, and the Bell system. There were few phones in camp from which one could make a long-distance call. When we answered on our system, we said "Deadly Red 6".

We were told that they were going to weed out all the "scrubs" in our outfit. All men over 35, all men with flat feet, those with heart trouble or exceedingly nervous, or those who got airsick would be transferred to other outfits. Having never flown, I didn't know whether I would get airsick or not. I found out later that I surely did. Our outfit would have to move fast, so they wanted the best of men – including me? We had the privilege of watching a few planeloads of soldiers parachute from their planes.

153

WORLD WAR II EXPERIENCES OF GERALD M. CUMMINGS – PART SIX

W e have shared part of Mr. Cummings' experiences during World War II in the Passage of Time. The itinerary from May 1942 to September 1945 will conclude this series.

My Itinerary – The War Years
May 28, 1942 – En route to Spencer to Ft. Thomas, KY
April 1-2 – En route from Ft. Thomas to Camp Clairborne, LA (Pullman)
July 14-26 – Furlough
Oct. 1-3 – En route from Camp Clairborne to Ft. Bragg, NC
Dec. 2-13 – Furlough
Feb. 4, 1943 – By jeep to Maxton, NC
March 6 – Returned to Ft. Bragg
April 18 – En route from Ft. Bragg to Camp Edwards, MA (train)
April 26 – From Camp Edwards to New York (train) at New York boarded 15,000-T "Santa Rosa"
April 29 – May 10 – En route from New York to Casablanca
May 10 – Hiked some 4 miles from Casablanca to Camp Don B Passage
May 14-15 – En route from Camp B Passage to Marhia (truck)

June 24 – En route to El Alem, Tunisia (4 1/2-hour plane ride)

Aug. 16-17 – Vacationed near Enfidaville

Aug. 26 – Moved a few miles west of Bizerte (about 450 yards from Mediterranean Sea)

Sept. 7 - Moved to Mateur Airport No. 2 (3-hour ride)

Sept. 8 – Flew to Cosimo, Sicily, then took a 49-minute plane ride to Castlevetrana (Mateur to Comiso flight was 1 hour 57 minutes)

Sept. 13 – Flew from Castlevetrano to Licata (32-minute flight). Loaded on LCI

Sept. 14 – Docked at Palermo

Sept. 15 – Landed at Salerno Beach, Italy

Sept. 16 - Hiked some five miles to our bivouac area

Sept. 18 – Moved 15 or 20 miles by truck (probably no more than seven miles from where we were).

Sept. 20 – Moved to "Red" Branch near ancient city of Pasteum

Sept. 21 - Moved by LCI to Maiori

Sept. 22 – Move about 400 yards to lemon grove

Sept. 24 – Moved to the side of a mountain

Sept. 29 – Moved to the town of San Egido

Sept. 30 – Moved to within two or three miles of Castellare

Oct. 3 – Moved to Naples by truck. In Fascist Hq Building

Oct. 12 – Moved to nice apartment building

Nov. 18 – March two miles to pier. Loaded on landing barge that took us to the "James O'Hara"

Nov. 18 – Dec. 9 – En route from Naples to Belfast, North Ireland

Dec. 9 – By train from Belfast some 35 miles. Then by truck to Portglenone

1944

Feb. 13 – By truck to Ballymena, then by train to Belfast.

Feb. 14-15 – En route to Liverpool, England on "SS Dempo"

Feb. 16 – By train from Liverpool to Scraptoft near Leicestor

Mar. 18-April 3 – Furlough in London

April 8-10 – Aldermaston Airport (training)

April 20 – Flew from Balderton to Rearsby by glider

May 6 – Rode buses to spot near Nottingham (division exercise)

May 29-June 6 – At Alderson Airport waiting to go into combat

June 7 – Crash landed in Normandy by glider. CP set up SE of St. Mere-Eglise

June 9 – CP in stone house near Canquigny

June 11 – Moved SW some two miles. CP in stone house

June 13 – CP in tent not far from Picauville

June 14 – CP in building west of Etienville

June 16 – CP in mayor's house in Rauville

June 18 – At advanced CP in Etienville (probably the only intact room in town)

June 19 – CP in farmhouse south of Douve River some two miles from where we were the night before

July 8 – Moved some five miles to Forward CP

July 11 – Moved to beach in preparation for return to England

July 12-13 – Crossed English Channel on LST. Landed at Southampton

July 14 – In same old tent at Scraptoft

Aug. 14 – To Saltby Airport for problem

Sept. 1 – To Folkingham Airport in preparation for Belgium mission

Sept. 4 – Back to Scraptoft by command car

Sept. 15 – To Folkingham Airport

Sept. 23 – To Halland by glider

Sept. 24 – In German barracks south of Groesbeek

Sept. 29 – Moved CP about a mile west. Set up in German barracks in the woods.

Oct. 1 – Moved CP to farmhouse near Mook

Oct. 3 – Moved to forest north of Groesbeek

Oct. 6 – Moved to a spot about two miles from Groesbeek. (on Oct. 15, CP was split into two sections. I was at rear CP).

Nov. 13 – Traveled 18 miles to Oss by jeep

Nov. 14 – By jeep 240 miles to Camp Sissonne, France

Dec. 3-5 – Three-day pass to Paris

Dec. 18 – Left Camp Sissonne for what became known as the "Battle of the Bulge"

Dec. 19 – Near Werbomont (We took 20 hours to make 150-mile trip).

Dec. 21 – Moved CP generally south 18 miles to Verleumont

Dec. 24 – Moved CP to village of Trou de Bra

Dec. 26 – Moved CP to village of Au Hetre

1945

Jan. 1 – Moved to top of pine-covered mountain

Jan. 3 – Moved off mountain and set up CP in farmhouse

Jan. 4 – Moved to spot near Noirfontaine

Jan. 6 – Moved to town of Odrimont

Jan. 10 – Moved by truck to town of Pepinster

Jan. 26 – Moved to Born

Jan. 27 – Moved to Valendar

Feb. 2 – Moved by Bullingen to place not far from German border

Fec. 6 – Moved to Vielsam

Feb. 8 – Moved to Smithof, Germany

Feb. 19 – Moved to Camp Sissone, France

April 2 – Moved to Cologne, Germany via Aachen, and Duren

April 17 – Moved to estate just outside Gymnich

April 27 – On the move. Stayed at German youth camp at Weidenbruck for the night.

April 28 – At Himbergen

April 30 – Moved to Bleckede

May 2 – Moved to Ludwigslust

May 20 – Moved to town of Eldena

June 2 – By jeep from Eldena to Weidenbruck (214 miles)

June 3 – From Weidenbruck to spot near Liege (209 miles)

June 4 – From Liege to Camp Sissonne

June 14 – Moved by jeep to Epinal

June 21 – Moved to Luneville (Now in 194th Glider Infantry)

July 28-Aug. 4 – Furlough to Switzerland (Basel, Bern, Interlaken, Lucerne, Zurich)

Aug. 28-30 – By "40 and 8" from Luneville to ST. Victoret Staging are near Marseille

Sept. 9-14 – From Marseille to Boston on the "Wakefield". Stationed at Camp Myles Standish.

Sept. 18 – To Fort Meade by train.

Sept. 28, 1945 – DISCHARGED! To Charleston by train.

154
HISTORY OF MEMORIAL UNITED METHODIST CHURCH, SUMMERSVILLE, WV

This history of Memorial United Methodist Church was written by the late Rev. A. F. Gregory about 1955. The late W. G. Brown, a Nicholas County lawyer and historian contributed to the history.

The following ministers served Memorial United Methodist Church since 1955: Rev. Riker Bennett, Kenneth Watkins, Virgil H. Ware, Paul R. Beal, Andrew C. Agnew Sr., Calvin McCutcheon, Steve Runnion, Thomas Clark, Damon Rhodes, James Malick, and presently serving Memorial is Rev. David Lancaster.

Memorial Methodist Church

The first Methodist church in Nicholas County was a substantial log structure built in 1810 and used until after the Civil War. In 1867, it was replaced by the present Bethel Church at Poe on Laurel Creek. The people of the Methodist faith, as well as other religious hungry Protestants, came from all parts of Nicholas County and borders of the surrounding counties to attend Bethel. They were regular in their attendance even though the distance was often great, the weather bad and their mode of travel was horseback or on foot. Church services were regular and often held by laymen because the pastor was able to meet with them only at intervals. The regular services maintained by the church members were Sunday school, prayer meeting, and protracted revival meetings. And so, it was that the people then living at Summersville attended Bethel from 1810 to 1848 when they were able to construct their first church.

In the early Methodist Church, the service was started at dusk or "early candlelight." The women were seated on the right side of the church and the men on the left. There was no organ or musical instrument, and no hymn books, except the one used by the pastor. The pastor, using his hymn book, would "line hymns" which meant he would say a few lines of the song and the congregation would sing the words. He would read more, they sing, until the song was finished. There were a few basic tunes and the verses of the song were fitted to these tunes. A tuning fork was used by the leader to get everyone in the right key to sing and everyone present usually sang with much spirit and conviction.

In 1844, the Baltimore Conference divided the church on the question of slavery and from that time we had the Methodist Episcopal and the Methodist Episcopal South; and in 1848 the Methodists established their first church in Summersville. It occupied the site where the present Nazarene Church now stands.

Forty years later, in 1888, a new Methodist church was built on the same site. This church, however, was really a Union Church rather than a Methodist church because those contributing to the support of the church were Methodist congregations, Baptist and Presbyterian members. The different denominations did not hold joint services with only one assigned minister for all, but instead each was assigned to certain Sundays of each month at which time the minister of that faith conducted services for his group. However, each minister cordially invited the congregation of the other denominations, which resulted in the same people attending all services but with the alternate ministers presiding. The Baptists used this church because they were at yet unable to build their own church; and the Presbyterians, few in number, had been unable to maintain their established church.

In 1891, the county had been divided into three Methodist circuits and the Methodist parsonage which had remained near the Bethel Church was officially moved to Summersville. In 1906, the Methodist Episcopal Church was established on Main Street. The construction of the new church was made possible principally by four members: John Stowers, John Brock, Dan Brock and William G. Brown. This church was dedicated in 1908 by the district superintendent, Rev. Ressegger, and was in use for 40 years.

The pastors serving the Methodist Episcopal Church South after the Civil War were as follows: Samuel Black, Adam Given, H. D. Thompson, Robert Wise, Edward Murrell, Joseph Smith, G. W. Brisceo, B. A. Wynne, W. R. Chambers, G. W. McClung, M. V. Bowles, C. W. Shearer, J. A. H. Barrett, Harry Auvil, C. N. Coffman, C. A. Powers, R. G. Walker, W. M. Reid, J. B. F. Yoak Sr., F. N. Nutter, N. L. Nutter, C. C. Lambert, L. W. Peters, Karl Scott and Rev. Scraggs.

The pastors of the Methodist Episcopal Church after the Civil War were: Louis H. Jordan, George C. Wilding, Alfred Beckley, F. H. J. King, George H. Williams, A. J. Morriston, S. D. Smith, Levi Cross, W. M. Hunter, A. S. Arnett, A. D. Adams, J. W. Carroll, H. D. Mahone, V. W. M. Ocheltree, R. D. Hall, W. R. Ross, C. A. Powers, E. C. Bedford, J. H. Hampton, N. S. Hill, E. G. Hutchinson, W. W. Sleeth, L. C. Harris, O. E. Elkins and J. A. Fitzwater.

In 1939, after 95 years of division, there was unification of all branches of Methodism and the two Methodist groups in Summersville which already were practically united were officially united. The ministers who served the United Methodist's Church were: H. L. Phillips, F. F. Neel, W. H. Gilmore and A. F. Gregory.

In 1946, the Nicolas Circuit was again divided into three charges: the Summersville Circuit #1, Summersville Circuit #2, and the Summersville Church was made a station church and a few years later the Summersville Circuit #2 was renamed Bethel Circuit.

In 1949, a new and modern church was begun and completed in 1950. The dedication service was held by the resident bishop, Lloyd C. Wicke, the district superintendent, Dr. R. S. McClung, and the pastor, Rev. A. F. Gregory on Oct. 1, 1950. Shortly after, the completed church was dedicated, the Methodists erected a matching brick parsonage close by the church for its pastors. After Rev. Gregory, the pastor was Rev. Ray Wilson, and the present pastor is Rev. E. S. Wilson.

In 1955, the membership of the church is about 343. The regular services are Sunday school and church services each Sunday morning, a weekly prayer meeting, choir practice and Methodist Youth Fellowship. There are also monthly meetings of the Wesleyan Guild for the young women of the church and the Women's Society of Christian Service for other adult women. Annually, in the summer, a vacation bible school is held for the children. The local Methodists help with the support of West Virginia Wesleyan College in Buckhannon, the only Methodist college in the state; and they also help to maintain Methodist missionaries in several foreign countries.

Rev. A. F. Gregory
Mr. W. G. Brown
Brochure of Methodist Church
History of Nicholas County, W. G. Brown

Memorial United Methodist Church, Summersville, WV

155
HISTORY OF SUMMERSVILLE CHURCHES

Nicholas County, named in honor of Gov. Wilson Cary Nicholas, was formed in 1818, and Summersville, the county seat, named for Judge Lewis Summers, was established in 1820.

Some 20 years before the county was organized, settlers chiefly from Virginia and Pennsylvania, had been coming into this wilderness region, bringing wives and children with the purpose of building permanent homes. They were mainly the descendants of the Scotch-Irish Presbyterians and German Mennonites who had fled to the New World to escape religious persecution. They brought their Bibles and hymnbooks and in their rude pioneer homes trained their children in their religious beliefs and gave them the rudiments of learning.

The early history of these pioneers gives us an insight of the hardships through which we have our present-day churches. How in their cabin homes, their camp meetings, and their first church buildings of rough logs and dirt floors, they steadily maintained and built up their religious societies and laid the foundation for the succeeding generations to develop the denominations and build our present-day churches, is a long story that can be told only in the history of the past century and a half.

We can only sketch briefly from scant records and tradition the history of the Methodists, Baptist, Presbyterian, and Catholic churches now the leading denominations in Summersville.

It is interesting to note that several denominations met for services in the Summersville Methodist Episcopal Church, south on Broad Street before getting a building of their denomination.

In the 1950s, four new church buildings were erected in Summersville. Summersville Memorial Methodist Church on Webster Road held the dedication on Oct. 1, 1950.

December 1952, Summersville Presbyterian Church held the first service in the new building on Water Street.

The present Summersville Baptist Church held opening services on Sept. 19, 1954 with a note burning ceremony held in 1955. The church is located on Main and Spruce Streets.

St. John the Evangelist Catholic Church on Webster Road celebrated the dedication of the new building on Aug. 4, 1957.

Since the 1950s, other denominations have been established in Summersville, West Virginia.

156
HISTORY OF SUMMERSVILLE BAPTIST CHURCH

March 13, 1861, elders met at the Methodist Episcopal Church, south and organized the Summersville Baptist Church, which was to meet once a month. The Civil War disrupted the services and the next meeting was held August 12, 1865, at Enon. The Rev. A.N. Rippetoe was secured as pastor. At the regular meeting in October 1866, the name was changed to Enon and that ends the history of the first organization.

June 27, 1882, the members of the Summersville Baptist church met in the Methodist Church and after a sermon by the Rev. J.L. Huffman and recess until 2 o'clock p.m., they met the appointed presbytery. Mr. Huffman appointed as moderator and W.A. Peck was selected as clerk. A covenant was adopted, and the name of Summersville Baptist Church was chosen. The pastor, A.N. Rippetoe was paid a salary of seventy-five dollars per year. Property was secured for a building in 1892 and completed and paid for by 1895 with a membership of fifty-three.

The growth of the church during the 1900's was slow, during the 1930's the depression caused setbacks financially. Growth with the membership in the 1940's helped the church financially. A new parsonage was built near the church in 1948. The Rev. L. Bruce Cooper who served until 1971 was the first to occupy the parsonage on Spruce Street. The present Summersville Baptist

Church held opening services on September 19, 1954 with a note burning held in 1955.

As the church membership grew so did the addition to meet the needs of a growing church. More property was obtained for parking and Family Life Center. A parsonage was built on Spruce Street after the first parsonage was removed for an addition to the church. The present minister of the Summersville Baptist Church is the Rev. Dana Gatewood.

The picture of the Baptist Sunday School Class of Adults of 1958 lists Jim Nichols as the teacher. Others listed are: Leonard and Mable Grose, John Simms, Dock Hinkle, Carl Holbert, Agnes Herbert, Mary E. Dooley, Alice Murphy, Ruth Kuhn, Daisy Coleman, Freda Nichols, Dorothy Brown, Retha Huff, Randall Huff, Sarah McClung, Mr. and Mrs. Barnett, Eva Fitzwater, Mary Lunter, Nona Hall, Leatha Heal, Marla Barron, Paul and Sylvia Cook, E.C. and Myrtle McDowell, Gladys Burr and Thelma Roop.

Summersville Baptist Church in early 1900's Main Street. Note the two front doors, which was a common entrance, one for men and one for women.

Summersville Baptist Church Sunday School Class 1958

157
HISTORY OF THE SUMMERSVILLE PRESBYTERIAN CHURCH

The earliest Presbyterians in Nicholas County seem to have been of Scotch-Irish descent who moved west over the mountains from the Shenandoah Valley into the Greenbrier area of Virginia in the 1700s. From that area of Lewisburg, missionary preachers made trips into Nicholas County, holding worship in homes or even under trees in good weather.

At the time of the Civil War, Presbyterians were farmers living in areas of Nicholas County. An organized church was established in the Summersville area in 1885 and later in Richwood in 1902.

The first Presbyterian Church in Summersville was located in a lot off Church Street. The limited membership in the early 1900s left only a few members. In 1918, the building was sold for $410 by the late Wallace Kincade who kept the money and added his tithing to the fund, which had grown to a nice down payment for the present Presbyterian Church on Water Street.

The Presbyterian membership expanded when the area of Summersville started to develop coal and related businesses. In the 1940s, the Sunday afternoon services met in the Methodist Episcopal Church, south on Broad Street. The reorganization took place in 1948 with the congregation meeting at the Nicholas County High School until the present church was built in 1952 on Water Street. An addition of the educational building was built in the 1960s.

In 1948, 15 members transferred membership from the Richwood Presbyterian Church to the Summersville Presbyterian Church. A Manse for the Presbyterian minister was later built in the Breckinridge section of Summersville.

It is interesting to note that the Summersville Baptist Church, the Summersville Presbyterian Church, and the Summersville Nazarene Church each met a period of time and organized their respective churches in the Methodist Episcopal Church, South on Broad Street, Summersville.

Summersville Presbyterian Church

158

HISTORY OF ST. MARTIN'S IN-THE-FIELD EPISCOPAL CHURCH, SUMMERSVILLE, WV

The history of the Episcopal Diocese of West Virginia records that Bishop George W. Peterkin visited in Nicholas County in August 1887.

In 1955, Bishop Wilburn C. Campbell held an organizational meeting at the home of Mr. Thomas and Eloise Atherton. Edith Breckinridge and Eloise Atherton were behind the idea of the establishment of an Episcopal Church in Summersville, West Virginia.

A small group decided to have Holy Communion the first Sunday of the month to make a beginning of St. Martin's In-The-Field. The Summersville Presbyterian Church permitted the newly formed congregation to use their church building for services.

Mrs. Edith Wright Breckinridge, widow of the late Attorney A.N. Breckinridge, wanted to see an Episcopal Church in her lifetime. She generously donated two lots from the Breckinridge Heights Property on McKees Creek Road, Summersville, WV.

The son of A.N. and Edith Wright Breckinridge, John Breckinridge, was elected Chairman of the organizational committee. Others who served were Percy Bright, Thomas Atherton and MaxeyAnn Tully.

St. Martin's continued to meet in the Presbyterian Church until November 1962 when the dedication of the new church building was held. The A-Frame Chalet of California redwood with solid glass front was 30 by 40 feet. An addition was later added to the building.

November 13, 1965, Mrs. Edith Wright Breckinridge died. She had experienced the realization of her desire for an Episcopal Church becoming a reality. She proved that one person can make a difference and through her efforts the Episcopal Church will serve more generations.

Edith Wright Breckinridge

159
THE FORMER SAINT JOHN'S CHURCH

In 1908, with money obtained from the federal government, as indemnity for the church destroyed during the Civil War, the above beautiful brick church was built. It was this edifice that was completely razed to the ground in a matter of minutes on that fateful and unforgettable day, Jan. 1, 1953 the Feast of the Circumcision of our Lord.

In the foreground is shown St. John's Cemetery in which many former members are buried.

The history of St. John the Evangelist Mission Church in Summersville is one filled with many trials and tribulations of the early Catholic settlers in Nicholas County. The parishioners of St. John the Evangelist Church Summersville can now look back and feel how great is their debt to those good and brave fathers who fought so hard during and after the Civil War to keep the faith and hand it down to their children as their heritage.

As early as 1818, some few Catholic families were already in what is now Nicholas County, near the present town of Summersville. The county of Nicholas was formed in 1818 from parts of Kanawha, Greenbrier and Randolph counties of Western Virginia. West Virginia was formed as a state on June 20, 1863.

There was no established mission until 1846, when a young Irish priest, Father Thomas Farrell, was appointed the first pastor by Rt. Rev. Richard Whelen, at that time bishop of Richmond, Virginia, to care for Catholics living in Nicholas, Braxton, Fayette and Kanawha counties.

Before the appointment of Father Farrell, the faithful would be visited by a priest that came up the Ohio River from the Diocese of New Orleans, Louisiana. This priest would say mass in one of the homes, baptize the children and administer the other sacraments.

Father Farrell died in Summersville in 1847, only one year after he came to this mission field. The Summersville Catholics continued to have regular services under Bishop Whelan, who in 1850 became the first Bishop of Wheeling. The first church in Summersville was a small log building that was replaced in 1848 by a brick structure through the efforts and sacrifices of John H. Duffy, a pioneer member of the church here.

CIVIL WAR A MAJOR CATASTROPHE

After a few short years of comparative order and peace, the little Mission was thrown into disorder by the rumblings of the Civil War. Nicholas County was on the dividing line between the North and the South. Some citizens of the community joined the Union, others fought under the Confederate flag. Both sides contested for Summersville, the Northerners finally becoming the victors. Both armies dug trenches on the hill where the present church now stands. The original brick church building was used as a fort and base hospital. The Union forces later destroyed the church by fire so that it would become useless to the enemy.

Bishop Whelan, as head of the Wheeling Diocese during and after the Civil War until his death in 1874, had great difficulty in finding priests to supply the needs of his growing diocese. It was during this time that priests from the surrounding parishes in Charleston, Orlando and Weston came into Summersville a few times each year to fill the religious needs of the few remaining Catholics.

EARLY CATHOLICS WITHSTAND MANY TRIALS

It was during these trying times that the handful of zealous Catholics remaining in and around Summersville proved their worth by maintaining their faith in the absence of priests. They would gather together for prayer and instruction classes in Catechism for their children. Among the more prominently mentioned people of these times was Andy Horan, who taught religion classes many years among the faithful few. It was through his efforts that arrangements would be made for a priest to come from Charleston to offer Mass in his home. At other times, he would have the priest alternate in other homes in the county in offering Mass and administering the sacraments. In this way, the Catholics continued the practice of their faith through many years without the benefit of a full-time mission priest.

It was during the time of Rt. Rev. Joseph Kain, second Bishop of Wheeling, that a little frame church was erected near the site of the present church. Father Stenger, assisted by Father Boutelot, came from Charleston on horseback several times a year to offer Mass. He remained for weeks at a time to instruct and baptize the people and administer to the sick and needy.

MARIST FATHERS ARRIVE IN 1902

In the fall of 1902, Father Nicholas Hengers of the Society of Mary was appointed the first pastor by the Most Reverend P. J. Donahue, then Bishop of Wheeling.

When he arrived, he found about 25 Catholic families scattered far and wide around Summersville, in Nicholas, Braxton, Upshur and Webster counties. Father Hengers was assisted in making a survey of the vast territory by Fathers Glodt, Capesius and Delaire.

In 1902, the Fathers of the Society of Mary established their residence at Richwood, and from that point served six or seven communities. Summersville at this time was having Mass offered in their church one Sunday a month.

NEW CHURCH IN 1908

In 1908, through the inspired and Herculean efforts of Sen. Frank Duffy and Andy Horan, the United States government awarded the parish an indemnity for the destruction of the original church during the War Between the States. The original plot of ground was enlarged by the donation of John Duffy of an adjoining lot. On this large plot of ground was erected a beautiful brick structure, which was the pride and inspiration of the faithful for miles around. This church was to serve the Catholics of the community for many years.

Father Hengers served as pastor of St. John's until 1920. During these many years of his devoted pastorate, his assistants were the Rev. Fathers: Bellwald, Halbwachs, Schmitt, Keltus, and Hoff. The Rev. Andrew Keltus, from 1913 to 1922, took care of the Summersville Mission along with the other Richwood missions.

In 1922, Rev. John J. Swint became Bishop of Wheeling. In the beginning of his administration, a parish was formed in Buckhannon from the Richwood missions. Father Hengers was the first pastor to serve the Buckhannon parish.

SOME INTERESTING FACTS OF OLD ST. JOHN'S CHURCH

Father Nicholas Hengers, S. M. first pastor of Holy Family and Missions, had written, "A primitive shanty church stood there at my arrival. A new church was built around 1909, St. John the Evangelist's."

A copy of a report by Reliance Insurance Company of Philadelphia, submitted April 14, 1952, read, "Summersville, St. John's Church. This is a two-story brick without basement. Building is heated by coal fired red hot air furnace with individual registers. Walls are common brick and roof is slate. Main section of the church measures 48 x 30 feet and the balance of the building is small, plain furnished classrooms. Wall height is

16 feet. Building was completed around 1909 and is in fair state of repair. Estimated insurable value is $29,800.00."

An interesting side in connection with St. John's was the beautiful stained-glass windows, four in number, which were installed when the church was built. These windows, originally from Germany, had been on display at an Exposition in San Francisco where they were bought by Father Hengers. One depicted the Agony in the Garden, another the Immaculate Conception, a third the Annunciation and the fourth the Coronation.

In 1950, four stained glass windows were brought from St. Joseph's Cathedral in Wheeling, given to Father Fijal by Archbishop Swint. These windows were cut down to size and fitted into place by Fathers Fijal and Emerick. Once depicted St. John, Apostle and Evangelist, another St. Matthew, a third the Sacred Heart and the fourth the Immaculate Heart of Mary. All eight windows were destroyed by the fire.

Beside the shell of the old St. John's is St. John's Cemetery, about the beginning of which there is little information on hand. Here some of the outstanding pioneer Catholics are buried. Among them are James and Michael Duffy, brothers, who bequeathed a 94-acre tract of coal land, to be used for St. John's, and Andy J. Horan, catechist.

A final note to the end of a chapter and the beginning of a new one: when the flames had died out and the embers had cooled, the alter stone and chalice and ciborium kept in the tabernacle could never be found. The chalice used today for saying Mass was a gift of His Excellency, Thomas J. McDonnell, Coadjutor Bishop of the Wheeling Diocese.

The Former Saint John's Church

160
THE CAMPBELL BROTHERS
FORD GARAGE – 1927

1927: The Campbell Brothers Ford Garage,
Main Street, Summersville

Man on left: Herbert Campbell; four other men are unknown.
Child in front is Joan Campbell, daughter of Howard and
Catherine Campbell. Howard Campbell was a partner at the
Ford Garage. Photo courtesy of Mary E. Campbell Adams

161

ELIZABETH HUFF BROWN'S KITCHEN

E lizabeth Huff Brown always wore an apron while doing housework and cooking in her kitchen. She also found many other uses for the apron, such as dusting, carrying firewood for the kitchen stove, as a potholder for removing hot pans and to save dresses from being washed so often.

Elizabeth and Dr. F. H. Brown were parents of nine children: four sons were medical doctors; three sons were dentists, and two daughters, Elizabeth Ann Brown (Jacobson) and Alice Marie Brown Juergens who is the living survivor of the Brown family.

Dr. F. H. Brown Sr. (1878–1945) and Elizabeth Huff Brown (1889–1978) raised their family and contributed much to the community of Summersville.

The following story was written by Alice Brown Juergens who resides in Morgantown.

OUR KITCHEN WAS THE HUB OF OUR HOUSE

The kitchen was large, noisy, inconvenient, and delightful in the house where I grew up. What it lacked in convenience was made up for by the many activities that took place there. My childhood home was on a farm, and the two-story house sat on a knoll surrounded by white oaks. I am the youngest of a family of nine, so every room in our house was well used, but the kitchen was our favorite gathering spot.

The walls in the kitchen were always painted yellow on the upper half and blue on the lower half so it was as cheerful and bright as the sun in a summer sky. There was a large linoleum rug in the center of the floor, and the only cabinet was a small one under the sink. The dining table was long and could seat 12 people. Beside the table were three windows that looked out onto the upper lawn. Outside these windows was a window box filled with red geraniums in summer and holly and greenery in winter. The big cook range reigned supreme over the kitchen, and my mother treated it like royalty. She had a can of polish called "stove black," and she often rubbed it on the stove to keep it looking like new. The space behind the stove was where I kept a cardboard box that was a "recovery room" for injured or sick pets.

There was also a drying rack where wet socks or mittens could be hung to dry.

Our kitchen was used for cooking, eating, and just about everything else! Sometimes it became my dad's outpatient clinic, as often some of his patients stopped by for medical attention. I remember the sound of needles clinking in a pan of boiling water on the stove as he prepared to give a shot to a patient.

Other times, the kitchen became a beauty shop where home perms and haircuts were given. Sometimes the dining table was used as a library table where we did our homework and sat to read. Often, we played games on this table — checkers, dominoes, or card games.

On ironing day, we always set up two ironing boards in the kitchen. When my brothers were away in college, they mailed their laundry home to be done. My mother always ironed the shirts, and some of the rest of us ironed the other things. She said that one week she ironed 54 shirts. Each white shirt was starched, dampened down, and rolled up for overnight before being ironed. Saturday evening was the time to get our clothes ready for church the next morning. So the ironing boards were set up again and my brothers pressed their trousers, and we all sat round the kitchen polishing our shoes.

Just off the kitchen was a pantry, and in it was the kitchen cabinet. It had a flour bin that held 25 pounds of flour and a metal pullout tabletop where piecrusts or biscuits were rolled out. I have wonderful memories of the kitchen at my old home place where food for the body and soul were always plentiful.

- Alice Brown Juergens

Elizabeth Huff Brown's Kitchen

Made in the USA
Columbia, SC
22 November 2023

26955194R00296